D0673465

IDEAL FOR THE HOME OR OFFICE

Panasonic's 'Mini Office' launched earlier this year to coincide with National Work at Home V

Weston Sixth Form College

small office ev.
machine can fax,
kit that includes a. ...

This versatile fax machine benefits from a small business or home working environment. Wit.. ....
software as standard, this multifunction machine has a scann... ...
600 x 600 dpi and is TWAIN compatible. The KX-FLB751 is also a fla.
scanner, making high-quality scanning of flat documents easy, (being a flatbed
design means you can scan pages from books or other bulky items).

The copier feature can reduce or enlarge images from 50-200%, collate and
produce multiple copies of up to 99 pages. Whilst the telephone feature is caller
ID compatible, has 100 speed dialling, 5 x 2 one-touch dial, electronic phone
directory and electronic volume control.

Other features include a modem speed of 33.3 Kbps and Quick Scan Memory,
with a rapid printout rates of 10 ppm. The machine also benefits from a monitor
button to verify that the fax is received at its destination and a useful jog dial
control – a simple way to access pre-programmed fax and telephone numbers.

The KX-FLB751 comes with a powerful 2 MB memory function, which enables
documents to be stored without paper, as well as a monitor button, and a
150-sheet paper tray – all in a compact and attractively designed small footprint,
ideal for home office or small department use.

The memory function enables storage of around 170 pages, depending on the
resolution and transmission mode of the documents. This document storage
capacity means faxes can be received even when the machine is out of paper.

Available now with a typical buying price of £549

www.panasonic.co.uk/faxes

Reader Enquiry Number: 08700 100 464

Digital image available upon request

For further editorial information contact:
Jane Hinton, Press Office
Tel: 01344 853855 (please do not publish this number)
Panasonic UK, Panasonic House, Willoughby Road, Bracknell, Berks. RG12 8FP

START UP & RUN YOUR OWN BUSINESS

START UP
& RUN YOUR
OWN BUSINESS

JONATHAN REUVID & RODERICK MILLAR

**KOGAN
PAGE**

First published in Great Britain in 2003
Reprinted in 2003

Kogan Page Limited
120 Pentonville Road
London N1 9JN
United Kingdom
www.kogan-page.co.uk

© Jonathan Reuvid and Roderick Millar, 2003

The right of Jonathan Reuvid and Roderick Millar to be identified as the authors of this work has been asserted by them in accordance with the Copyright, Designs and Patents Act 1988.

British Library Cataloguing in Publication Data

A CIP record for this book is available from the British Library.

ISBN 0 7494 3862 2

Typeset by Saxon Graphics Ltd, Derby
Printed and bound in Great Britain by Thanet Press Ltd, Margate

HOW TO MAKE YOUR SMALL BUSINESS RIVALS FEEL EVEN SMALLER.

Grow. Business Link services offer an unrivalled range of business support. From independent advice and information on legislation, finance, marketing and staff development to help with things like starting up, expansion and networking, all tailored to suit your business. Last year we helped over 300,000 small businesses from mechanics to florists boost their profits, increase productivity and stay competitive. To make sure your rivals look up to you, call Business Link.

Business Link

0845 600 9 006
www.businesslink.org
THE UNFAIR ADVANTAGE

ACCESS TO FINANCE

Whether you are just starting out or looking to grow your business, one of the most critical issues is finance. There are many different types of finance available for small businesses, and below we highlight some of the more common types of finance that are available and may be suitable for your business:

- ## Overdrafts

An overdraft is a flexible bank facility, which allows you to borrow up to an agreed limit, usually arranged for a period of up to a year and possibly with interim reviews. You pay interest only on the amount outstanding, which can go up or down according to your needs. This may be repayable on demand and you will be charged an arrangement fee, plus interest on the funds used.

- ## Factoring/Invoice Discounting

This is an alternative to an overdraft. Factoring companies may advance you up to 85% of the value of invoices issued while you re waiting for theses invoices to be paid. As your business grows and your sales ledger increases, the factoring facility grows with you, so long as the factor believes that your customers are a good credit risk.

- ## Short Term Fixed Loans

Short-term loans over one to three years could be used to fund working capital. Capital repayments are fixed and interest can be variable with changes in base rates or fixed for the term of the loan. These loans may be secured.

- ## Leasing/Hire Purchase

Leasing and Hire Purchase are used to finance an asset over the period the asset is likely to be in use. Leases take different forms and should allow you to obtain the use of an asset with minimum initial outlay. They are usually calculated at a slightly higher interest rate than a bank loan, but may be more easily obtained.

- ## Fixed Term Loans

Term loans are bank loans over a fixed term, usually between one to ten years. These are usually secured and full repayment terms are known at the outset. Capital repayments are fixed, which helps your to forecast your cash flow, and repayment holidays may be possible.

- ## Small Firms Loans Guarantee Scheme (SFLGS)

The SFLGS is for raising bank term loans of up to £250,000 where you have insufficient assets to offer the bank as security. The Government, through the Small Business Service guarantee a percentage of the bank loan, to encourage banks to make loans available.

- ## Small Firms Training Loans (SFTL)

The STFL are term loans available form some banks – Barclays, National Westminster, the Co-operative and the Clydesdale Banks. Loans can be up to £125,000, but may only be used for specific training costs that would other wise not be afforded.

- ## Business Angels

Small businesses will generally find funds from a private investor (e.g. Business Angel), and are suitable in the early stages of their development. The Business Angel will often want to become involved in the management of the business, and will offer their considerable experiences and skills.

- ## Venture Capital

Raising finance through venture capital involves selling a share in your business. Large sums of finance are potentially available.

For more detailed information about the different types of finance available and where to obtain specific help and advice, you can request unlimited copies of the 'Sources of Finance for your Business' publication from DTI by telephoning 0870 150 2500 and quoting ref no. URN 01/1413. You could also contact your local business link on 0845 600 9006 or via the web at www.businesslink.org who can also offer help and advice to determine the most suitable source of finance for your business.

OUR MISSION

"We strive to build and maintain lasting relationships; relationships built on trust and sustained by our dedication for excellent client service, individually designed integrated solutions enables us to create more opportunities for our clients to enhance their foundation"

WEALTH → Creation → Maximisation → Preservation → Distribution

Financial Dimensions
104a Park Street, Mayfair, London W1K 6NG
Tel: +44 (0) 20 7495 6000
E-mail: ask@fdadvice.com
Fax: +44 (0) 20 7495 8000

Does my business require a financial adviser?

Financial Planning is often overlooked when starting a new business. This is an important element to ensure that the partners and employers are protected and provided for in later years.

Research indicates that whilst the need for protection against loss or damage to the material assets of a business namely, buildings, plant, machinery etc is understood, the extent to which a business depends on individuals is often undervalued and unrecognised. A Key person is any individual whose critical illness, premature death or total disability would cause financial difficulties for the business because the individual cannot be easily replaced causing problems such as loss of profits, expense of replacing that person.

What is Key person assurance? Key person assurance is the life cover effected to provide protection against such losses. Examples of key persons are proprietors, managing director, sales manager, production manager, research & development staff or individuals closely involved in the development of specialised projects. Other major problems That could occur are repayment of loans made to the company by key persons (directors' loan accounts), loss of important business connections, loss of existing contracts, loss of goodwill and the list go on.

What happens if I am a shareholder/director of a limited company? A limited company will not be dissolved upon the death of a major shareholder/director but the surviving directors run the risk of the deceased's shares passing to someone with no interest in the company, or even into the hostile hands of a potential corporate predator. It is preferable then that there should exist a pre-arranged scheme for the surviving directors to purchase the shares of the deceased director from his estate. There are various methods this can be arranged ; cross option agreement, the buy and sale agreement and Keyman Insurance. When setting up these type of advice will be given concerning the tax treatment of products and their benefits which are based upon our understanding of current tax law and Inland Revenue practice. Levels and basis of, and reliefs from, taxation are subject to change.

Other areas of financial planning for the corporate sector: - Pension Planning, Permanent Health Insurance, Private Medical Insurance, Death-in-Service benefit for employees.

Contents

Simply Effective

Before you invest in your company website:

☐ know what it can do for your business

☐ make sure it includes everything you need

☐ make sure it can grow to suit your needs

☐ make it easy to manage

Step by step
Give us half an hour of your time, we will find out about your business, recommend the solution that suits your needs and get you online - *fast*.

A professional website solution from £149
It couldn't be simpler - our solutions are tailored to the specific needs of small businesses and include everything you need to get online - including hosting, domain name, web mail, technical support and even content.

Get your online presence working for you now, call us on **01925 286400**

www.freecom.net

freecom·net

What can your Web presence do for **your** business

A website can be a valuable asset to any business. Most companies in the UK today could be using the Internet more effectively; in fact for many business sectors, customers expect to be able to access a company website as a first point of information.

In the early days of the Internet companies developed websites because it was the 'fashionable' thing to do. As experienced business people, we are all aware that for any web presence to deliver real benefits, business processes and objectives need to be fully reviewed and understood.

Key Objectives

To be effective your Web strategy must concentrate on your business objectives, you must decide exactly what you require from your Internet presence and the role of the website within your business; both now and in the future.

Many companies use their website as a purely marketing or promotion tool whilst others use it as an additional route to selling their products and services.

Alternatively you may be looking to increase efficiency by reducing telephone and printing costs by replacing these with e-mail. There are many interactive tools that are now available for your website, that will offer your business the facility to record data and measure feedback from the Internet visitors that are interested in your business and products. From this information, you will be able to create an invaluable marketing database that can be used for marketing campaigns and Improved customer service through faster and more interactive communication.

You may feel your industry is not in a position to take advantage of the Internet, your competitors haven't invested in a website so why should you? – why not gain competitive advantage by being the first to use a website as the fastest and most efficient route market. Remember, building a web presence needn't be expensive; with the right solution, you will have the flexibility to experiment with different approaches until you arrive at a strategy that works for your customers.

Building your Web Presence – What do you need to consider
There are a number of practical considerations that need to be addressed before your can publish your company website. Everything from how to get online: reliable Internet connectivity, e-mail and domain names, to content and functionality, online promotion and integration with your traditional marketing and customer relations strategy.

You could approach a web design company for the website, an ISP for hosting, a marketing company for content and a whole raft of Internet suppliers for services such as search engine positioning and e-commerce. This is fine if you have the time and the experience; but you need to ask yourself whether all these services will be able to you in the future and who will take responsibility for ensuring everything works together as it should. If you want an easy life – choose a supplier with the expertise to provide you with a one-stop-shop for the solution, and importantly the backup and ongoing service you need.

What makes a good website
A good website is a great leveller, if it's the first contact a potential customer has with your company, it can enhance credibility if it is professional and easy to use.

Make it fast to download so visitors don't get bored and move on; easy to navigate so customers can access the information they want without having to work too hard; finally, make it interactive and content rich, if the website is regularly updated and contains news and information that is valuable to your potential customers, they will keep coming back.

Stephen Clitheroe
Business Development, Freecom.net

Introduction

Setting up your own business is not for the faint-hearted. Keeping a thriving business afloat and managing growth are equally challenging, and entrepreneurs should not expect that the burdens of running their own business will ease with the passage of time. Nor will the excitement and satisfaction, which are the reasons for setting out on what may prove to be a stony road.

The authors of this edition have both started up and run businesses, with varying degrees of success, and can attest from experience to encountering most of the problems and difficulties discussed in *Start Up and Run Your Own Business*. The book is intended more for entrepreneurs who have resolved to start up and grow their business into an enterprise serving a solid customer base and employing staff than for self-employed sole traders who prefer working for themselves to salaried employment. There is plenty of advice applicable to sole traders in Parts One and Three, but Parts Two and Four will not apply to them unless their aspirations are raised.

Part One helps readers to carry out an objective evaluation of their business concept and the positioning of their business in the market they have identified. At the same time, some rigorous self-assessment is encouraged, to determine that the entrepreneur has the mindset and aptitudes to set up his or her own business. Part Two, written by Kevin R Smith, the independent financial consultant, outlines the funding alternatives that may be available to those setting up their own businesses, and the sequence of steps necessary to raise finance.

Part Three is devoted to the essential management functions that are critical to the operation of your own business from the moment it is up and running. It focuses on the operating roles that you will have to perform yourself or supervise closely in the early stages of developing your business. We are grateful to Paul Waite, senior partner of chartered accountants Aspen Waite, for his concise summary of the current taxation regime, which should be reviewed in the light of any amendments in future Finance Acts. Our thanks are also due to Chris Hutber, Commercial Director of Object Group, for his instructive chapter on IT and management communications.

Finally, in Part Four, the book moves on to the issues that will emerge as your business grows and becomes more successful. Again, we acknowledge our thanks to Paul Waite for his contribution on ownership issues. In the final chapter readers are invited to revisit their original objectives when they set up in business and to confront the ownership issues which arise when planning for the longer-term future of the business and their own and family financial interests.

Whatever stage you may have reached in your deliberations, your preparations for start-up or the further running of your business, we hope that this book will help you to crystallize your plans and, hopefully, strengthen your awareness in key decision-making areas. May good fortune accompany you in your big adventure.

Part One

Setting Up Your Business: Key Considerations

1 Defining and Analysing Your Business

In *Twelfth Night* William Shakespeare wrote, 'Be not afraid of greatness: some men are born great, some achieve greatness, and some have greatness thrust upon them.' The same is probably true of those who set up and run their own businesses: some are born entrepreneurs whom no other form of occupation would satisfy; some build their own businesses slowly and prudently from a modest base; others are driven to start their own businesses because they lose their jobs, their employer fails, they inherit a family business, or the routine jobs into which they are locked are unrewarding and frustrating. Whatever the motivation for wanting to strike out on your own, you will be wise to study first the overall experience of other small business start-ups and closures before taking the plunge and beginning to plan your own.

AN OVERVIEW OF RECENT BUSINESS START-UP EXPERIENCE

A recent survey conducted by the bank Barclays reveals that mainstream business starts in England and Wales totalled 342,000 in 2001, a fall of 15 per cent on the previous year. The first half of 2001 was especially weak and, after seasonal adjustment, the closing months of 2001 in fact reveal a small pick-up in business starts towards the end of the year. For the purposes of the survey, 'mainstream businesses' are defined as full-time businesses set up with the intention of making a profit as opposed to part-time, second job and small not-for-profit enterprises.

The main factors which impacted the timing of people starting up a new business in 2001 are thought to have been:

I   generally low business confidence and perceptions of a slowing economy throughout the year;
I   the knock-on effect on personal wealth of a deteriorating stock market;
I   relatively high employment levels up to, at least, the last quarter.

Indeed, Barclays found a reverse correlation between strong economic indicators, especially GDP growth, and a reduced stock of mainstream businesses. In the year 2001 business closures totalling 410,000 represented a 4 per cent increase on 2000, and were thus an even stronger factor in the overall net reduction in the stock of mainstream businesses by 67,000.

Nevertheless, it is important to remember that businesses closing by no means equate to the number of businesses failing. Many businesses close simply due to retirement, a return to salaried employment or a lifestyle change. Some are sold on to a new owner, thereby creating a new business start-up. Another reason why people act early in closing down or delaying start-up plans is a vivid memory of what happened to themselves, families or friends a decade ago in the recession of the early 1990s.

In 2001 the regional pattern of start-ups and closures was clearly affected by the incidence of foot and mouth disease, which was a major factor in many rural areas. However, some regions were like the North-West, where the impact of a heavily depressed start-up market in the rural areas was partly offset by a more active economy around Liverpool and Manchester, so that the regional decline was in line with the national average (down 16 per cent). Typically, the regions that were hardest hit were those that had seen the largest increases in new businesses in the past: notably Greater London (down 22 per cent) and the South-East (down 18 per cent) where the end of the computer services and IT boom played a part.

A sectoral analysis of mainstream start-ups in 2001 reveals that the winning sectors were construction (up 3 per cent: the fastest rate of growth since 1997) and manufacturing (up 14 per cent). In the construction sector, where house building thrived while commercial and industrial building was sluggish, repair and maintenance was more buoyant than new building, reflecting a high incidence of new businesses in the construction trades such as plumbers, plasterers, joiners and electricians. The increase in manufacturing start-ups appears to be an anomaly against the sectoral recession in 1991, but represents a rebound from the very low level of manufacturing start-ups in 2000.

On the downside, property/finance was down 29 per cent in 1991 while hotel/catering start-ups fell 25 per cent as a direct result of the foot and mouth outbreak at the beginning of the year and the fall-off in visitors to the UK after 11 September. The sector that was hit hardest was business and professional services (down 36 per cent). Advertising and recruitment agencies suffered their first real decline since the early 1990s recession, with knock-on effects on other businesses within the advertising sector such as graphic designers, printers and communications consultancies. The Recruitment and Employment Confederation (REC) reported that in December 2001 permanent recruitment had been in decline for eight consecutive months, while temporary recruitment billings fell for the third month in a row. National newspaper recruitment advertising expenditure, a reliable indicator for the executive search market, declined throughout 2001, to stand 40 per cent below its level a year earlier at the end of 2000.

PROFILES OF BUSINESS START-UP ENTREPRENEURS

Men and women take the decision to set up and run their own businesses at all ages, but there are three groups that Barclays has profiled as among the most active: those over 50, those under 25, and the growing sector of women in business. These findings may be relevant to your situation if you are in any of these three groups, and may still assist you in making your personal decision if you are instead in the 25 to 50 age group.

Third age entrepreneurs: the over 50s

Described by Barclays as third age entrepreneurs, those over 50 now account for an estimated 15 per cent of all start-ups in England and Wales, an increase of 50 per cent over the past 10 years.

The motivations of third age entrepreneurs are compared with those of the under 50s who start a business in Table 1.1.

Table 1.1 Main reasons for starting up: percentage within age grouping

Reason	Age when started business	
	Under 50	50 +
Made redundant	10	17
To make (more) money	20	16
Freedom to be own boss	16	11
Retired from previous job	3	11
Develop hobby into something money making	4	7
Job satisfaction/dissatisfaction with last job	4	6
New challenge	6	4
Supplement pension	–	4
Enjoyment and fun	4	3
Saw an opportunity	1	3
Realize an ambition	3	2
Unemployed	1	2
Time on hands	–	2
Business passed on through family	11	2
Experience in particular field	4	2
Could not find a job due to age discrimination	–	1

The primary motivation for 20 per cent of both groups is to make money (or supplement a pension in the case of third age entrepreneurs). Redundancy (17 per cent) is the next rated reason among the older age group, followed by 'freedom to be own boss' and 'retirement from previous job' (11 per cent each). Among the under 50s 'freedom to be own boss' ranks second (16 per cent) followed by inheritance of the family business (11 per cent) and redundancy (10 per cent). A tenth of both groups rank greater job satisfaction and the challenge of running one's own business collectively as the principal reason for start-up.

The long-term expectations of older and younger entrepreneurs differ significantly. While 26 per cent of the under 50s do not expect to retire before they die, 19 per cent have no idea and 37 per cent expect to retire between 60 and 69, 14 per cent of the third age entrepreneurs do not expect to retire, while 28 per cent have no idea when and 38 per cent expect to retire before the age of 70. However, 40 per cent of the over 50 group expect to close the business down when they retire compared with 22 per cent of the younger group, perhaps because third age businesses are less likely to be a full-time occupation and are therefore less marketable.

Characteristics of third age businesses

Around half the over 50s starting businesses (51 per cent) do so in a similar area of work to their previous activity, and 49 per cent come from professional jobs such as management and teaching. By contrast 51 per cent of under 50s starting in business previously worked in manual, clerical or secretarial jobs, compared to 26 per cent of third age entrepreneurs. Only 3 per cent of the over 50s (6 per cent of under 50s) were unemployed in the period preceding their business start-up, indicating that most of those who were declared redundant took the decision to 'go it alone' during their redundancy period rather than waiting to become unemployed.

Thirty-two per cent of third agers have previously run their own businesses, of which half have run one, rather more than 40 per cent two to five businesses, and 7 per cent six or more businesses. Among the under 50s, some 73 per cent were previously employees.

In the Barclays survey the average turnover of businesses started by under 50s was £104,000 compared with £70,000 for those started by the older group, which may be partly a reflection of the shorter time that the latter group have had to grow the business. It also suggests that third age businesses employ fewer people.

Third age owners are more likely to view their businesses as a part-time occupation, with 51 per cent running the business to supplement their pensions, while for 52 per cent of younger business owners the business is the only source of income.

The sectors in which these businesses operate also differ. The highest proportion (34 per cent) of businesses started by third age owners are in property, finance and professional services, with only 10 per cent in the retail sector, compared with 19 per cent of under 50s starting in business. This pattern reflects the business backgrounds from which third agers come and their preference for sectors where there are more opportunities to balance work and leisure.

Third age business owners coming from management jobs are more likely to be computer literate (71 per cent) and to have invested time and effort in undertaking research and detailed planning involving the use of a computer before launching their businesses. They are also heavy users of computers in running the business for word processing, record keeping and accounts, but slightly less likely than under 50s to use them for e-mails or Internet access.

Sources of finance

Third age business owners are also likely to be better prepared for start-up, having spent time preparing a budget, business plan and cash flow forecast, as well as researching the market, their competitors and pricing. They are also more likely to use more of their resources to fund their start-ups, such as savings, redundancy money, a pension lump sum, or proceeds from the sale of a previous business or property. With these sources providing 75 per cent of start-up finances for third age businesses, compared with 66 per cent for others, over-50 business owners are less likely to have recourse to a bank or building society loan.

Whether you are an over- or under-50 entrepreneur, how does your situation compare with those of the business owners described above? If you are in the third age category, take comfort from the further survey finding that 95 per cent of the over 50s interviewed did not regret their decision to start a business.

Under 25 business entrepreneurs

An increasing proportion of under 25s start their own businesses. Although they represent a decreasing section of the population, due to the lower birth rate of the 1980s and more remaining in the education system beyond the age of 16, their share of start-ups in England and Wales has held steady at 7 per cent, and every week around 550 businesses are launched by young entrepreneurs under 25. Not surprisingly, 63 per cent of those interviewed in the Barclays Bank survey identified Sir Richard Branson as the businessperson they admire most.

Almost two-thirds of the under 25s interviewed identified the opportunity to make money and the urge to be their own boss as the drivers for starting their businesses. Nearly half of them develop business plans, research what their competitors are doing and pay attention to the pricing of their product or service. When starting up and in the early years of running their businesses, more than half of the 18–24 year olds do not undertake any training. Of those that do, nearly two-thirds choose a course that is business-specific.

Businesses with higher turnovers (two-thirds of those with sales above £500,000) or that have been operating longer tend to have their own premises, but 49 per cent of young entrepreneurs either work from home or use their homes as the 'hub' for their activities.

Although only 13 per cent of young owner-managers have a degree or higher qualification, 36 per cent were students and 42 per cent were in full-time employment before starting their business, and young people are more likely to start their own business if there is a family history of entrepreneurial activity. Ethnic minorities made a strong showing at 9 per cent among the young business owners interviewed, against 7 per cent of the overall population.

Types of business started by young entrepreneurs

Nearly one-third of young entrepreneurs' businesses are service-based, ranging from graphic design and media services to gardening and child minding. Other significant activities are: production or construction (20 per cent), retail (16 per cent), professional services (14 per cent) and catering and leisure (12 per cent). Young business people have a preference for dealing with their own age group, and tend to define their target market on the basis of their product's or service's appeal to that age group, rather than their personal product or service preference. Around one-third of young owner-managers run their business part-time in the first year, but this proportion falls to 13 per cent by the time that a business is five or more years old.

Although the majority of businesses are small (51 per cent have sales of less than £20,000 a year, with 20 per cent between £20,000 and £50,000 and 9 per cent between £51,000 and £100,000), 11 per cent of those interviewed in the Barclays survey were generating a sales turnover of between £100,000 and £1 million.

Type of business entity

About 55 per cent of young entrepreneurs run their businesses as sole traders, 29 per cent operate limited companies and 18 per cent are in partnerships, including sleeping partners. People skills become increasingly important as 11 per cent of these businesses employ at least three members of staff. Although 42 per cent of those employing staff claim that the age of a prospective employee is irrelevant, 34 per cent would like to employ people their own age.

Sources of finance

Only 16 per cent of the young entrepreneurs surveyed had required £10,000 or more to set up and launch their businesses; two-thirds spent less than £5,000 and 30 per cent spent what they described as 'very little'. For half of those questioned the purchase of equipment was the biggest initial cost; for a further 17 per cent the premises were the most costly element.

Access to finance is not considered a constraint; over two-thirds found it easy to secure the funding they required. Only 8 per cent experienced great difficulty. Unlike the experience of older entrepreneurs, finance from banks, building societies and friends has tended to replace savings, and the proportion which these sources account for had risen from 20 per cent to 48 per cent between 1997 and 2001, perhaps reflecting lenders' efforts to make start-up funding for young people more accessible. However, 38 per cent still use their savings and 25 per cent manage to persuade family or friends to provide most of the finance, with 5 per cent benefiting from a Prince's Trust loan.

The problems that young owner-managers describe as most prevalent, in order of importance, are age discrimination by customers, suppliers, institutions and government agencies; not being taken seriously by colleagues or business contacts; difficulties in attracting funding; and lack of support from family or friends.

If you are under 25 and are planning to set up and run your own business, you may wish to heed the advice of others who have gone before you. Over 70 per cent of the young entrepreneurs surveyed by Barclays said 'stick with it', 'plan thoroughly' or 'get professional advice'.

Women in business

Although discrimination is still an issue for women in business, women now own over one-third of small businesses with a turnover of up to £1 million a year and account for a similar proportion of business start-ups (33 per cent overall compared to 27 per cent in 1996). The proportion of women among third age entrepreneurs is rather less: 26 per cent against 43 per cent for businesses started by those under 50. Among under 25 owner-managers, women account for 44 per cent.

The reasons for wanting to set up in business cited by women and men are generally very similar. However, men are more likely to quote earning more money as a prime reason, while for women, factors such as wanting more control or a better lifestyle rate strongly behind the chance to be their own boss.

Women appear to be more adventurous in starting out on their own, with only 41 per cent having prior experience in the same kind of business compared with 71 per cent of men. As one would expect, family and domestic issues are a stronger influence among women, with 35 per cent saying that the decision on timing the start of a business was affected by whether they had children as opposed to 18 per cent in the case of men.

Men's and women's perceptions of the main challenges in starting up a business differ. For men the focus tends to be on financial resources and cash flow. Women are more inclined to rate not being taken seriously, as well as sexual discrimination, as the main barriers. The Barclays survey revealed that women place greater emphasis on skills such as being better organized and having the ability to do more than one thing at the same time when citing their strong points. More than 20 per cent of male respondents felt that women are 'better with people' and have a better image, which gives them an advantage in starting a business.

Women appear to be more resolute than men in starting a business. Although 37 per cent of women in the Barclays Bank survey reported experiencing actual discrimination during the previous five years, it seemed not to hold them back. Of the 2 per cent of women in the UK who are thinking about setting up a business at any one time, 63 per cent actually go on to do so compared with 51 per cent of men. Women business owners wanting to grow their businesses also demonstrate their confidence and positive outlook. They are more likely than men to employ staff to help run their business, and there has been a substantial rise in the proportion of women who have undertaken formal business training, from 31 per cent in 1996 to 57 per cent in 1991. Women are also keener to build a business they can ultimately sell.

Use of business support organizations

Women turn to the same range of sources for business support and advice as men, but are more likely to turn to business support organizations (18 per cent) than men (10 per cent). They believe that such organizations should provide more information and publicize themselves more effectively, a view that the Small Business Service has no doubt taken on board in formulating strategy to encourage more women to start their own businesses.

DEFINING YOUR BUSINESS

It is worth trying to position yourself within the profiles of start-up entrepreneurs described above. If you conclude that your situation and outlook differs widely from the group in which you fall, male or female, under 25, 25 to 50 or third age over 50, you may be wise to revisit your concept and consider whether you are likely to succeed in a start-up business. In Chapter 2 we offer a self-assessment programme which addresses your personal qualities, skills and aptitudes. But first, you should define your business concept and subject it to rigorous analysis.

Whatever the product or service at the core of your business idea, the first question to be asked which will test its strength is, 'Who will want to buy the product or service I plan to sell?' The viability of your business idea will depend crucially on the answer to this question. There are two elements to the question: 'What is the market for my product or service?' and 'What price should I charge?' You need to answer both parts at the outset.

The market for your product or service

Confirming whether there is a strong potential or existing demand for your product or service requires some rigorous, objective evaluation, and poses more questions :

- Are any others selling anything like it?
- How are they doing?
- Is there room for another business?
- Is there anything special about your product or service that makes it better?

If your past business experience has been working for a company that offers a similar product or service, you may be in a stronger position to answer these subsidiary questions. Experience will tell you whether the product you propose to sell is better than the product you have experience of, or whether your proposed service is superior (does it answer product defects or customer complaints?). But don't assume that your past experience of a market is comprehensive. Many companies operate in a blinkered environment, living on an established customer base and strong brand, without exposure to the more competitive marketplace that faces a newcomer. Confirm that your perception of a market conforms to today's reality.

You can gather facts and figures about your target market from Internet Web sites, by contacting trade associations and publications, or from your local library. Your local Business Link, Chamber of Commerce or Enterprise Agency are also useful sources. If your bank has a Small Business team, like Barclays, it may have a

business opportunity profile which provides background information on the business sector which you are targeting. From this
research you should be able to develop a clearer picture of the
competition you will face and be able to confirm whether you are
offering something special. Just offering good service and after-
sales care may be enough to provide you with a unique selling
proposition (USP).

If there is no direct comparison to your business idea or
no competitors in the marketplace offering your product or
service, you may have to carry out a limited market survey
to satisfy yourself (and anyone whom you ask to back your
business idea) that there really is a market. Guidance on undertaking market research yourself to a professional standard is given
in Chapter 3.

What price should you charge?

The more competition there is, the more pressure there will be on
the prices you could charge and, for your business to succeed, the
price for your product or service must give you a decent profit.
Your basic research will identify what are the market prices for
comparable products or services and what your strongest
competitors charge. If you do carry out formal market research,
include questions about price.

All you need to do at this stage is to identify what price your
market will bear and to see if it looks likely that you will make
sufficient money from selling your product or service to cover your
personal financial needs. Instruction on how to make profit and
cash flow forecasts is given in Chapter 5.

What sort of business structure do you want?

The right structure for you will depend on your plans for the future
as well as the nature of the product or service you will provide. The
alternative structures are sole trader, partnership or limited
liability company. If you intend to work on your own for the foreseeable future, operating as a sole trader will avoid all the regulations that apply to limited companies; you just need to inform the
income tax and social security authorities that you are working for

yourself. If two or more of you will be running the business, you may want to form a partnership.

Before doing so, be sure that you understand the full implications – each partner is personally liable for any debts incurred by the business even if they were run up by another partner – and agree now among yourselves how the business is to be run, how profits are to be shared and what will happen if you need to wind it up. All these matters should be covered in a legally binding partnership agreement to be drawn up before the business starts. If you intend to run your business as a private limited company, you will need help from an accountant or solicitor to complete all the formalities of setting up the company before you start trading.

ANALYSING YOUR BUSINESS NEEDS

Having identified that your business idea is viable in market terms, it is time to put some flesh on the skeleton by defining the resources you will need to get started. Generally, the three most immediate resources that you will need to consider are start-up funds, staff and location.

Start-up funds

Even if no investment in assets or significant pre-start-up expenditure is required, most new businesses have to wait a little time before income from sales starts to come in. Therefore, you will need the availability of cash to pay wages or buy supplies in the opening months. The preliminary cash flow forecast will be sufficient to give a clear idea of the cash needed for this opening period. If your own savings are not enough to cover the cash requirement you will need to use someone else's money.

There may be grants available to you as a start-up business, and information will be available from local agencies via Business Links and Chambers of Commerce. Funding alternatives and the whole process of raising capital are addressed in Chapters 4 and 5.

Employing staff

Employing staff from your first day of trading will add greatly to your operating costs and is to be avoided unless the type and size of your chosen business demand that you do so. For entrepreneurs who start up as sole traders but need some administration back-up, your first recourse could be to your family and any available time they may have.

If you do have to employ staff at the outset, there are immediate employment law requirements, and you will need to involve yourself in PAYE and national insurance administration and to have employer's liability insurance in place. The whole area of employment regulations and good practice is a complex minefield to which much of Chapter 14 is devoted.

The location for your business

If your business does not involve face to face contact with customers and you are starting as a sole trader, then location will not matter; you should consider running your business from home if there is sufficient space, your family will accept the arrangement and you will not contravene any restrictions imposed by your mortgage lender, landlord or local authority on the work you can carry out. You may be subject to business rate council tax or capital gains tax if you sell the property, although the latter can normally be avoided.

Otherwise, if you do need separate business premises, you may be in an area where there are special grants for start-up businesses or where the local authority offers low-cost small business premises or workspaces. Convenience for staff and suppliers may be a consideration in the choice of premises, as will the nature of the area if your business will depend on attracting passing trade.

Some guidance on real estate assets is given in Chapter 15, but be sure to take professional advice on any lease or rental agreement that you take out. Ensure that you have the flexibility to adapt to unexpected changes in your level of trading. If the business does well you will probably want to move out into larger premises during the period of your tenancy agreement.

YOUR FIRST SWOT ANALYSIS

Once you have answered the basic questions surrounding your business idea, it is time to apply the well-worn but reliable management tool of a SWOT analysis, which is the acronym for the assessment of a business in terms of its present condition and future prospects from opposing standpoints :

- strengths;
- weaknesses;
- opportunities;
- threats.

List all the features or factors that you can think of objectively under each heading, and ask any member of the family, or a business friend with whom you have discussed your business idea, to review them. At this stage, before you complete your market research and business planning, the lists of strengths and opportunities should be taken as provisional, but you should not wait to address weaknesses and threats.

Spend as much time as you need in deciding how to correct the more serious weaknesses where you can. Develop and articulate a strategy for pre-empting or combating each threat. If you cannot see how to overcome weaknesses or to draw up a contingency plan for addressing the threats, you should revisit your basic business idea. This may be the first moment of truth when you decide to abandon the original business idea or amend it significantly.

The same SWOT analysis can be applied at any stage in the development of your business to check progress and identify any limitations to future growth.

Checklist

- Be aware of the business start-up environment and recent start-up experience. Start-ups in England and Wales fell 15 per cent in 2001 to 362,000, while closures rose 4 per cent to 410,000.
- The hardest hit regions in 2001 were Greater London and

the South East where increases in new businesses had been largest in the recent past.

▌ The most buoyant business sectors for start-ups in 2001 were new house building and associated trades and manufacturing. Business and professional services start-ups were hardest hit, down 36 per cent, followed by property/finance and hotels/catering.

▌ The main reason for starting a business among both under and over 50s is to make money or supplement pensions, but long-term expectations differ.

▌ 51 per cent of third agers (over 50s) start their businesses in a similar area of work to their previous job and 49 per cent come from jobs such as management and teaching. 32 per cent have run one or more previous businesses. 34 per cent start their businesses in property, finance and professional services; only 10 per cent in the retail sector. Average turnover is £70,000 compared with £104,000 among businesses started by under 50s.

▌ 75 per cent of start-up finance for third age businesses comes from own funds, compared with 66 per cent from under 50s.

▌ 36 per cent of young entrepreneurs who started their businesses aged under 25 were former students and 42 per cent were in full-time employment previously. Only 13 per cent had a degree or higher qualification. Two-thirds spent less than £5,000, 30 per cent spent very little in starting their businesses and only 16 per cent needed £10,000 or more. 48 per cent used third-party finance.

▌ Women owners account for one-third of small businesses with turnovers up to £1 million and 33 per cent of business start-ups. They appear to be more adventurous in starting out, with only 41 per cent having experience in the same kind of business. Domestic issues affected the start-up timing of 35 per cent.

▌ Test the strength of your business idea by asking the questions 'What is the market for my product or service?'

and 'What price should I charge?' Together they will tell you 'Who will buy the product or service I plan to sell?'

▌ Evaluate your market and competition objectively. If you have been working in a similar business, do not rely on experience alone. Use available information sources and carry out a limited market survey if needed.

– Analyse your business needs: start-up funding, staff requirements, where you will locate your business.

▌ Carry out your first SWOT analysis. Focus on any weaknesses and threats. If you cannot see how to overcome weaknesses or plan to address threats, amend or abandon your basic business idea.

$\boxed{2}$ Limitations to Growth

Among the weaknesses and threats which the preliminary SWOT analysis of your business concept will pinpoint are a variety of limitations to growth which may impact your business idea either at its launch or over a longer period of time. Broadly speaking, they can be divided into those due to external factors which may be totally outside your control or influence, and those due to inherent characteristics of the product or service derived from your business concept.

External factors could kill your concept stone dead at the outset if you cannot find a way to overcome or bypass them before the start-up. Alternatively, if they pose threats and therefore add risk to the business, you may be able to address them by contingency planning with a blueprint for changing the character of the business or how it operates if disaster strikes. Adverse factors, in the form of inherent defects, barriers to entry or especially onerous demands on operating management, may be more responsive to planned solutions; however, you may not have the personal capability to implement the solutions. Indeed, you should supplement the SWOT analysis with rigorous self-assessment. The self-assessment model that Barclays recommends to its customers is examined later in this chapter.

EXTERNAL WEAKNESSES AND THREATS

External weaknesses and threats come in all shapes and sizes. The following are some of the more common:

- market size and rate of growth;
- environmental change;
- registration and/or qualification barriers;

▌ pending legislation / regulation;
▌ technology developments;
▌ intellectual property.

Each of them may have a severe impact on your ability to get your business started or to sustain it as you seek to grow over the coming years. It is easier to discuss each type of factor in terms of practical examples.

Market size and rate of growth

The research you carry out to answer the question 'Who will want to buy the product or service plan to sell?' should also provide you with insight into the future outlook for the market you seek to enter. Desk research will establish the size of the market nationally, regionally and locally, and its historical rate of growth.

If your product or service is intended for a sub-market of a larger market in which there are alternatives, you should research the wider market as well. For example, if you are planning to open a keep-fit centre the market which you are addressing is not just the established market for keep-fit centres but the broader leisure market of alternative sports and exercise, including home users of keep-fit equipment. Evidence that the rate of growth in the use of fitness centres nationally exceeds the growth in sales of exercise equipment to home users would strengthen your view of starting up. The converse would be a deterrent.

You should also investigate the characteristics of the local market where you are planning to set up your business in comparison with the national market. For example, if you were planning to open a fitness centre and you find out that the local authority has a forward plan to build 10,000 new starter homes, while a new telephone call centre is about to open bringing 1,500 new jobs to the area, then you might uprate the opportunity. Alternatively, if you find that the local population is ageing, a new fitness centre opened last year and that the largest local employer is in liquidation you would probably look elsewhere. As noted previously, competitor activity is also a key aspect of the investigation.

Environmental change

This kind of external factor can be the effect of a natural phenomenon or a human-induced change to local conditions. Its occurrence may be unexpected and the effect may be temporary or permanent. For example, if you had invested in holiday cottages in Cornwall in 2000, your business would have suffered in 2001 as a result of the BSE livestock crisis but benefited in 2002 from the terrorist destruction of the World Trade Center in New York which deterred British holiday-makers from flying abroad (both short-term effects). On the other hand, the noticeable change in the British climate where summers are wetter and shorter is a long-term phenomenon which may have an increasing effect in reducing the demand for holidays at home. Other obvious examples of environmental change of the human-induced variety are road bypass schemes which disrupt the pattern of local trade or airport construction which impacts residential property values.

Registration and qualification barriers

In spite of what politicians tell us about the reduction or abolition of red tape, most of us are aware that businesses of all kinds, small or large, are increasingly subject to regulation. (Just ask farmers what they think of the increasing burden of paperwork generated by completing returns and maintaining records to satisfy government requirements.)

Some of these measures are introduced to protect the consumer or to raise standards of practice and customer accountability. Although regulation on these grounds is generally beneficial, it does impose barriers for new entrants into a number of business activities. Suppose, for example, that after 25 years working for a national pensions, life assurance and mortgage provider you are planning to set up in business as a financial consultant. Today you are required to register with the Financial Services Authority (FSA) which involves satisfying the FSA of your competence. Although your work experience may be more than sufficient, you may need to acquire an additional qualification which will delay your business start-up.

There are other occupations that are less demanding in terms of qualification, but in practice you may find it very difficult to get started in your own business without taking out membership of an accepted trade association in that field. Trade association membership is what elevates a construction worker or amateur carpenter into a skilled building trades practitioner. Membership of some trade associations requires qualification through recognized training programmes. For example, a building society will not recognize the work carried out to roof timbers to remedy infestation or rot unless the contracting firm is a member of one of the recognized trade associations.

Management consultancy is a field into which many experienced businesspeople are drawn, either as sole traders or in partnership, and remains unregulated, although the Institute of Management Consultancy (IMC) is a well-established body with professional standards and entry qualifications. This is not altogether surprising since many managers out of industry set up their consultancies on the back of assignments from established contacts including, quite often, their previous employers. However, unless they operate in a very specialized field, the credentials of IMC membership may prove increasingly important in growing their consultancy business. Fortunately, it is possible to gain IMC membership while practising as a management consultant, since admission qualifications are awarded more on the quality of work and experience, including past employment as an internal consultant or project manager, than on academic achievement.

An alternative way to surmount qualification barriers is to join forces in a partnership or limited company with an associate who already has the necessary qualification to satisfy registration requirements and provide the firm's credentials.

Pending legislation/regulation

Part of the threat of pending legislation is the long period of uncertainty that it generally causes. Election manifestoes, government inquiries, white papers and budget speeches all give hints of forthcoming legislation, but uncertainty remains until a Bill is laid before Parliament and becomes law. Therefore, pending legislation may be a deterrent to starting a business before the legislative playing field has been redefined. A case in point is the field of life assurance and pensions, where some form of legislation and/or regulation seems certain in respect of both the content of pension schemes and life assurance policies, and marketing and sales. Setting up in this business as a consultant or broker would seem unwise in 2002. On the other hand, established brokers and advisers in this field are becoming discredited as the victims of underfunded pension schemes and endowment policies multiply, and there may be opportunities for new firms to enter the market, offering a new generation of more user-friendly products. In this instance, entry timing could be all important.

More mundane examples of changes in regulations are local planning consents that impose (or remove) restrictions on the location of specific types of business.

Technology developments

The effects of developments in technology are often uncertain and can be seriously misread. The latter half of the 1990s produced two interrelated examples with unforeseen consequences. The Internet bubble was fuelled by marketing assumptions as to how the Internet could be exploited commercially and how consumers would react which proved to be mistaken. Except for a few well-defined products and services (eg books and online banking) the Internet has not proved to be the infallible growth channel to market on which a whole generation of e-economy start-ups was based. The logistical problems and costs of physical delivery to fulfil customer orders were wholly underestimated, and most of the brightest stars have crashed or gone into non-growth orbit. However, the Internet has proved itself as a highly cost-effective medium for the delivery of information, and 'old economy' companies have learnt to use the new capability in their global business operations.

The second current case of over-reach through misappreciation of technology benefits has been in telecommunications, where the national industry leaders underestimated the time and cost of developing the broad band telephony infrastructure, resulting in exorbitant prices for 3-G licences, while the growth in mobile telephone usage of WAP technology has failed to occur. Consequently, the global market leaders have been laid low.

Major developments in technology could have a similar impact on your business start-up if you have misread market trends, but the e-business hype is long over, and sources of finance rely once again on the traditional balance sheet and profit and loss account parameters rather than trendy paradigm shifts.

Intellectual property

One by-product of the IT and Internet revolutions has been that companies have learnt to value their intangible intellectual property rights (IPR) more than before. Outside the publishing industry, the focus previously had been on patentable designs, technical drawings, processes and products; documentation that is protected by copyright; and brands, corporate logos and marketing aids protected by trademark registration. Computer software is now treated as a further category of product eligible for copyright protection.

In setting up your own business you will be aware that you must not employ these kinds of tangible IPR without a licence from the owner. You must also be careful not to infringe the IPR of other businesses, particularly a former employer, in know-how or 'knowledge assets', that they have articulated and packaged into hard copy, disk, CD ROM or electronic format for delivery as in-house training or to customers, suppliers or other third parties, perhaps under licence. Knowledge assets may also take the form of management systems, training programmes, marketing and customer relations techniques.

However, other people's knowledge assets are not necessarily a barrier to entry. There is no copyright in intellectual concepts, only in the form in which they are expressed and published. Therefore, there is no reason why you should not use the same marketing techniques or sales pitch as your former employer or competitors, provided that you avoid their branding and the use of the same promotional literature, graphics, slogans or catchphrases, and wording in your printed material. The test here is whether anyone examining your product or service might believe that it was your competitor's offering; if so, you are vulnerable to a claim of 'passing off'. Conversely, you should pay attention to the protection of your IPR by making your product or service offering as distinctive and unique in its presentation as you can.

INHERENT WEAKNESSES AND THREATS

The SWOT analysis will certainly reveal the inherent problems in your business concept – those that are inbuilt and an integral part of the concept. For example, if your proposed business is the mail order sale of fashion garments, of which you have to hold stock and market through catalogues, success depends upon your flair in choosing seasonal stock ahead of time and your skill in contracting with reliable suppliers. The element of flair in judging market demand is an unavoidable risk at the core of your business, but the identification and management of suppliers demands a set of skills which you can hire or develop.

If your business is a telephone call centre, then a key element is the availability of operators who are readily trainable and an ability to retain staff. For that business, choice of location is paramount, since it will help provide a local supply of well-educated, articulate staff without too much competitive employment. In addition your ability to train staff and your people skills in building a working environment that encourages loyalty will be essential ingredients.

What is crucial in confronting inherent weaknesses is to work out in detail how to overcome them, to identify the resources needed, and to build them into your business planning.

At the heart of your decision making is your own resourcefulness, initiative, imagination determination and resilience – the personal qualities that are fundamental to success and without which any limitations to the growth of your business are likely to prove insuperable.

If you are unsure of your personal strengths and weaknesses, you might like to subject yourself to the self-assessment questionnaire and scorecard which Barclays offers to its small business customers:

Self-assessment questionnaire

1. I often feel I'm the victim of outside forces I can't control	Yes	No
2. I often work later than planned	Yes	No
3. Some days seem to go by without me having achieved a thing	Yes	No
4. Given a bad situation, I'll always try to get something out of it	Yes	No
5. I think a well ordered pattern of life with regular hours suits me best	Yes	No
6. I'm much happier not having to rely on other people	Yes	No
7. I'm prepared to take risks only when I've thought through all the consequences	Yes	No
8. There's no point in starting something unless you're going to see it through	Yes	No
9. People often tell me how good I am at seeing things from their point of view	Yes	No
10. I tend not to be too ambitious to avoid being disappointed	Yes	No
11. It's very important to me that people recognize my success	Yes	No
12. When I find myself talking to a telephone answer machine, I usually hang up	Yes	No
13. I've never been one to follow the crowd	Yes	No
14. All that matters is how much I earn regardless of how hard I work to get it	Yes	No

Scoring

Score 2 points if you answered Yes to questions 2, 4, 7, 8, 9, 11 and 13, and 0 points for questions 1, 3, 5, 6, 10, 12 and 14. Score 2 points if you answered No to questions 1, 3, 5, 6, 10, 12 and 14, and 0 points for questions 2, 4, 7, 8, 9, 11 and 13.

The maximum score is 28 points. The higher your score, the better equipped you are likely to be for your future business venture. When you have completed the exercise, even if you achieve a respectable score, you should ask yourself the question objectively, 'What limitation does my involvement impose on the likely success and growth of the business?'

Limitations in skills are less serious than in personal qualities. Most management skills can be acquired through self-education or formal training, and technical or specialist knowledge and expertise can be added to your business through selective recruitment. Limitations in personal qualities can sometimes be compensated for by association or partnership with others who are strong in the qualities you lack and, perhaps, weaker in those attributes where you are strong. However, the most compatible partners may be those who share the same deficiencies as yourself, and such combinations are generally fatal to the business.

Checklist

▮ The SWOT analysis will pinpoint threats and weaknesses that may impact your business idea at the launch or over a longer period of time.

▮ Weaknesses and threats are due to external factors outside your control or influence or to inherent characteristics of your product or service.

▮ The more common external weaknesses and threats are related to :
  – market size and rate of growth;
  – environmental change;
  – pending legislation / regulation;
  – technology developments;
  – intellectual property.

▮ If your product or service is intended for a submarket, investigate the wider market as well. Include competitor activity in the investigation.

▮ Registration and qualifications are not generally insuperable barriers but may delay your business start-up. Membership of a trade association or professional body adds to your firm's credentials but may require qualifications as well as experience.

▮ Pending legislation / regulation may be a deterrent to starting your business but may give an advantage to new entrants.

- Take care not to misread the impact of technology development on your business market.
- Avoid claims of 'passing off' by taking care to distinguish your product or service from competitors', and developing different literature and material if the fundamental business concept is similar.
- Confront inherent weaknesses by planning to overcome them and identifying the resources needed.
- Test your personal strengths and weaknesses through self-assessment. Address the question, 'What limitation does my involvement impose on the likely success and growth of the business?'

3 Researching Your Market

In Chapter 1 we discussed the core task of defining your business in terms of the market for your product or service and referred to the dangers of relying on past experience of the industry, however well you think you know the business or the territory, without carrying out basic research to confirm your belief that your core business idea is marketable.

At this stage, it is possible that there is sufficient information available from publications, business agencies, trade associations, providers of finance and Internet Web sites to give a clear picture of the competition and enable you to affirm that your business idea has a USP. However, if your product or service is truly distinctive you will probably need to do more to convince yourself and any potential financial backer of the market opportunity.

DIFFERENT TYPES OF RESEARCH

Broadly, there are two types of market research: desk research and field research. Desk research is the process of tapping into information sources of the kinds described, which can be carried out from home by accessing published information and interrogating sources by telephone, fax and, increasingly, via the Internet. The aim is to develop a profile of the market you are seeking to enter, and the past history and product offerings of market leaders who serve it.

Field research, as its name implies, involves person-to-person research 'in the field' – either by face-to-face or telephone interview, or sometimes, and usually less successfully, by fax or e-mail questionnaire. (The resistance to floods of incoming junk mail has hardened the resistance of fax users to questionnaires.)

Field research is conducted with potential customers and suppliers, or with product users in the case of research into new product design or packaging.

Of course, professional market research can be purchased from a market research agency, but this is not an expense you would wish to incur while your business is in the design and planning stage. However, you can achieve much by carrying out the research yourself, provided that you follow the basic rules for researching objectively and thoroughly.

One research avenue you should not neglect is established competitors in the same line of business, but operating in locations outside the territory you have chosen. You will find that most people are happy to talk about how they have developed their businesses, current problems and opportunities, provided that they do not view you as a direct competitor.

RESEARCH OBJECTIVES

The starting point is to construct your research brief, specifying the information you need to evaluate your target market and the opportunity for you to gain entry – the same brief as you would give to a market research agency to develop its proposal.

The following are 10 key questions that you need to answer:

1. What is the value of the market you propose to enter?
2. Is the market growing or shrinking?
3. What and where is the main competition?
4. What are the market shares of your main competitors?
5. Are your competitors profitable?
6. What are consumers/customers looking for?
7. Where in the market should you position your product/ service?
8. What is the profile of your average target customer and what market share could you capture?
9. How can you fulfil consumer/customer demand profitably?
10. How can you promote economically to your target audience?

Depending on the nature of the business and its scope there will be more or less information that you can gather by desk research before you begin to consider how to survey the target market yourself through field research.

CARRYING OUT DESK RESEARCH

Let's consider two completely different kinds of business, both service industries, one a specialized form of consumer retailing, the other a service to industrial and commercial clients. Business A is the operation of a local fitness centre, for which you have no prior experience except as a keep-fit enthusiast. Business B is a consultancy to audit health and safety (H&S) standards in businesses and to advise on remedial action and the installation of H&S routines to conform with government regulations and national standards. (Suppose that before deciding to work for yourself you were a qualified H&S officer in an industrial area).

For Business A, desk research will enable you to answer just a few of the 10 key questions on a national basis. You will be able to identify the overall value of consumer expenditure at fitness centres and on fitness products, and to confirm the rate of growth of the overall market. Local competition is readily identifiable – but not market share or profitability. There are a few listed companies engaged in fitness centre operations, which are obliged to file detailed accounts, and an inspection of these will provide some indications of how profitable these activities may be and whether their profitability is increasing or declining. However, in the context of planning a local business, desk research alone will not provide answers to the last seven questions.

For Business B, your prior work experience will help you to conduct desk research and to answer more of the 10 key questions. You should not rely on your experience only to answer Question 6 (What are consumers/customers looking for?) or Question 7 (Where in the market should you position your product/service?), although it may provide strong pointers as to the range of services you should offer and the market sector you should target, which can be tested at the next stage.

Indeed, there are two possible markets for your proposed H&S consultancy services: as an outsource provider of H&S management, or assisting clients to set up their own H&S functions in-house to best practice standards and training new or reallocated staff. Within the latter market, there are probably a number of niches in terms of size of company and the nature of its products or services. You will have to check out both markets by direct contact in your field research.

ENGAGING IN FIELD RESEARCH

Field research is only useful if it is completely objective. There is a great temptation, particularly if you are enthusiastic about your business concept, to wander round asking a few questions to possible customers and suppliers, perhaps people who know you quite well, and to fool yourself that you have conducted a useful research exercise. Worse still, you may phrase your questions so that the response you are hoping for is clearly evident, and people who know you and want to encourage you are likely to give you the answers you are looking for.

The best way to avoid these traps is to discipline yourself to draw up a representative sample of the market you are researching and to prepare formal questionnaires, whether you will be interviewing face to face or by telephone. It also helps to condition yourself to conduct interviews as if you were a professional researcher carrying out the assignment for clients rather than on your own behalf.

Sampling

A truly representative sample that reflects accurately the total market in terms of income and social groups, age groups, occupations and purchasing profiles is the ideal which researchers strive for when surveying consumer markets. But this is probably impossible to achieve. Instead, professional market research agencies often design 'quota' samples, and instruct their researchers to interview fixed numbers of respondents, whose circumstances and buying habits conform to various templates. (The preliminary questions of each interview are used to establish into which quota definition the respondent falls.)

Alternatively, the research agency may decide to adopt 'random' sampling. For example, if a survey of 100 households were commissioned in a neighbourhood of 1,000 houses, interviewers would be instructed to call on every tenth house. A random sampling approach might be more appropriate in our Business B example, where you decide to interview potential clients for H&S consultancy or outsourcing among a range of selected industries located within your local region. A simple way to pick your sample would be to refer to the telephone yellow pages or local Thompson's directory, and pick your interview targets according to the size of sample and number of companies listed in each business category.

What size of sample should you pick? Statistically, you might think the bigger sample the better. In practice, a sample of 100 is normally sufficient for consumer products or services if the sample is chosen carefully. For industrial products, as few as 30 interviews may suffice.

In the case of Business A, it should be possible to survey your local fitness centre market and produce unambiguous findings from 100 interviews of customers leaving local fitness centres, selected on a random basis. If there are two or three centres in serious competition, you should split interviewing between them.

For Business B, a quota of five or six extended telephone interviews in each of, say, six targeted industry sectors should give a clear picture of the market for your H&S services. If the findings are ambiguous, you may need to extend interviewing selectively.

Questionnaire design

Most of us have been interviewed from time to time, either in the street, in shopping centres, or at railway or bus stations – often when we're short of time and don't want to be stopped; so we know what the standard market research interview involves. Try to organize your questionnaire in a similar way to conventional interviewing techniques. Here are a few tips that may help you:

▍ Use short introductory phrases for each question to 'lead in' your respondents, such as 'I can see that you're a fit person – how often do you visit a fitness centre?'

▌ Arrange the topics for your questions in a logical order – proceed from the general to the particular. For example, in the case of research for Business A:
  - frequency of fitness centre visits;
  - weekend / weekday sessions;
  - with / without family or partner;
  - range of services and fitness products purchased;
  - seasonal variations in your fitness routines;
  - other fitness centres used;
  - other sources for fitness products;
  - customer spend per visit (range / average).

▌ Always position questions about money towards the end of the interview (they may be 'turn-offs' and cause the respondent to terminate).

▌ Try to ask questions in open-ended form first and so that they cannot be answered just 'Yes' or 'No', before offering structured alternatives: for example, 'How many other fitness centres do you visit regularly?' before 'Which of these other local fitness centres, a, b and c, do you visit regularly, sometimes or never?'

▌ Include a few personal questions at the end of the interview to establish the demographic identity of the respondent (eg age group, occupation, residential neighbourhood, size of family).

Other field research

Of course, you will want to carry out other fieldwork in addition to interviewing prospective customers or clients. For Business A, you will need to visit each competitor location, examine the layout, range of equipment, quality and pricing, ancillary services such as sauna and massage, clothing, point of sale material and promotional offers, and observe the customer traffic. You will also need to approach equipment suppliers to check the availability, lead times, prices and credit terms which you could negotiate. For Business B, you may want to sample the quality of the H&S management that potential clients have currently, in order to assess their needs for outsourcing or training consultancy.

USING YOUR MARKET RESEARCH FINDINGS

At this stage the market research you carry out yourself might throw up attractive niche market opportunities that you had not identified previously, or cause you to modify or extend your product or service offering. It will also deepen your understanding of the business opportunity, and provide much of the background data needed to support your business case at the next stage when you are seeking finance.

The Business B example differs from Business A in another important respect. Interviewing by telephone may establish your first list of actual business prospects among those who register a demand for the services which you intend to offer – in this case, H&S management consultancy. The same outcome is likely in the case of most business consultancy services you may research. You will be able to follow up on the prospect list later when your plan is complete, funding is in place and you are ready to launch your business.

The final test of objectivity, if your market research findings are negative in any important respect, is to decide whether you can overcome any weaknesses or threats to your business concept that they reveal. It is a good idea, in any case, to write up your research succinctly and to show the report to an adviser or friend who will give you an unbiased second opinion. As we counselled at the end of Chapter 1, if you are in any serious doubt yourself, abandon the original concept and go back to the drawing board. The research exercise has not been wasted. It will stand you in good stead next time.

Checklist

▪ Don't rely on your experience or perception of an opportunity without carrying out the basic research to support the business concept.

▪ Define your research objectives first in terms of the key questions you need to answer.

▮ Carry out desk research first from home by accessing published information and interrogating sources by telephone, fax and the Internet.

▮ Don't neglect others in the same line of business, but operating in a different location. Unless you are competing directly, they will probably be informative.

▮ Visit your competitor's location and investigate product range, quality, pricing and activity levels. Approach potential suppliers.

▮ Field research should be completely objective. Discipline yourself to draw up a representative sample of the market and to prepare formal questionnaires.

▮ Arrange the topics for your questions in a logical order. Always ask questions about money at the end of the interview.

▮ Ask questions in open-ended form first so that they cannot be answered just by 'Yes' or 'No'. Then ask them in structured form.

▮ Include a few personal questions at the end to establish demographic identity.

▮ If your research findings are negative, restructure the business concept – or abandon it and try again.

Part Two:

Capital Funding and Business Finance

4 Funding Alternatives

Kevin R Smith

When considering the options and funding alternatives available to assist with the establishment of a new business, it is all too easy for the owners or management to think that funding comes only in the form of equity or debt and that debt can only be in the form of a term loan or an overdraft.

This perception is often caused by the unimaginative approach of many banks, and sadly many of their small business advisers don't seem to know very much more than the businesses they are meant to be advising. Therefore, it is important that anyone considering how to set up their own business has a working knowledge of the many different funding alternatives and the wide range of potential funders which may be available.

If an informed approach is made, there is a whole range of different products available from banks and other more specialized providers of funding. What is the perfect solution for one company may not work at all for a very similar company, and structuring the most efficient, cost-effective financing package can make all the difference between the success and failure of the company. This is particularly true for new and growing businesses; at best, the wrong financing package can hamper growth.

The following may be numbered among potential funding alternatives.

Starting Your Own Business?
We can help make it a success

Starting a new business is a big decision. It's likely to be one of the most exciting and challenging times of your life. The success of your business is in your hands, but the people and the resources you choose to support you can make a real difference. Barclays was voted best UK Bank 2001 by The Banker Magazine, so with our support, you'll stand the best possible chance of realising your ambitions. We help thousands of people start up in business every year, so we know the potential pitfalls and will work with you to avoid them.

We believe we offer one of the most comprehensive start-up packages of any High Street bank including unique products and services, and the kind of support you simply won't get anywhere else.

Our research has shown that new businesses which tend to succeed are those that are run by people willing to get every bit of training, support and advice available. So to help you think through your ideas and plans we provide a programme of Start Right seminars run in an exclusive partnership with the National Federation of Enterprise Agencies. Start Right Seminars are run throughout the country and most are free of charge. They provide practical guidance from a wide range of experts, covering topics such as finance, business planning, management and marketing.

We are committed to investing time and resource to help you and your business through the crucial early stages, periods of growth and with planning for the future. That's why you will have the support of an experienced Start-up Specialist who has undergone award-winning training developed by Warwick University –

Starting your own business?

We can help make it a success.

Barclays was voted Best UK Bank 2001 by *The Banker* magazine. So how does that benefit you?

Every business starts with a good idea. Yet not every business starts with the advantage of a comprehensive support package from Barclays.

Our FREE Start Up pack has the essential information to help you get started. We also run unique Start Right seminars with the National Federation of Enterprise Agencies to give you help and support right from the very beginning.

So call us today, and get your new business off to a flying start.

Call 0800 028 4002* to claim your FREE Start Up pack and Start Right seminar information.

BP01

 BARCLAYS

one of the most respected business schools in the UK. They are available to talk through your plans and to share their experience and expertise.

We can help you with the funding of your business even before you start trading, with our unique business credit card. Provided by Company Barclaycard, voted 'Best Business Charge Card Provider' 2001 by Business Moneyfacts, it allows you to make essential business purchases, whilst enjoying up to 45 days interest free credit, and no transaction charges.

Most businesses need insurance from the day they start trading, but when starting your new business, the last thing you'll want to think about is what might go wrong. So it's good to know you're protected if the unexpected does happen. To give you and your family peace of mind we provide three months free accident, illness and life cover to new businesses through Barclays BusinessCare. A service you simply won't find anywhere else.

You can carry out your banking as and when it suits you through Businesscall telephone banking service, or if the e-world is for you, then join over 2 million customers who use the UK's leading Online Banking service. You may of course still need the human touch, so don't forget your Start-up Specialist is there to help you and you will have access to over 1800 branches throughout the UK.

If you are an online addict then you might be interested in clearlybusiness.com. This portal, developed jointly by Barclays and Freeserve, specifically for small businesses, provides a wealth of practical information, tools, services and advice. It can even help you set up your own website.

Barclays has a wealth of experience and knowledge to support you. So if you're ready to get your business off the ground or simply want to discuss your business idea call 0800 028 4002* to arrange for a Start-up Specialist to call you, or visit our website at www.smallbusiness.barclays.co.uk

* Calls may be recorded and monitored for training purposes.
Terms and Conditions apply – please ask for details.

BARCLAYS

PROPRIETORS' OR FOUNDER SHAREHOLDERS' CAPITAL

Any business of any size requires capital, and it is unrealistic for any entrepreneurs to expect others to provide funding for their new venture if they are not prepared to do so themselves. Proprietors' capital is important not just from a pure balance sheet perspective, but also because it demonstrates to others that the founders believe strongly in their own chance of success and are prepared to 'put their money where their mouth is'.

In overall funding terms, the percentage of proprietors' capital does not always need to be very large, but other funders will want to be certain that there is real financial incentive for the owners/managers to ensure the success of the business.

This type of capital is sourced primarily from the founders of the company (either reinvested savings or financed by personal borrowing), but often includes friends, relatives and associates who have faith in the entrepreneur's ability to grow the business.

As anybody that has set up a new business will testify, much time and expense is involved in the early stages, and it is often difficult to reflect this fully in the opening balance sheet. Unfortunately, very few funders give full credit for this 'investment', often disregard it and focus purely on the cash contribution. Many a new business has failed to get off the ground due to lack of sufficient proprietors' capital.

We shall look at other sources of equity and venture capital later in this chapter.

TERM LOANS AND OVERDRAFTS

All banks offer senior debt, and in practice many branches only offer senior debt finance. This is debt that is backed by some form of security (often a first fixed and floating charge on the assets of the company) and ranks before almost every other creditor. Banks' standard term loans and working capital or overdraft facilities invariably fall into this category.

This senior debt is normally provided by way of either a term loan and/or a working capital or overdraft facility, depending upon the needs of the company. For a new business the funder will probably require proprietors'/directors' personal guarantees as well as physical security on any assets of the company. Again, these guarantees are designed to ensure that the founders of the company have a tangible incentive to ensure the success of the business.

The type of facility will depend upon what the funding is to be used for. Term loans are provided for the purchase of specific assets (such as property, office fixtures, and computers) with a medium to long-term life. The term of the loan will reflect the type of asset, its value and expected life. Interest may be charged on either a fixed or floating basis, and repayments will typically be made on a monthly or quarterly basis, although semi-annual may be possible.

Normal trading fluctuations are best funded by way of an overdraft facility where the level of borrowing (and thus interest paid) varies on a daily basis. This ensures that borrowing costs are kept down, and the bank exposure is also limited. The bank will constantly monitor the level of an overdraft and expect it to fluctuate, including the account going into credit periodically. If this does not happen and a 'hard core' of borrowing is identified, the bank will often wish to separate this out into a short-term loan and structure a repayment schedule to reduce it to zero. One very important aspect for the borrower to remember is that overdraft facilities are 'on demand', which means that the bank can demand instant repayment at any time.

With most bank lending the borrower will be liable to pay not just its own costs but also those of the bank. Interest margins will vary depending upon the perceived risk, but are typically around 3 per cent above base rate for a small or medium-sized enterprise (SME) with a track record, or 4 per cent for a start-up company. Larger loans may be linked to LIBOR (London Interbank Offer Rate) rather than base rate. LIBOR fluctuates on a daily basis and varies depending upon the term, but is broadly similar to base rate.

Competition between banks is fairly fierce, and this may be shown in the level of service offered, reduced charges (at least in the first few years) or lower margins. It certainly pays to compare the terms offered by a number of potential funders. Unfortunately, this level of competition does not often lead to greater flexibility or one bank being prepared to provide facilities where another will not. As for any business service, though, it does pay to shop around.

ASSET-BASED FINANCE

Leasing is the most common form of asset-based finance. The major feature of asset finance is that it looks primarily to the value of the asset as security, rather than to the strength of the balance sheet. This can be particularly useful for start-ups and smaller companies with only limited balance sheets, or for companies that operate in asset-intensive sectors. Leases can be either on balance sheet (finance leases) or off balance sheet (operating leases), and depending on the equipment being leased, 100 per cent of the cost can be financed.

Leasing is most effective on assets with an easily assessed market value such as cars or computer equipment, but can be used in a wide variety of circumstances. It can also be useful simply as an alternative or additional source of funding to the main bank borrowing. Depending upon a company's tax and VAT position, certain leasing structures may also be more advantageous than bank loans.

All the banks have their own in-house leasing companies, but leasing facilities can also be obtained from specialist leasing firms.

Factoring or invoice discounting is another form of asset finance, as the lender looks towards the quality of the trade debtors and outstanding invoices as security, rather than the balance sheet. Again, this can be useful for smaller companies, especially during periods of rapid growth, as the facility advances a percentage of outstanding invoices and as such is more flexible. The funding is also available more quickly than a bank overdraft facility, which looks back in time rather than forward, and is far more related to the strength of the balance sheet.

Many start-up and early stage companies are restricted in their growth by lack of working capital, and factoring can often be the solution, although it is important for any company to guard against over-trading or growing too rapidly. Factoring facilities can be more expensive than bank debt, but as well as allowing the business more room to grow, these facilities can provide some cover against bad debts, and reduce administrative time and costs.

GOVERNMENT SCHEMES AND GRANTS

The area of government grants is complex and confusing, given the number of different schemes, the complicated nature of the majority of them, and the fact that what is available and on what basis changes constantly.

In simple terms, grants are normally associated with areas that are deemed to need assistance, whether that is due to geographic location, industry sector or some other criteria. The country is divided into areas, with the majority not eligible for regional grants. The more deprived areas are split into tiers, with the biggest and most wide-ranging grants available in the most disadvantaged areas. These grants can include investment and employment incentives as well as support in areas such as staff training.

Similarly, most sectors of the economy do not qualify, but certain economic activities such as the recycling of waste do. The grants available are often similar but assessed on different criteria. Details of these grants are available through the government directly or through the regional Business Link offices (for contact details see Appendix 2).

However, by far the most important government scheme to individuals considering setting up their own business is the Small Firms Loan Guarantee Scheme. This scheme guarantees loans made to small firms by commercial banks and certain other financial institutions where the firm lacks available security and/or a track record. In applying for a guarantee, the lender must satisfy itself that the commercial viability of the company is such that the lender would have made the loan but for the lack of security. If a Small Firm Loan Guarantee is made available, the bank is not allowed to take personal assets or guarantees as additional security, but may require a charge over whatever assets or security the company has available.

For a start-up business the guarantee covers 70 per cent on loans between £50,000 and £100,000, but this can rise to 85 per cent on loans of up to £250,000 for companies that have been established for more than two years. Not only does this scheme unlock bank lending that would otherwise not be available to young companies, it also reduces the cost of such borrowing. Information on the Small Firms Loan Guarantee Scheme is available through either Business Links or commercial banks that operate the scheme.

Small unsecured loans up to £5,000 are available to young entrepreneurs to start up a business under the Prince's Youth Trust. The applicant must be under 30 years of age and is usually required to show that funding has been refused by commercial lenders.

FORMAL AND INFORMAL VENTURE CAPITAL

Before we look at different sources of equity, it is important to underline the fact that there are also many different types of equity, because many people establishing a business will often be reluctant to part with equity. As well as 'normal' equity there can be different classes of shares with different voting rights; for example, preference shares which rank ahead of 'normal' equity in the payment of dividends, and many other variations on this theme.

It is also worth remembering that ownership of shares in a company and control of the company can easily be separated by using a shareholders' agreement, so that ownership of the majority of shares does not necessarily translate into control. This structure is often used when equity is injected by a venture capital firm that only seeks to own a minority stake, but needs to be able to exercise control in order to limit the risks on its investment.

External equity or venture capital can come from a range of different sources, some more formal than others. Many small firms are set up using equity provided by the founders and their friends, relatives and associates. These sources are often easier to access in many ways than more formal providers, but generally provide only relatively small amounts of money.

Raising small (ie less than £1 million) amounts of equity is often more difficult than raising larger amounts. Many of the equity funds and providers of venture capital take the view that the level of work involved is similar irrespective of the amount actually invested, and that it is not economic for them to invest less than £1 million.

The most common source of funding for start-ups and lower levels of funding is 'business angels'. These are typically wealthy individuals who have run businesses of their own and are looking to invest their own money. As well as their financial investment they often bring relevant experience. Business angels invest from as little as £20,000 but more commonly £100,000 plus. A number of networks exist, and through these, individual investors can club together to form a syndicate to invest larger amounts. Given the personal involvement, the investment decision is often taken partly with the heart as well as the mind, and investors normally stick to industry sectors in which they have experience. In practice, this makes the search for the right investor more difficult, but with the benefit that the investor once found can often display more flexibility and vision than a more professional investor.

Individual investors can obtain considerable tax relief on investments made of up to £150,000 if the investment qualifies under the Enterprise Investment Scheme. As well as tax relief on the initial investment, no capital gains tax is payable if the investment is held for at least five years.

Perhaps the best-known source of equity is the investment funds and venture capital funds run by City institutions. Investors in these funds are banks, insurance companies, pension funds and the like, and the funds invest in a portfolio of companies. Each fund will normally have a focus on certain sectors and on certain stages of a company's development, as well as other criteria such as minimum and maximum levels of investment. It is worth pointing out that very few venture capital funds are really interested in investing in start-up businesses, irrespective of what their marketing material might claim. Probably the most common level of investment is between £1 million and £5 million. Most funds look for an annual return on their investment in the region of 25 per cent to 30 per cent (this level of return includes both projected dividend income and forecast capital appreciation). The majority of investment funds are members of the British Venture Capital Association.

ALTERNATIVE CAPITAL STRUCTURES

The actual financial structure of a business will depend on many factors, and while getting the structure right is of paramount importance to the business both at start-up and in the future, there is no certain rule for what that structure should be, as the optimum will vary from one business to the next.

Equity will be more expensive than debt, but has the benefit for a start-up that it does not normally have the same cash requirement (ie interest needs to be paid irrespective of profitability; dividends do not) and it is available without the need for additional security. Too little equity will prevent the company from accessing loan funding, and make the company far more vulnerable to a downturn in trading and other financial shocks.

By using a little more imagination and identifying the strengths of the growing business's financial structure, an entrepreneur can construct a financing package that is both more flexible and more cost-effective than traditional funding. Finding such a funder (or indeed a combination of funders) may not be easy but it will always be worth the effort.

Kevin R Smith is Managing Director of AWS Structured Finance Ltd, international financial consultants, and can be contacted on 01892 667 891 or email kevin.r.smith@awsconsult.co.uk

5 | **Raising Capital**

Kevin R Smith

Once a business opportunity has been identified, market research carried out and the concept of a strategy and financing needs have been thought through, it is time to move forward and take the steps necessary to turn the concept into reality. There are clearly many steps to this process, but the most critical will be your ability to raise capital. To achieve this you will need a business plan. In preparing this document all necessary steps will need to be identified and your strategy clarified.

WRITING THE BUSINESS PLAN

Writing a good business plan is not only the first step but also the most important one. The business plan is the first real contact that the new business will have with potential funders, and not only will it say a lot about the business, but its presentation will also say a lot about the management. For any new business, funders are at least as interested in the management team as in the business. The plan will demonstrate how clearly the managers have thought through their business idea and how methodical and detailed their approach to the business is likely to be.

If the business plan is the most important document, the two-page executive summary at the front of the document is the most important section. Banks and equity investors are bombarded with business plans, and many potential funders will not read further than the executive summary unless it grabs their attention. If it

I'm ready to be my own boss.

'I know there's a lot to think about. Finding customers. Making sure they pay you. And then making sure they come back again and again. Money's just one of my worries. But I've talked to my bank and, amazingly, they can give me all the solutions I need.'

BANKING WORTH TALKING ABOUT

Talk to us about more than money on
0800 056 0056

Lloyds TSB
Business

How to...Set Up In Business
By Lloyds TSB

With more than three million small businesses in the UK, self-employment is already proving to provide a high degree of personal satisfaction, making it easy to see why it's an attractive proposition. Whatever the reason for starting out on your own, the rewards can be great. However, it can also be challenging, demanding and sometimes frustrating.

David Singleton, Managing Director of Lloyds TSB Business, has put together the following tips to help you before taking the plunge:

Your Objective

Decide your business vision and financial goals – it may sound obvious but ask yourself why you want to run your own company? Is it because you want to make huge profits or because you cannot stand the idea of working for someone else? Think also about how you envisage the progress of the business once it's up and running. Your ideas might be fantastic but have you got the patience and drive it takes to turn the dream into reality?

Your Skills

What experience do you have in the business you're looking to enter? Running a business also means running everything initially from financial management, marketing, operations and managing people. Do you already have contacts you can use for advice and support? Training, self-help and professional advice is available to you and you can talk to your bank about where to get the help and information you need.

Your Preparation

Good business preparation shows commitment and confidence in your business. It shows that you have thought out your plans, you know where you're heading and what it is you want to achieve – and that it's realistic.

Your Finance

Finding money to start-up is not always a simple task. There are a number of options available to raise finance including trade credit, bank overdrafts and loans, leasing/hire purchase and grants and you need to think about the type of finance that suits your needs. An overdraft can give day to day flexibility to business needs, as there is no fixed repayment, however, leasing and hire purchase are simple ways to fund the purchase of capital items like cars and computers whose value depreciates over time.

Your Premises

Where will you run your business from? Some businesses start out from the owner's living room but this may not always be possible. Premises are often a big commitment – there may be rent or mortgage and maintenance costs to consider, including insurance and security.

Your Marketing

Marketing is about winning customer preference – you need to have enough demand for your product or service to warrant running the business. Businesses often struggle with promotion and may decide to advertise in the press and on the radio. This is the obvious option but can be expensive. An alternative is to launch your business with an event, inviting press and prospective customers. It goes without saying that good 'word of mouth' recommendations can bring in the best and most loyal custom.

Bearing in mind these tips can help increase your chances of turning your entrepreneurial dreams into reality. Although it's hard work, running your own business can also be one of the most rewarding things you ever do.

Our business Starter pack guides people through the process of setting up a business, and includes Start-up RouteMap. This is available for free along with further information on Lloyds TSB's range of products and services from Lloyds TSB branches, or by calling us on **0800 056 0056** and visiting our dedicated website at www.lloydstsb.com/success4business

does not, all the time and effort put into developing the rest of the plan will be wasted.

The business plan should be split up into logical sections, and each section should be broken down to ensure that all the important points are covered. The following areas are critical:

I **Executive summary.** Describe the key elements of the business, the market in which it will operate, key reasons for success and barriers to entry. Identify risks and how they will be managed, outline strategic objectives and potential for growth, state key strengths of the management team and past successes, present headline financial projections and, lastly, indicate how much finance is required and what it will be used for.

I **Background.** Provide a history (if one exists) of the business. Describe the industry (ie size, major participants, growth potential, barriers to entry, outside influences etc).

I **Market.** Demonstrate that a market exists for your product/service, estimate market share, assess competition, describe your customers and how you will obtain them, and outline competitive advantages.

I **Product/service.** Describe the product or service and advantages over existing providers, outline future development and detail any patent or intellectual property issues. Outline production/delivery issues and expected future requirements and premises.

I **Management team.** Identify key management and their roles, outline background and skills. Identify any weaknesses in the team and how they will be addressed. The managers will be expected to demonstrate their financial commitment to the project.

I **Business strategy.** Demonstrate deep understanding of the market and business in the proposed strategy. This should be demanding but realistic. Outline areas such as capital expenditure, staff recruitment, marketing and selling, together with proposed timing.

I **Financial planning.** Demonstrate careful thought in the financial projections and the assumptions but be concise (use appendices where necessary). Provide external corroboration of forecasts and assumptions where possible and for an existing business include historic accounts. Provide sensitivity analysis.

The business plan should be well presented and logical, and if a lot of detailed information is to be included this is often best done by using appendices. If the plan is muddled, has gaping holes in the information provided, has many typing or grammatical errors or anything else that undermines the professional feel of the document, this can often be enough for it to be rejected irrespective of the quality of the underlying business proposal, because the reader will have lost confidence in the management team.

TAKING PROFESSIONAL ADVICE

The biggest problem that affects people wishing to establish a business is the limited amount of financial resources available to them. Trying to raise funding is much easier said than done. It is important that all aspects of establishing a business are properly understood, and the business case must be presented professionally when trying to raise funding.

One area in which some entrepreneurs look to save money is the use of outside experts and paying for professional assistance. Unfortunately this can all too often be a false economy. Professional assistance can make the difference between success and failure in raising funding or in the business itself.

What professional advice is needed will clearly depend upon the areas of expertise of the management, the type of business and a range of other issues, but there are a number of core areas such as accounting and legal issues.

Financial advice is often needed to build up the detailed financial forecasts and to ensure that they are accurate, realistic, and that all the issues have been properly considered. Mistakes are most commonly to be found in areas such as tax and VAT. Missing out costs or not timing cash flows properly can totally undermine the economic viability of a business case, and at the very least does not instil confidence in the business or management as a whole.

In addition to the general areas of professional advice there are a number of specific areas on which funders will ultimately require a professional opinion. These include matters such as intellectual property rights, copyright, certain employment and tax-related issues, asset and property values, environmental impact and other areas requiring specialist knowledge.

Independent professional advice or corroboration of parts of the business plan will greatly increase the impact of it and demonstrate that a thorough approach has been undertaken in its preparation. For all these reasons, careful expenditure on advisers should reap dividends.

IDENTIFYING EXTERNAL EQUITY SOURCES

As we have seen in other sections, there are a number of different sources of equity available, from high-net-worth individuals to multi-billion-pound investment companies. While not all of these potential sources of equity are members of an association, the majority tend to be. Identifying individual sources of equity funds can be a slow and painful process, but this can be made much easier by identifying the associations first.

Probably the largest such organization is the British Venture Capital Association (BVCA), with 298 members that include most of the biggest and best-known investment funds in the UK. The details of all the members of BVCA can be obtained through the BVCA (see Appendix 2). All investment funds provide an outline of the type of investment that they consider, which stage, sector, size of investment and similar details, but this should be viewed more as marketing material than as something that should be relied upon. Relatively few investment funds advertise that they invest in start-ups, and experience shows that many fewer will be interested in doing so when contacted.

Once possible sources of funding have been identified, there is no substitute for making direct contact in order to discuss whether your requirements fit with the funders' present requirements. In order not to waste too much of your or their time, it is generally preferable to have an initial conversation and then if a funder is interested in principle, send a written executive summary. If the

AWS STRUCTURED FINANCE LTD

INTERNATIONAL FINANCIAL CONSULTANTS

Need assistance with *debt, equity* or other aspects of *financing* your company?

We can help at any stage from *concept* or *business planning* through *writing a business plan* or advising on *strategy*, to *structuring* the most effective and bankable financing structure.

Our approach is a very *practical* one, based on real *experience* of what works and how to make things happen.

We offer a very *personalised service* and develop long term relationships with our clients.

High quality assistance but at a very *competitive cost.*

Improve your business opportunities.

Call us to see how *AWS* can make a difference.

Tel: 01892 667891   Fax: 01892 610891
Email: kevin.r.smith@awsconsult.co.uk

funder remains interested it is then necessary to exchange a confidentiality agreement and, once this is returned, to send the full
business plan and arrange a meeting.

There are a number of large associations of business angels (ie
high-net-worth individual investors) around the country, and these
can often be located through the local Business Link or similar
organizations. Many of the business angel networks provide a
service that allows the company looking for funding to prepare a
brief presentation, which is then circulated to the association
members by way of a regular newsletter. Alternatively they may
hold investment fairs where companies are invited to meet with
potential investors. The whole procedure with business angels is
rather less formal than with investment funds, and as the decision
is often made partly with the heart, the process is rather more hit
and miss.

Like most aspects of starting a business, identifying external
equity sources can take much more time and effort than may at first
be appreciated. Once potential sources have been identified the
next steps also drag on, and the whole process can take many
months, so it is best to accept this and to allow for it at the outset,
rather than hope that matters will progress very quickly.

As with any other 'quote', it is best to obtain more than one initial
offer in order to ensure that the best possible deal is obtained. A
decision will need to be made as to which offer looks most suitable,
prior to spending any time or incurring any costs.

FIRST ROUND FINANCE

First round finance, as the name would suggest, is the first tranche
of investment into a new company. As with many definitions,
though, it can mean different things to different people. Does the
capital put in by the founders and their friends and family count as
first round funding or not? Here we will look at first round funding
as the first time a company has sought to attract external equity in
order to establish a new business.

Of all the times that a company will look to raise outside
investment over its life, none will prove to be more difficult than
first round funding. This is because there are very few sources of

such funding and a lot of demand for the limited supply. The reason that there are so few investors prepared to invest in start-ups is because the risks are much higher and there is no real track record. From the investors' viewpoint, of course, when they get it right the rewards can also be much higher.

In addition to the difficulties of raising first round finance, raising small amounts (ie less than £1 million) of equity is often more difficult than raising larger amounts. Many of the equity funds and providers of venture capital take the view that the level of work involved is similar irrespective of the amount actually invested, and as such it is not economic for them to invest less than £1 million.

The most common source of funding for start-ups and lower levels of funding is 'business angels'. (See page 52 for more information on these.) However, perhaps the best-known sources of equity are the investment funds and venture capital funds run by city institutions (see page 52).

Since 1983 over £35 billion has been invested by the UK private equity industry in around 20,500 companies in Britain. However, for the 298 member companies of the British Venture Capital Association, over 50 per cent of investments are for expansion of existing companies (ie second and third round financing) and the next largest type of investment is for acquisitions, management buyouts and the like, leaving only a very small amount for first round financing.

PREPARING FOR DUE DILIGENCE

Once a potential investor has been found, any investment decision will be subject to due diligence. Due diligence is the process that covers all aspects of the funder getting comfortable with checking out what they have been told about the company, the marketplace, legal titles, ownership of assets and so on. Investment funds will have a well-practised, comprehensive procedure for making these enquiries, but business angels are likely to be rather less formal.

The due diligence procedure will often include external accountants and lawyers as well as other specialists able to provide an unbiased, detailed report. The better prepared the management team is for this process, the quicker and easier it will be. It is worth noting that while the due diligence process will be run by the potential funder, and all experts will be appointed by, and report to, the funder, the costs will be borne by the company requiring the investment. (Payment will be made from the investment proceeds, and can quite easily amount to a considerable amount.)

NEGOTIATION AND CLOSING

There is an almost infinite number of different variations on how the equity can be structured, and as such plenty of scope for negotiation. As with any negotiations, there needs to be a degree of flexibility on both sides and a desire to find the middle ground.

It is important for the SME to work with trusted advisers to assist with the negotiations, as the investor will have much more experience in such matters, and it is easy for the SME to fail to push for the best deal simply through lack of knowledge.

The structure of the deal and the negotiations will shape the future cooperation of the parties, and can also lead to a massive difference in the value the founders get for selling a stake in their business. As such it is extremely important.

The final closing meeting will almost inevitably involve more people, take longer and be more fraught with last-minute issues than is often imagined. Not only will the SME and the investor be present, but so too will accountants, lawyers and other advisers from both sides, as well as any other funders (such as banks) that are involved. Once all the documentation has finally been signed, the management team will be free to concentrate on growing the business until the next stage of funding is required.

Kevin R Smith is Managing Director of AWS Structured Finance Ltd, international financial consultants, and can be contacted on 01892 667 891 or email kevin.r.smith@awsconsult.co.uk

Part Three:

Essential Management Functions

Marketing

There is a lot of confusion about marketing. This stems from two sources. First, the definition of 'marketing' must be clarified. And second, the amount of resources a small business should allocate to it needs to be addressed.

The definition is simple to deal with. To marketing professionals and academics, marketing can be summed up as 'making what you can sell'. To the public it is more usually thought of as 'selling what you can make'. If you are to run a successful business, the first definition is the better one to be guided by, and so a more holistic approach is necessary, involving what those in the trade refer to as the four 'P's: product, price, place and promotion. To this the public relations industry also adds a fifth 'P': perception.

The amount of resources you can and should allocate to marketing is much more subjective. There is no empirical test to tell you what you must spend in time or money in order to achieve any specific level of return. The marketing industry, in all its many forms from advertising salespeople and trade show organizers to copywriters and PR agents, will make cogent arguments for the necessity of using its services. And being salespeople they will often make you worry that you will be left behind if you do not use them. The bottom line should never be 'Can you afford not to?', but always 'Will the marketing return justify the costs?' No doubt everyone would like to take full page colour spreads in the weekend supplements backed up by television and billboard campaigns, but clearly that is not an option to those on a limited budget. This chapter will try to indicate some of the options available to those on a small business budget.

MARKET RESEARCH

The beginning of your marketing process should begin long before you start trading your new product. This applies as much to Microsoft's latest software as to the new hairdressing salon on the high street. They must both establish if there is a market demand for a new product and what exactly the demand is for; they must conduct market research. The difference is that Microsoft has rather larger marketing resources than the hairdresser does.

Established businesses have a huge advantage over start-up businesses in carrying out market research. They have an enormous exposure to market sentiment and reaction every day through their current business activities. Added to this is their database of past and current customers which they ought to be able to analyse and, should they wish, contact for views and opinions. This information can also form the basis for extrapolating their current data to build up likely market information for different geographic areas or market sectors.

The brand-new start-up company is unlikely to have any of these resources readily available to it, and while discussion among like-minded competitors is often a lot more open than you might expect, you will not be handed databases and customer views by your future competition! As such, the prospective businessperson must try to build a picture of what the market for the intended product or idea is currently like, and whether there is sufficient demand for the concept with its benefits. This can be done by collecting either brand new data direct from the marketplace specifically for your own purposes (primary data) or data already gathered by others that you can shape for your own use (secondary data). Obviously primary data will be more relevant, more current, and you can assess how reliable it will be, as you will know how it was collected and collated. Secondary data may well require you to make some assumptions as to how and where it was gathered and how reliable it is; it may be slightly out of date, and also is likely to be only partially about the information you require. However, it will be vastly cheaper to acquire.

In today's economy there is no shortage of information available. The trick is to sift out the wheat from the chaff. Identifying the correct questions to ask is important. You must think carefully

Get more done in a day without 'upgrading the caffeine potency'

Perhaps it's not the people who need to work faster. It's the technology. Business broadband from BT enables heavy data to be quickly downloaded, uploaded and shared. The 'Always On' connection means no more waiting to access the internet. And because it's un-metered, you can spend all day on it without it making any difference to your phone bill. And right now, place an order for an Internet Business Pack and any product from the BT Openworld Business PLUS range* before 30th September 2002, and get £130** cash back. To stimulate productivity without the stimulants **Free***fone* **0800 389 8707** or connect to **BT.com/business**

BT.com/business   **Connections that get results. BT**

Technology made simple

When starting a business you are often faced with decisions that you have never had to consider before. Technology can be one of those decisions which seems expensive, time consuming and complex – but in fact the process is much simpler and less costly than you think.

Communicating through technology is essential for any business, regardless of size, but for a start-up it is crucial to choose wisely before investing. The time you save in the long-term by choosing the right technology from the start can be significant, such as faster automated order processing, administrative tasks carried out online and updates to customer records being possible via the PC. This can clearly have a positive effect on your business overheads and can cut costs dramatically in terms of more productive man-hours. There are also cost savings to be gained from paying one bill for one package of products and services. It allows you to keep track of and plan for additional technology changes as you grow.

Here are a few guidelines to consider before taking the plunge:

Be clear what you get for your money
Before buying, ask what is included in the offer and what is extra. For example, system down-time can lead to lost business, so a package that offers around-the-clock technical support, such as BT's Digital Office (see below) provides peace of mind and expert advice whenever it is needed.

Get the right connection
Higher bandwidth connection through broadband technology is easy to install and cost-effective. It means you can use web and phone at the same time, from a single telephone line – and all for a flat fee. You need never dial the internet again as access is immediate.

And keep it simple
Technology does not need to be complex – it is possible to have one, easily integrated system. BT SME – the specialists in helping small businesses – has identified a variety of solutions which you can choose from, in the form of BT Digital Office solutions, a raft of technology packages, services and support

designed to enable the small business to make best use of, and get most business benefit from, information and communications technology (ICT). It also ensures you do not have to deal with multiple suppliers and requires no up-front capital outlay, which is ideal for those businesses working to tight budgets or who don't have large amounts of capital to invest upfront.

BT has developed these packages in partnership with highly reputable companies, including Cisco, Dell, Microsoft, O2 and Nortel.

The BT Digital Office team will work with you to find the very best solution to meet your specific business needs but all Digital Office packages offer:

- Internet Access – ISP service offers "pay-as-you-go" and "unmetered" access options.

- Digital Lines – offers a range of high-speed Internet access methods, via ADSL or BT Highway.

- Business PCs – these range from standard desktops to ultra-slim laptops for mobile computing.

- Printer – a choice of printers from inkjets to network printers.

- Website – a two page website to help promote the business.

- Installation – the system is professionally installed and concludes with a full tutorial to brief users on the equipment and how it all works together.

- Support – whether the business needs help with a PC, applications, Internet. connection or line, there is just one single point of contact, one telephone number which you can call for immediate assistance.

- Finance – flexible and easy payment options to help spread the costs.

Microsoft business software comes with every package and helps you reduce the time you spend on reports, letters, analysing figures and creating brochures, flyers and newsletters. It can also be tailored with e-store so you can create an online store where customers can browse purchase products easily and securely.

BT works with over one million SMEs every year and understands the needs of new and growing businesses. If you would like to know more about getting your business online, making the most of technology and how BT can work with you to help your business, visit www.bt.com/business or call us on **0800 400 400.**

what factors you need to sell your product or service successfully. This will include the profile of your potential customers (age, spending power, where they live, family status, sex), a profile of the market (whether it is growing or shrinking, which sectors of the market are doing best and why, the long-term trend), and some marketing research (what your competitors are doing to sell their products, what is working and what is not).

If you intend to sell locally then your market research can be done more on a primary than on a secondary basis. You can go out and speak to potential customers; you can observe the competition. The more disparate your potential customer base, the more difficult it will be for you to track customers down and have a useful dialogue with them. In this case secondary data collection will become more important, and for tracking sector trends it will be your only option.

- Trade magazines and financial press will offer some information but probably unsystematically – that is, it will be pot luck what you find.
- The information you seek will most likely be somewhere on the Internet, but sourcing can be difficult, and assessing its reliability and how up to date it is, is often a problem.
- Larger libraries will have a range of market research books that can give you useful information.
- In addition to these sources you may find that your local authority business advice unit will have current information available to you, as will the local Chamber of Commerce and Business Link office.

Most of these sources of information will be either free or inexpensive to access. If you still require more information, you can purchase market information from market research and business information companies. The British Market Research Association will be able to provide a list: visit www.bmra.org.uk.

SEGMENTATION AND STRATEGY

Having gathered the relevant market information for your concept's sector your next marketing task is to identify where exactly your product or service fits within the sector. The most basic division is whether you want to sell to businesses or consumers. Consumers are more numerous and normally will pay higher prices, but they are more difficult to reach (they do not list themselves as companies do in trade directories and magazines, or the Yellow Pages with contact names and numbers), more fickle (most companies will not change their suppliers just because a new one comes around), and purchase in smaller quantities less regularly.

As a small business you will need to focus on specific segments of the market, as you will be unable to offer all things to all comers. Are you going for high-end users willing to pay for quality and/or uniqueness, or are you trying to provide a service locally where none currently exists? What is your 'unique selling point', or USP in marketing jargon, which differentiates you from the competition?

With your sector knowledge and your segment identified, you must now design your marketing strategy and thence plan. The information gained will indicate what is the best way to reach your potential customers:

- trade magazines;
- local press;
- national press;
- radio;
- bus advertising;
- promotions;
- trade shows;
- leafleting;
- direct mail;
- inserts.

You will have an idea of how generous or frugal your marketing budget can be, so you will have a feel for how much advertising and PR you will be able to afford. The research you have carried out to this point in identifying your gap in the market, who you should be selling to and what in particular it is they want, will provide a clear indication as to what type of media you should be using.

If your target market is well-paid young individuals who purchase goods for their image and lifestyle associations rather than pure value for money, then your advertising must be in media that project image and lifestyle. While this is obvious from the unpressurized standpoint of writing the business plan, when you are in the thick of trying to get some media exposure you can easily start to lose control of the original plan. Even the smallest business will be approached occasionally by sales departments wanting it to spend its money on promotion in their publications, on their products or at their shows. It is for this reason that it is very important to design a clear marketing strategy that you can refer to and keep as a controlling influence over the media offers that will come your way. Amend and update the strategy as an ongoing project certainly, but in your own time, not because someone else tells you to!

The strategy you build is like a road map – it will show you where you are and where you want to get to. It will also show the preferred route for getting there, and the most comprehensive strategies will also be able to show you how to get back on track if you lose your way or are detoured by events beyond your control. The first task is to set your targets – where you want to go – whether that is to increase sales by 15 per cent or open a new outlet. Then plan a timetable of marketing 'events': these can be any marketing action such as a press release, placing adverts, leafleting the local area, a trade show or whatever you choose. All will be chosen because they reach out specifically to your target market, and you believe they will bring in more in sales revenue than they cost.

Critical to all these 'events' is the evaluation process that you must go through after each one of them. Especially for a new business where the response to any event is fairly unpredictable, it is vital to know which types work and then work out why. The simplest way to track the success of events is to note down all responses you get from potential customers from the event and how many positive sales this leads to. It is very easy not to ask customers enquiring about your product where they heard about you, but it is also very foolish. Nobody will mind being asked, it gives an impression of a well-organized company, and vitally, it provides you with critical information on which to base future marketing events.

Beauty is in the detail.

Attention to detail. That's the beauty of the C-40 zoom digital camera. 4 megapixels, for sharper images.

Aperture and shutter controls for more creativity. And a 'my mode' feature, which remembers all your customised settings. Like they say, it's the little things that count.

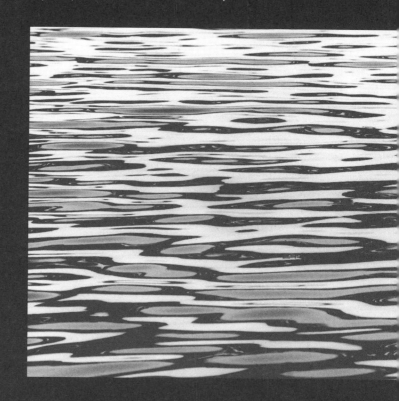

OLYMPUS DIGITAL C-40 ZOOM

Pictures taken on palm-sized C-40Z digital camera with 2.8x Olympus optical zoom.
4 million pixels (effective pixel number); 7.7 million pixel recorded image, up to 3200×2400 pixels.
www.olympus.co.uk or call 0800 0720070.

Make an impact and save money at the same time with digital photography

IMAGE IS EVERYTHING

Portraying your business and products in the best possible manner is essential to the success of any new venture. A picture may paint a thousand words - but if you can't paint then you have to get someone to do it for you, and that costs. In real terms, this has meant that, until recently, it was necessary to employ a photographer to take the required images for your marketing materials.

This incurs their fees, plus film and processing costs followed by an arcane art called reprographics. This is where you really are at the mercy of the experts. For reasons that never seem clear, it is essential to part with cash to have your perfectly good picture put into a form that printers can use. Worse still, you pay by the millimeter according to the size of the picture that is to appear.

IMAGES ARE EVERYTHING

Unless you are writing a thesis on theoretical physics, photographs make all the difference in most business communications. Quickest to catch on to accessible digital photography were probably the more upmarket estate agents. Digital images could be on a website in minutes, emailed to a key potential client, or dropped into one-off copies of details. In short – a digital camera gave them competitive advantage.

The Internet has been key in this development and digital cameras, even early on, provided images at a fast rate - a key for website success.

However, most companies still produce conventional material and those that do it regularly know the cost of conventional photography, but do not feel there is a good enough alternative.

IMAGES ARE EVERYWHERE BUT ARE THEY GOOD ENOUGH TO PRINT

Things have moved on fast even in the last six months, so let's get a few popular misconceptions out of the way first. Lets not worry about the terminology – it will become familiar.

Affordable digital cameras can't take photographs that are good enough for printed promotional material.
Wrong.

Providing the lens is good and the CCD sensor is over a certain size it is quite possible to use digital images from a model under £200.

The Olympus C-220Zoom is the latest entry level zoom compact that offers all this at under £200. It has a 2 million pixel CCD that is capable of excellent reproduction, up to at least A5 size, and is excellent for general use. It even comes with simple to use software that allows you to manipulate, resize and catalogue images you have taken.

You have to know about photography, computers and publishing to take brochure quality material.
Wrong again - Providing you follow a few simple rules you can take perfectly acceptable photographs for many uses. Naturally a flair for photography helps if you are going to try something a bit more adventurous. For more professional or stylised work you can still use a photographer, but specify that the material is digital to save money on reproduction and film costs.

Models like the Olympus C-3020 Zoom offer 3 million pixels and with a range of exposure functions to give you more control and flexibility. At under £500 it is perfect for more demanding use and can produce excellent prints up to full size A4.

Designers and printers are sniffy about digital images.
Sure, the front cover of Vogue is a major affair but most designers will happily use digital images. One designer in particular uses digital images regularly for that staple of the company brochure - the pack shot. In their case the printer didn't believe the images were from a relatively modest digital camera, proving that many people are still unaware of how fast things have progressed.

Take a practical example of something that depends on quality images - a car magazine. A publisher was concerned that he spent £30,000 a year on film processing and repro (transferring the film results to the designer's computer). He recognised that his photographer knew what he was doing and had no intention of taking the pictures himself. However, he felt that a lot of the basic shots - close ups, wheels, trim, accessories etc could be done digitally. He tried the Olympus C-4040Zoom and E-20 P, the current 4 and 5 million pixel models, and was amazed. The photographer loved them, took even more shots for them to choose from, while the publisher saved money on film and repro as the images could be transferred direct to the design process.

SO WHY WAIT?
No reason at all – the time is perfect.

Just think – presentations on computer or in print, email shots using html and images for impact, fax shots, brochures, newsletters, cd's, adverts, training programmes! You name it, if photographs are involved you can have more material prepared quicker. With spectacular quality available right now it needn't cost a fortune – after all your image is everything.

IMAGE

Part of the marketing function is to build your business's and products' image. As a small business you will have very limited resources to address to this area of marketing. You should be focusing your product trading on a homogenous sector of the market, and your goal should be to present as coherent an image for your business as possible, across all its aspects. Essentially, all companies do this. If we look at the Ford Motor Company, their Ford branded cars are placed so as to be attractive and affordable to the mass market, but Ford also owns Jaguar and Aston Martin, executive and super-luxury cars, which it keeps very distinct from the Ford name in their marketing, although it is well known that many components are shared between the different cars in the group range.

It is therefore important to consider the impact that every marketing event you undertake will have on your entire range of goods, not just the single item you are promoting. The quality of the material used in your advertising or promotion will underscore the message you want to get across. That your business's reputation takes years to build but can be destroyed in moments is no less true for being a well-worn cliché.

DIRECT MARKETING

Direct mail is often considered to be the black sheep of the marketing toolbox. However, it is really a victim of its own success. If the response rate to direct mail was not so high, in terms of cost to increased sales, then it would not be as prevalent as it is currently. It is this prevalence that leads to the problem of 'junk mail' piling up behind your door every morning.

The advantage of direct mail to the marketer is that it is very flexible. You can choose your recipients' geographic area, their income level, their leisure preferences and so on. You can also choose how much you wish to spend on any given mailout with great flexibility. The drawbacks are in choosing to whom the mailout should be sent, the expense and the legal implications. For the start-up business, purchasing a list can be relatively expensive, and also requires a degree of specialist knowledge in selecting your list broker and the criteria by which the particular list is built up. It is worth researching the use of direct marketing carefully if you intend to spend a significant percentage of your marketing budget on it. The British Direct Marketing Association (www.dma.org.uk and 020 7291 3300) can provide much useful information. For overseas information, Kogan Page publishes *The Directory of International Direct and E-Marketing* annually.

If your business is well established you are likely to have built up a database of past customers' details. If your business is not of the type where you collect your customers' details as a matter of course, it is worth considering methods by which you might be able to gather such information through a loyalty card, notification of sales offers or similar schemes. When you have a list of customers you are in a position where not only can you re-contact them, but you may be able to trade your list with other companies in your area. However, there are increasingly strict data protection laws governing notification of customers (at the time of taking their details) if you wish to share their details, in any way, with other bodies. Again the DMA can guide you with this.

ADVERTISING AND PR

It should be so simple to get your message across. You know your product or service inside out, you understand the benefits and you recognize the quality. What is more frustrating is you also know that people will enjoy using your product – all you have to do is persuade them to try it. And that is the problem.

The situation is difficult because all your competitors are trying to gain the consumer's attention as well. There is a lot of 'noise' out there in the marketplace and your job is to make sure you are heard above everyone else. Advertising and PR are your routes to doing this, but be aware that the market in the UK is very sophisticated and it will take a fair amount of expertise to make your business stand out. This chapter is not able to cover the vast range of skills and advice needed to ensure that your advert or press release is eye-catching, but the basic principles are simple enough, although the details are where the difference is made.

- ABC – accuracy, brevity, clarity – make good copy.
- Avoid jargon and formality.
- Never bend the truth (this includes phrases like 'once in a lifetime chance' if it is not): it cheapens the message and damages your reputation.
- Keep it interesting and relevant (if you are writing a press release, open with an idea that will work as a headline).

The ability to write good adverts and press releases is gained more through experience than natural skill. If you have the time to learn about it then it will be time well spent; if not, it may well pay you to find an expert to help you out. If you have any contacts in the media they may be able to help draft the copy for you and show you what makes the difference. If this route is not available and you feel your attempts with only a book to help you are uninspiring, then it may be time to use professional help – the PR agent.

The problem with PR agencies is that you have to pay them! That in itself is not surprising, but quantifying their success is awkward. Most agencies will be keen to get you on a monthly retainer. If your marketing budget can afford this, then it will probably serve you to sign up to a limited-term contract, as you will then be able to set out exactly what you expect the agency to provide, over what time period, and discuss with it what it hopes to achieve in this period in terms of copy placed or extra sales achieved.

The advantage of PR agencies, beyond their ability to write successful copy, is that they should have a good selection of media contacts through which they can get your message heard. Your business is to produce and sell a successful product; often this will not give you much space to build relationships with the media, and your PR agent is there to overcome this barrier. Agents' businesses are based on their ability to get their clients' messages into the media, be it local press, national press, radio or any other medium that works, through an established network of contacts.

In choosing an agent or agency you must therefore make sure of a number of key points:

- The most important is that you trust the agency. This means that you should get hold of references from their existing clients and see what the agency has done for them.
- You should also feel completely comfortable working with the

agency. Do you have a rapport? Does it understand your business implicitly? Does it have time for your business? How quickly do staff return your initial calls?

▮ Beyond your relationship with the agency staff, you need to know how effective they are. What are their copywriting skills like? Not all are as good as each other by any means. What are their media contacts like, especially in the area of the media you are interested in?

▮ Get a limited-term contract written up that sets out your requirements and budget.

▮ Keep a very tight rein on costs – often the retainer fee will be small while the 'extras' can mount up quickly.

Towards the end of the limited-term contract (you may need six months before any real progress can be judged), evaluate what difference to your profit margins the PR agency has made. If you feel that it is negligible, then discuss this with the agency and, if needs be, be prepared to leave it.

DAMAGE LIMITATION

An area often overlooked in small businesses is a damage limitation or crisis management plan. PR agents should be good at helping develop these, but they are essentially straightforward and you should be able to create a plan yourself.

No business wants a crisis, but inevitably, they will appear from time to time, in varying degrees of severity. If you have taken time to consider what you should best do in various disaster scenarios before they occur, you will be very much better placed to deal with them should the scenario become reality. Not only will the plan give you a clear idea of how to progress, but its very existence should reassure you and give a sense of calm.

Crisis management falls into two parts. The first is how to deal with the practical side of the problem, whether it is power or machine failure that stops production, transport problems that prevent distribution to customers, accident or injury to personnel or – perhaps the most business-critical – a problem with the product that causes illness, injury or significant financial problems to the customer. Your plan will identify each different scenario and then follow it through certain stages: action to stop further damage and action to restore service. The second element is the communications side. There should be clear procedures to inform your customers what the problem is, how long it will continue, what measures are being taken to rectify the problem, and what measures are being taken to ensure it does not occur again. With health and safety issues you will also need procedures to notify relatives of injury or, heaven forbid, fatality.

You will also need to have a plan for dealing with the press. This is, from a marketing point of view, where the plan comes into its own. The reputation of your business will rely on a single coherent message being put out about the crisis. A single senior person, essentially the owner or chairperson, should be the spokesperson. That individual should unambiguously give out all the known facts, avoid any conjecture, indicate how the problem is being contained, and ensure that any essential safety information is clearly provided. The silver lining to crises is that the media attention can be turned to the business's advantage if it is correctly handled. The eradication of panic and chaotic reaction will go a long way to doing this.

THE INTERNET

The limitations of the Internet as a transforming marketing tool have been seen clearly in the last two years. The reality that the Internet will not instantly create an endless stream of cheap sales has been clearly, if belatedly, understood. With hindsight, it is becoming clearer that the Internet is good as a very effective means of providing information about businesses. It is not so good at directly selling products or services.

In a way this is good news for the small business. It is relatively cheap to establish a simple Web site for your business, but expensive to set up a transactional site. A simple Web site should provide as much information as possible, without running the risk of becoming quickly out of date. So give a brief description of what your business does as a necessary opening requirement, and take the opportunity to show where the business originated from and

STAY AHEAD OF THE COMPETITION

As competition for new and existing customers grows, businesses need to gain an advantage over their rivals and find alternative ways of generating new trade. he Internet is one of the most accessible tools to do this, as it opens doors to both a wider national and international marketplace.

Companies can overcome traditional barriers of distance, nationality and time zones by using the Internet to buy and sell products and services. A web site is accessible 24 hours a day, seven days a week, offering customers around the clock access. This is a key benefit to international commerce as your business may be operating over several different time zones.

A user-friendly, accessible web site is key to developing a wider customer base both in the UK and overseas. This will attract potential customers and also encourage visits to translate to sales. There are a number of steps businesses can take to do this.

- Design a web site which displays as many products and services as possible, as the web site may be the only point of contact that customers choose to have.

- Include password protected areas on the web site, so customers can check order progress or account status.

- Develop a multi-lingual site that customers around the globe can read and understand. Start with one key market and look to develop as trade increases.

- Introduce facilities for multi-currency payments and a currency converter. Ensure your customers are aware of the online security measures you have in place.

- Make international trading terms clear on the web site, with pricing, payment, duty, delivery options, and returns policies spelt out for overseas customers.

UK online for business is a partnership between industry and Government that aims to help firms make the most of the business opportunities the Internet can offer them.

Through a network of local business advisers, UK online for business can offer cost-effective, impartial advice, helping you find the right information and communication technology (ICT) solutions for your business.

UK online for business can also help you adapt your e-commerce strategy for both national and international marketplaces. The publication "E-Commerce — How Trading Online Can Work For You" offers advice on how to make the most of opportunities made available through e-commerce and "Doing International Business Online" demonstrates how you can enter the international marketplace.

Both these publications are available free — together with case studies and additional resources — from www.ukonlineforbusiness.gov.uk

For more information on how UK online for business can help your business, call the Infoline on 0845 715 2000 or visit www.ukonlineforbusiness.gov.uk

why, as this draws the reader in. Include a clear list of what products or services you offer, with greater detail available if possible. Given that your Web site is primarily an information rather than a dialogue portal, it is important to provide a postal address and telephone contact numbers. It is also useful to provide a guide to 'who is who' in the business so that the appropriate person can be contacted, although be aware that this can also act as an open invitation to every salesperson, recruitment agency and e-mail spammer in the country!

The expensive element of the Internet comes into play if you wish to conduct sales over the Net. You can acquire simple Web trading packages for substantially under £1,000, but sophisticated sites require a much greater investment in computer hardware and software, which will need a substantial volume of transactions to make them profitable. Many companies are now realizing that the consumer primarily wants information from the Web site and is happier to make purchases by traditional means. Clearly this does not apply to all products and businesses, and there will be many successful Internet sales businesses in the future, but unless you intend to be an Internet specialist you must cost carefully the investment required (and time involved in developing and maintaining the software and equipment) against your expected return.

Luckily there is an enormous amount of detailed information on Internet marketing, both freely available on the Internet itself and in printed form.

TRADE SHOWS AND EXHIBITIONS

Trade fairs and exhibitions are great opportunities to showcase your business and increase your sales, but like all other parts of the marketing equation you have to know why you are there and what you want to get out of the event. Just turning up and 'being there' will be an unrewarding experience. Therefore you must go through the – now hopefully familiar – routine of asking yourself what your objectives are from being at a trade fair. They might be to launch a new product; heighten your profile in a particular geographic area; increase sales to a specialist sector. Evaluate a realistic target for the exhibition: get 200 new potential customer names; sell £10,000 of product; get a profile in the local press, and so on.

Having identified your specific objectives you will find it much easier to decide whether or not the trade fair is appropriate. Ask for the media pack from the organizers to see who goes, where they are from and what you can expect them to spend. Time and money invested in an unsuccessful trade show can easily be avoided by a little research at this point.

Once at the exhibition hall, as with other advertising, you must make yourself stand out from the crowd. A little money invested in bright and clear display materials will pay dividends quickly if the alternative is an amateurish look. Probably the most important task is to make sure that your staff are enthusiastic and knowledgeable. An upbeat and animated person on the stand will be more successful than a bored and embarrassed person, regardless of the product or quality of display materials.

Finally, the post-exhibition follow-up is vital. Throughout your marketing process any lead that is not followed up is a lost lead, and therefore money wasted. With trade shows you should plan your follow-up procedure before you go to the show, so that you can get it dealt with swiftly afterwards. This avoids the risk that you delay it too long so that it never happens, or happens too late, and also ensures that your follow-up, whether it be an enquiry form or telephone call, gets to the customer before anyone else's.

Checklist

▮ Do you 'make what you can sell' or try to 'sell what you can make'?

▮ How carefully do you collect your sales data and analyse it?

▮ What are the key research objectives you need to answer? Have you carried out any primary research? How objective have you made it?

▮ What is your ideal customer profile? Does it exist in your area?

■ Have you clearly identified your USP? What sort of potential market does this direct you to? Does it exist in your area?

■ Have you considered all potential markets in your area? Are you going for the most accessible and / or lucrative? If not, are you happy why this is the case?

■ How can you best reach your customers? Do you have any experience with this form of media? Do you know how best to utilize it?

■ Are you confident your cost of marketing for any event is less than its minimum likely return? If not, do you know why you are spending money on it?

■ Does your product or service lend itself to direct marketing? If not, are you sure there is not an angle you are missing?

■ Have you considered investing in a PR agent? If so, do you have a mutually agreed list of targets and timetable to achieve them by?

■ Are you maximizing your profitable exposure to the Internet? This can mean, are you spending either too much on it or not enough?

7 | Sales and Customer Relations

Conducting sales is the pivotal moment of the business process. However, it can turn out to be incidental after all the toil and preparation that has been involved to get you to that point. As we stress throughout this guide, your likelihood of achieving a good performance in any area of business management is greatly enhanced by thinking through the process, setting your objectives and creating a plan to realize them. It is no different with sales.

In fact, building a plan is probably more important for sales than in any other area. This is not because it is a particularly complex task but because the plan will help keep you focused and committed.

REJECTION, PERSISTENCE AND THE SMALL BUSINESS FACTOR

There are several key factors that drive the success of any sales strategy or salesperson. Foremost among them, is that it is important that all those involved in the act of selling are aware that they are being 'paid to be rejected'. That is the salesperson's function. The continuation of this thought is that until the salesperson has been rejected, he or she is not actually doing any selling, just offering. It is the ability to manage the rejection, turn it to his or her advantage and be thick-skinned enough to persist after a string of rejections that marks out the good salesperson from the poor one.

Being rejected is a wearisome business, and the fear of being rejected often a considerable barrier to overcome. If the salesperson cannot view the possibility of rejection in a positive manner then it will be very difficult for him or her to make another sales attempt, and the fear of further rejection will make the person awkward and reticent – the very factors that attract rejection. In sales like nowhere else, success breeds success and failure begets failure.

If rejection is the salesperson's function, then persistence is his or her watchword. If the salesperson does not make another sales call then he or she cannot hope to get another sale. The statistics are well documented, that the more persistent the salesperson, the more successful he or she will be. The well worn Pareto Rule or 80:20 ratio works well here. Eighty per cent of your sales will come from 20 per cent of your customers. Furthermore, 80 per cent of your sales will come from 20 per cent of your salespeople.

This is where the small business factor comes in. If you are Unilever then these 80:20 statistics will apply. You can afford a mass of below-average customers if you have a hard core of excellent ones. Similarly, you can cope with less able sales personnel if you have an elite team of excellent ones. If you are a small business then there is absolutely no room for this under-performance. You must use all your management skills to achieve the highest return possible from your sales. (Of course, Unilever do this as well and with larger resources – but their margins for error are more generous.)

BUILDING A STRATEGY AND THE SALES PROCESS

Your sales strategy and your marketing strategy are inevitably closely connected, and will frequently be part of the same document. The sales strategy will be based on the same set of objectives and data from which your marketing strategy was built. The key to your sales strategy is keeping it simple. If it is too complex then it may well become entangled and unfocused. Presuming that you have correctly identified your target market, sales success is largely based on hard work and persistence. If your strategy is simple then following it up, consistently and persistently, will be straightforward. If it is complex then you are likely to lose clarity on who you should be following up.

So identify your objectives. What are the key markets and timescales you are going to pursue? Set realistic targets for numbers of prospects to contact and the level of sales increase to be achieved.

You should have already identified from historical data which are your best-selling lines, who buys them and how the market's development may alter this in the months ahead. Given that you have focused your marketing in this direction, you should already have 'softened up' the reception you can hope to get when the sales force begins. For the purposes of the strategy your sales force may comprise a team of trained sales personnel or it may be just yourself. This does not alter the structure of the strategy.

You have already identified your customer profile, so targeting a list of 'prospects' should be relatively simple. Match your potential prospects as closely as possible to the ideal profile. Having assembled a prospects list you must work out how best to attract each one. Will they all respond to similar benefits, or are some cost-led and others function-led, while others are perhaps more time or service-led? With most prospects this knowledge will only come from speaking with them, so it is now necessary actually to make contact. The earlier you do this the better – there is no advantage to be gained by prevaricating.

Arrange a meeting if at all possible; buyers will think you less opportunistic if you can plan ahead and give them some time. The arrangement can be made by letter, which is slow and impersonal; e-mail (if you can get their address), which can be more personal, but also can be interpreted as lazy; or preferably by telephone. This establishes a voice contact; you can gauge reaction immediately, and if you are confident, it is most likely to gain you a meeting. The rejection will also come more swiftly, if it is going to come. Consider this as being a positive thing as you no longer need to spend time wondering.

The rejection is a sales opportunity. If it is handled correctly, very few customers will say 'no' to your parting question, 'Do you mind if I contact you again in X months?' Attached to your 'prospect list' should be a 'prospects sheet' where you note how many times you have tried to make contact, when you finally do make contact, what the reaction was, and what action is to be taken in the future. From this you will be able to determine if there is a pattern to the sales approach. Does time of call, type of customer, or some other factor make a difference to the sales result? What are the most common reasons for rejection? Do you have a good response to these reasons? Can they be improved?

The sales plan will therefore comprise a list of objectives, a timescale, targets, and then prospects and notes on what features of your particular product or service may be attractive to them. It will also contain past 'prospect sheets' with the analysed sales data.

MOTIVATING AND REWARDING THE SALES TEAM

As we have noted, selling can be psychologically draining. Without some form of incentive the salespeople can quickly lose that vital edge that makes them successful. As soon as the hunger to close a sale disappears, the chances of a successful conclusion fall significantly. It is therefore critical to keep the sales team motivated and well rewarded.

Your initial task is to discover what motivates the sales force. If you do not offer sufficiently attractive rewards they will not act as good incentives. The motivational rewards do not have to be in the form of cash. It may well be that time off, travel vouchers, car parking spaces or meals out are more welcome. Offer a list of alternatives to your salespeople and let them gauge what they would like. It is often a good idea to offer different levels of reward so that there is an incentive for coming second or third, or showing certain levels of improvement, as well as for being the best.

The timescale for any motivational scheme should be clear, both at the beginning and at the end. This creates a sense of excitement and energy at both points, as the participants try to gain a good start or improve their finish. If you sense a flagging of interest during the scheme you can re-engender enthusiasm by showing how each one is doing and offering some additional sales material to stimulate the drive.

The measurement of success must be based on easily quantifiable data that is not open to manipulation. The scheme is intended to increase total sales, so you are looking for all participants to maximize their sales. As such, percentage rates of improvement are probably better than gross sales as a measurement unit. This way everyone starts on a relatively even basis. It is up to you to choose the best unit to suit your business, but an open discussion with the sales force before the scheme begins will give them an opportunity to put their views and allow them some 'ownership' of the scheme.

Finally, it is worthwhile making a bit of a splash about the handing out of awards. For example, if it is a regular monthly scheme, you do not want to hire a room and invite guests, but it may be worth gathering everyone together to announce the distribution, or at the very least, putting the results up in a staff area and so letting the month's winners get some recognition.

The risk with motivational programmes is that those who do not 'win' are disincentivized and feel themselves to be 'losers'. Clearly this is not desirable, so you must structure the scheme so that people are not made to feel stigmatized. The easiest way to do this is to ensure that there is not a small minority that gets nothing, with the majority being rewarded.

CUSTOMER SERVICE

Once you have made the sale, the next most important task is to retain the customer. There is an overwhelming argument for trying to improve your customer retention, but the principal factor is that it costs five times as much to attract a new customer as to retain an existing one. Research at Harvard Business School tells us that reducing customer defections can improve your bottom line by 25–85 per cent. The theory of how to do this is simple: make customers continue to feel cherished. The practice is often a lot harder.

Improving customer service is the major way to improve your customer retention. The more tangible factors of product price and quality, presuming they are not a long way out of line with the rest of the market, are significantly less important factors in retaining your customers. If the product has broken but the problem was solved quickly and without fuss, then you are likely to retain the customer. It the product breaks and the solution is drawn out and ineffective, you surely will lose the customer.

Your opportunity to offer excellent customer service comes in two phases. The first is at the point of sale. Whether your business is selling a product or a service, the efficiency with which potential customers are seen to have their various options explained, and the level of empathy and understanding for their particular needs, will be significant factors in whether they use your services or not. This clearly goes beyond the basic, but by no means always present, level of customer service that requires the salesperson to be polite, knowledgeable and enthusiastic.

If your product or service requires some degree of after-sales service, then your opportunity to offer a positively attractive level of customer care is made easier, but the risk of failure is higher. If there is no such after-sales need, then it is very simple to let your customers disappear forever.

First, let us look at the after-sales service element. This may be because your product requires installation, periodic servicing, or more probably delivery, spare parts, refills or other consumables, or a repair. In a small business the level of customer care is assumed to be higher anyway. The cynic would say that this is because there are fewer opportunities to pass the buck. More positively it is because the chances of the staff knowing how to deal with the problem are higher, as in small businesses staff tend to cover a variety of roles. What this analysis tells us, however, is that knowledge of the business structure and how it deals with customer problems is the first task in creating a successful service environment.

If you can create a system that deals efficiently with customer enquiries and problems, and ensure that all personnel who come into contact with customers understand the system, then you are well on your way to achieving good customer care. The system should have certain key elements:

- All enquiries should be directed to a single central point, whether that is an individual or dedicated telephone line.
- The responsible person should be as senior as the potential

time involved allows. That is, if you expect only occasional enquiries or complaints, then the owner or senior manager can deal with them. If you expect a constant stream of enquiries (hopefully not complaints) then the duty manager or equivalent may be the best qualified to deal with them.

▌ Promptness in all actions is always appreciated, from answering telephone calls and returning messages, to providing answers and repairing faults.

▌ If a delay is unavoidable then make sure the customer is notified and the reasons for the delay explained.

▌ Ensure that customers always know who is dealing with their enquiry and that they are provided with contact details for that person.

▌ Always accept responsibility when it is your fault. Passing the buck impresses no one and will not solve the problem.

▌ Give realistic and honest information about costs, timescales and reasons for problems.

To summarize the above, it is always advisable to keep the customer as informed as possible, and to deal honestly. Mistakes occur and, generally, customers accept that they will happen. What they will not accept is not being told what is going on, not being told the truth, and responsibility not being taken for errors.

Should your product or service not present the opportunity to have continued contact with customers, you may still be able to keep them in mind of you. If you can get their names and addresses, then occasional mailouts to inform them of your latest products or sales will be an invaluable resource.

TELESALES AND CALL CENTRES

By far the most powerful tool in direct marketing and customer service is the telephone. While the Internet has revolutionized parts of this sector and has very powerful applications in gathering usage information, it does not allow person-to-person familiarity between the business and the customer. This arm's length interaction is why the Internet is great for promoting information about your products or services, as it allows a customer to make enquiries without being actively sold to. However, as we noted above, a salesperson is not really 'selling' until he or she has been told 'no'. The telephone allows you to get past this initial rejection point. It is probably for this reason that telesales have gained a bad impression in the world at large; so much so that the word is little used nowadays and the function is referred to by its location instead – call centres.

It would be a pity if the power and benefits of the telephone were to be ignored because of the poor image that telesales has conjured up over the years. Successful and non-intrusive use of telesales can be achieved and utilized within a small business environment to good effect. Indeed the very fact that you are a small business will make the negative aspects of telesales less significant. An enthusiastic and knowledgeable caller will be more appealing and convincing than a script-reading employee of a vast call centre.

Although we are all very familiar with using the telephone these days, successfully using it for a sales and customer care function is a skill that needs to be practised as much as any other in the sales repertoire.

Telephone sales work best in the business to business market. They will also produce the largest return on effort and time expended with existing or known customers. Cold calling is much harder work, your reception will be more variable, and your success rate will be lower – but at the end of the day these are the calls that provide your extra margin of profit. Cold calling for retail sales is the most difficult area of telesales, and for the small business is probably not a high priority. It requires the accumulation of a large number of leads or prospects, which can be expensive, and demands a significant allocation of time and even more skill to produce results.

Not all businesses can benefit equally from telesales. Intangible services, such as insurance or advertising space, do not require any physical inspection before purchase and so lend themselves ideally to telesales. But you should not limit your view of telesales to this kind of operation. Businesses with physical products can benefit from contacting their customers and strengthening their relationship.

To focus on business to business telesales to existing customers: this need not be a hard-sell tactic. You can use the call to:

▌ Arrange a face-to-face meeting, which assures you of actually seeing someone when you arrive. It shows planning and organization, which reassures customers, and allows them to have their say when you arrive, which empowers them.

▌ Discuss any new products or services you have available that may be of interest, thus re-establishing your presence in customers' minds, and creating the opportunity to discover any areas on which you might be able to capitalize.

▌ Enquire if customers need to reorder, so prompting them to do so.

▌ Let them know of any special offers you currently have available.

When making telephone calls to customers it is important to create a positive image of yourself to them. This can only be done by the sound and delivery of the voice and what you say. From this perspective, that is a lot less to work on than if you go to meet the customer in person, when your clothes, mannerisms, and even the car you arrive in will all add to their impression of you.

It is a plain fact that conversations where neither correspondent can see the other one are more likely to be misinterpreted. It is therefore hugely important to ensure that your speech is clear, so ensure you do not speak too fast or incoherently. Make sure you are sounding animated about your subject, even if it is to arrange a meeting; so banish the monotone and try to sound as natural and relaxed as you can. If you make sure you are smiling when you speak it actually changes the way you sound. Try it.

Having mastered how you sound, it is equally important to manage what you say. Out goes jargon and waffle. Keep all relevant information easily accessible so you can answer queries quickly and accurately, and make your points straightforwardly and succinctly. It will not be possible to acquire an expert telesales technique overnight; it requires practice and training. (See *Selling by Telephone*, published by Kogan Page in association with *The Sunday Times*.)

If you wish to carry out a concerted telesales campaign it may be worth outsourcing the work to a call centre to help you out. They will have already made the considerable investment in equipment and technology, will have trained staff, and access to large volumes of prospect lists should you want them.

Checklist

- ▌ Have you accepted that in order to sell you will encounter frequent rejection?
- ▌ Do you know how to motivate yourself and your sales staff to ensure they persist in going for the next prospect?
- ▌ Have you thought through your sales strategy from core objectives to the marketing details?
- ▌ How up to date is your customer profile? Has it changed? Can the product be changed to better meet your existing market?
- ▌ Do you have a clear and well-understood customer complaints procedure?
- ▌ Do you know what your competitors' customer service is like? Are you better than them?
- ▌ Do you and the rest of the sales team have good telephone skills? Is it worth investing in training to improve this?

8 Procurement and Purchasing

More attention is given in most books about managing small businesses to sales and marketing than to purchasing and procurement, and this book is no exception. However, as the reverse side of the commercial coin at the heart of your business operation, the procurement and purchasing function merits similar if not equal attention.

When starting up in business you will probably act as purchasing officer yourself; certainly, you will not want to delegate authority to commit the business financially to an employee until you have established a formal purchasing function within the business. This will mean that you select products and suppliers, negotiate the terms and sign the orders in the early start-up phases. Initially, the task may not seem too onerous; unless your business is in manufacturing or retailing, daily purchasing requirements will be quite modest, related to office consumables, except for the setting-up phase when you will be procuring more expensive capital items – office equipment, furniture and maybe vehicles – and entering into contracts for insurance, telephone and cleaning services, and the supply of utilities.

Even at this stage, it is important that you distinguish between procurement and purchasing activity. Procurement encompasses the setting of specifications which you require products and suppliers to meet, selection of shortlisted suppliers against specifications, and negotiation of purchase and supply terms, from prices and minimum order value to payment and credit terms, and from delivery times to returns procedures. Purchasing is the more mundane activity of placing orders against agreed terms from approved suppliers on a timely basis, progress chasing of undelivered product, rejection and return of sub-specification product, and approval of invoices for payment. As the business grows you will be able to set purchasing guidelines and to delegate the clerical purchasing duties with confidence, but it will be some time before you will feel able to delegate the decision-making procurement role.

CIVIL LAW AND THE BUYING AND SELLING OF GOODS

Civil law lays down quite clearly your rights as a purchaser and seller, which are the same as those of your customers and suppliers. Most activity in business, as well as our personal commercial relationships in the community, is governed by civil law. Aside from employment law, which is covered in some detail in Chapter 14, only two aspects of civil law – contract and tort – will concern you most of the time in running your business.

Contract law

Breach of contract arises when one party to a contract fails to perform the obligations which it has undertaken. In the context of purchasing, your supplier is in breach of contract if it fails to supply the product or service which you have ordered to specification and within the agreed delivery time. In such circumstances you have a claim against your supplier for the damages or cost that you have incurred through their failure to supply you to your contract, which may include the cost of any claims your customers may have against you for your failure to perform your contracts with them as a result of your supplier's failure. In practice, most claims of this kind are settled between the parties for a lesser sum than the original claim without a court action, since neither party will want to incur the costs of litigation, which often represent a substantial proportion of the value of the claim.

Contracts between purchasers and suppliers of goods and services can be verbal or embodied in a formal legal agreement. The latter is more common in the case of contracts to provide services, such as the design and installation of computer software or an outsourcing contract to provide facilities management. In the case of orders placed to provide a tangible product, it is more common for the parties to rely on their standard terms and conditions of purchase and sale, which are typically listed in the small print on the reverse side of offer documents and acceptance forms. The main purpose of small print terms and conditions in a vendor's offer document is to limit the liabilities of the seller and to reject responsibility for consequential loss. We will discuss the issues of what constitutes a contract and standard conditions of buying and selling later in this chapter.

Tort

First, the second element of civil law that may impact your business is the law of tort (French for 'wrong'). Tort actions arise from the commission of any of the following civil wrongs:

- **Conversion:** selling stolen goods, even if purchased innocently.
- **Defamation:** damaging a competitor's, supplier's or former employee's reputation.
- **False imprisonment:** for example, detaining on suspicion of theft a visitor or employee who is later acquitted.
- **Negligence:** failure to repair damaged equipment or buildings and their fittings which results in accidents to staff, customers, suppliers or any other third party.
- **Nuisance:** such as making noise or smells or blocking access to neighbours' premises.
- **Passing off:** maintaining that products were made by someone other than their manufacture.
- **Trespass:** entering property without authority or invitation.

The form of tort that businesspeople meet most often is negligence. Third party personal accidents may be covered by your employer's liability insurance, but the policy could be nullified in the event of negligence on your part. Employee accidents as a result of negligence are also likely to give rise to prosecution by the Health and Safety Executive for breach of the laws requiring you to provide safe working conditions.

Contract essentials

There are three necessary elements for a contract to be in force:

▮ **Offer** of goods or service from the vendor.
▮ **Acceptance** by the purchaser.
▮ **Consideration.** There must be a payment of some kind, not necessarily money, in exchange for the goods or service supplied.

A contract may be made on specified terms, such as, typically, delivery within 10 days and payment within 30 days of invoice. In practice the contract exists and is legally enforceable when agreement is reached over what is offered and at what price. Although agreements made verbally are enforceable, it is clearly much easier to prove what was agreed if there is a written, signed document. The only common exceptions to the validity of verbal agreements are land sales in England, Wales and Northern Ireland which must be in writing, and cases where members of the public place an order or sign an HP or credit sale agreement in their own homes or at their place of work, when there is the legal requirement for a 'cooling off' period in which the customer has a right to cancel the agreement.

There are also implied conditions in all contracts, which do not have to be spelt out, that:

▮ the seller has the right to sell (ie that the goods are not stolen or already on HP);
▮ the goods comply with the description (eg if reconditioned, not described as new);
▮ the goods are of 'suitable quality' and 'fit for use' in the way that the customer expected;
▮ the sample corresponds with bulk.

It is the third of these conditions that tends to be at the core of most disputes between vendors and purchasers, where the meaning of words is ambiguous or uncertain. Legal actions on these grounds are time-consuming and likely to be profitable only for the legal profession.

Terms and condition of buying and selling

This chapter focuses on your procurement and purchasing activities, but remember that there is a 'do as you would be done by' element in this discussion, since the terms and conditions that you seek to impose on your customers may be the converse of those that your suppliers try to use when selling to you.

With your buyer's hat on, it is important to specify what you want the goods to do as a part of placing the order, and to place an official written order on which your terms of trade are entered (printed, if you use a standard order form). Your standard terms may differ significantly from the standard terms of which the supplier has already advised you on their quotation or order confirmation, and the rule is that the last one wins. Therefore, you should make sure, whenever possible, that you are buying on your terms. The terms on your official order will prevail provided that the seller does not send an order acknowledgement on which its terms are specified.

Remember that even if the supplier's sales rep promised you that a particular condition would not apply in the case of your order, there is probably a disclaimer somewhere in the small print that staff have no authority to agree any variation.

Another area of the supplier's small print to which you should certainly pay attention is the procedure for complaining if the goods are delivered damaged, or in some other way are not what you ordered. Unless you process your complaint as instructed and within the specified time limit, you may still have to pay for defective product.

With your seller's hat on, the following are some of the terms and conditions of sale that you might consider adopting for your business. As a buyer, you may expect to find them among the terms and conditions of a 'reasonable' supplier (another ambiguous term on which lawyers are happy to charge their 'taxi meter' fees in litigation).

Terms and conditions of sale

1. Descriptions shown in brochures, advertisements, and by way of samples, are correct at the time of going to press, errors and

omission excepted. They are liable to amendment at any time without notice.

2. Prices will be those ruling at the date of despatch and exclude VAT, which is due at the current rate in force. We may revise prices without notice. Any invoice query should be made in writing with 10 days of the date of invoice.

3. Quotations and estimates remain current for one month.

4. All accounts are payable in full within 30 days of invoice date.

5. No liability is accepted for delay in despatch or delivery.

6. Orders for goods may be cancelled only with the written agreement of a director of this company.

7. Carriage may be charged in addition to the quoted price, except for orders over £100 which will be delivered free within 30 miles.

8. Liability cannot be accepted for non-delivery of goods unless written notification is received within seven days of the date of invoice.

9. Shortage of goods or damage must be notified by telephone within 48 hours of delivery, and confirmed within seven days of delivery, or no claim can be accepted. Delivery of obviously damaged goods should be refused.*

10. No liability is accepted for any consequential loss or damage whatsoever.

11. Acceptance of the goods implies acceptance of these conditions which may not be varied except in writing by a director of this company.

12. Under some circumstances we may cancel the contract without notice or compensation. Such circumstances would include: strikes, lockouts and other forms of industrial action or dispute, fire, flood, drought, weather conditions, war, civil disturbance, act of God or any other cause beyond our control making it impossible for us to fulfil the contract.

13. We reserve our title in goods supplied until they have been paid for in full.

14. Any invoice unpaid in full by the due date shall attract interest charges accrued at base rate plus 5 per cent from the due date.

15. A 'quotation' given is a firm price for the job but subject to these terms and conditions. An 'estimate' is our best estimate of

the final cost but may be subject to fluctuation due to the unforeseeable exigencies of the job.
(*This condition should mirror your carrier's conditions which you accept, including identification routines and the retention of damaged goods for verification.)

PRODUCT SELECTION

Purchasing decisions for capital and high-value items are necessarily more critical than for lower-value items of current expenditure. Some guidance on the former is given in Chapter 15 on asset management, and the methods of financing the acquisition of capital equipment and vehicles, both on and off balance sheet, are described in Chapter 4 'Funding alternatives'. Although the choice of make and model of any kind of equipment, whether PC or motor vehicle, is largely subjective, you should consciously apply certain business criteria in the selection process:

▪ **Fitness for purpose.** Don't consider buying equipment that is unnecessarily refined or of a capacity in excess of your business needs (eg your choice of motor car or telephone switchboard). On the other hand, be sure that it will do the job for which you need it. In particular, if you are financing a capital item by leasing or rental, be careful not to commit yourself to inferior specification or lower-capacity equipment than the business will need a year or so before it can be replaced.

▪ **Cash flow.** Some equipment manufacturers may offer financing packages that demand lower monthly payments than others, or that can be procured from third party finance providers. If the product specification and quality are acceptable, this may determine your ultimate choice. However, preferential payment terms may not be sufficient to offset the risks of an inferior guarantee, high servicing costs, or an unreliable product, which can disrupt your business and cause expensive repairs and replacements. The net effect on cash flow, including lost sales, could be severe.

▪ **Net profit effect.** The higher the net price of the capital equipment, the greater the charge against profit is likely to be –

however preferential the financing package. This is a similar consideration to the impact on cash flow with one important difference. Remember that, in addition to running/operating cost, there is the cost of depreciation charges which must be taken against profit if your business is purchasing the asset. If the expansion of your business depends on maintaining healthy financial results, depreciation may be a significant factor.

■ **Competitor practice.** If in doubt, check what equipment your most effective competitor uses in its business. Maybe you can gain a product advantage by using improved equipment which will justify the incremental cost. Of course, the argument could go the other way. If you spend less on equipment, you might be able to afford to offer your customers additional service benefits which would be still more appealing.

Purchasing consumables does not generally demand so much deliberation. The critical factors in the decision are, of course:

■ price;
■ quality;
■ reliability of supply;
■ delivery time;
■ payment terms.

In the early stages of running your business, payment terms may be more important than the last 5 per cent of discount. Cash on delivery for a 10 per cent price advantage is no substitute for 30 days credit when cash flow is critical. In some product areas, like office stationery, direct purchase from national or regional wholesalers can give you all the advantages of good quality, low prices, excellent service and credit; but this is not so in all areas. For example, land line and mobile telephone services, or professional services, are such 'no-brainers'.

Purchasing via the Web

Using the Web to source your consumables will probably waste more of your time than the value it might gain in identifying new sources of supply or keener prices. However, the Web will give you useful price comparisons and could produce serious savings on higher-value items. For the main part, you may be able to use the prices of products on the Web to elicit matching offers from your local suppliers.

PURCHASING PROFESSIONAL SERVICES

Possibly the most difficult procurement and purchasing activity is the selection and engagement of professional services. This is one function which you will probably wish to reserve to yourself so long as you occupy the chief executive position in your company. You may well share the reluctance many businesspeople have in investing time and money with professional advisers beyond the bare necessities of the annual audit, completion of your tax return or entering into a commercial lease. That reluctance extends to areas like fundraising, human resource requirements and pension planning.

Practical selection and engagement

Finding a professional adviser through personal introduction is a traditional route, but requires caution. An adviser who is suitable for one business may not be appropriate for your business because of differences in outlook, objectives or cultures. Alternatives are a search among local professionals or direct contact through the national directories of the Law Society or Institute of Chartered Accountants. Whatever route you choose, do not be embarrassed to interview and evaluate several firms, having provided each with a brief, as you would in any important procurement area. Aside from technical expertise, experience and the capacity to take on your assignment, satisfy yourself of the compatibility of those who would be working with you before arriving at a decision. Before making a binding commitment, take up references. Any excuse or attempt to avoid giving references should be regarded as a disqualification.

Implementation is as important as any advice that may emerge from the reports of professional firms you engage. Therefore, before making your final choice of advisers, be sure that they will be able to help you to carry out their recommendations with their own staff or by transferring skills to members of your staff.

Be clear about the fee basis and how any additional costs may be triggered. Agree in advance details such as invoicing frequency in writing, together with the exact scope and timing of the work. You should insist that any changes in fees, schedules and phasing are advised promptly and fully justified. Avoid agreeing extensions to the assignment or new tasks until the original assignment is completed to your satisfaction.

PURCHASING PRACTICE

As we suggested at the beginning of this chapter, you will probably want to delegate the routine part of the purchasing function as the business expands. The best way of doing this securely is to draw up a set of rules for your purchasing officer, which anyone in the firm, including yourself, should observe. The following are among the most important:

▪ No commitment to a supplier of goods or services without a formal purchase order issued by the purchasing officer.

▪ No commitment to purchase outside the expenditure budget except with the express approval of the managing director.

▪ Quantities purchased to be determined by usage and negotiated terms (for consumables, no more than two or three months' usage at a time).

▪ Orders to be placed only within limits of authority (any expenditure above authorized expenditure to be sanctioned by the managing director).

▪ Selection of any new supplier or supplier of capital equipment to be against quotation from alternative suppliers (typically, two alternatives).

▪ Annual review of every supplier's terms and prices against competition.

Quality, delivery performance, and the incidence of defects of every supplier should be monitored and logged. Equally, you should remain aware of your own firm's performance against agreed payment terms. Even the most reliable supplier's service can become unsatisfactory if it is alienated by your failure to pay promptly.

_____

Checklist

■ Understand the distinction between procurement and purchasing. As the business grows, set guidelines and delegate clerical purchasing duties, but retain the decision-making procurement role for some time.

■ Aside from employment law, contract law and tort are the only two aspects of civil law that will concern you most of the time in running your business.

■ Your supplier is in breach of contract if it fails to supply the product or service you have ordered to specification and within the agreed delivery time. Contracts between purchasers and suppliers can be verbal or embodied in a formal legal agreement. In practice, the parties commonly rely on their standard conditions of purchase and sale.

■ Negligence is the most common form of tort in business. Employers' third party personal accident liability insurance may be nullified by negligence.

■ The necessary elements for a contract to be in force are: an offer of goods or service; acceptance by the purchaser; consideration (payment) in exchange for the goods or service. Among the implied conditions, 'suitable quality' and 'fitness for use' represent the most common causes for dispute.

■ Whenever possible, make sure that you are buying on your terms. The terms on your official order will prevail unless the seller sends an acknowledgement on which its terms are specified. The rule is that the last one wins.

■ To ensure that you do not have to pay for defective product, follow the supplier's procedures for complaint, and return goods within specified time limits.

■ Select and purchase capital expenditure items by reference to fitness for purpose, the effects on your cash flow and net profit, and competitors' practice.

▌ Purchasing consumables on the Web probably wastes more time than the value gained in keener prices, but Web prices may help you to secure matching offers from local suppliers.

▌ When selecting and engaging professional advisers, pay attention to compatibility as well as technical expertise and experience. Any excuse or attempt to avoid giving references should be treated as a disqualification.

▌ Before choosing your advisers make sure that they will help you to carry out their recommendations or transfer skills to members of your staff. Do not agree extensions to the contract until the original assignment is completed to your satisfaction.

▌ As the business expands, draw up a set of purchasing rules which everyone in your organization, including yourself, must observe.

9 Transportation

Your customers will judge the quality of your products and the physical services your firm provides in terms of their delivery, as well as by their intrinsic value. This is partly a matter of fulfilling orders promptly, delivering to schedule and carrying out service calls on the due date and at the agreed time, and partly the personal service that your staff or your contractor's personnel give at the delivery point. It is not possible to provide prompt delivery or efficient service without quality transportation, and that is the theme of this short chapter.

CONTRACT DELIVERY OR OWN TRANSPORT

When you start your business, one guiding principle is to keep fixed costs to a minimum so that any investment in vehicles, whether it involves interest and repayment of principal on bank loans or hire purchase, leasing or rental charges, is unwelcome if it can be avoided. If you are supplying goods over a wide area, perhaps nationally, contractor services will offer the most appropriate means of delivery. There are a multitude of courier and parcel services available whose charges are based on the size or weight of the package and distance delivered. If you are able to invoice your customers for delivery charges, it should be possible for you to convert your contractor's tariff into a scale of charges which you can quote on your order form and your customers can check on their invoices received.

Whatever terms you may negotiate with your selected contractor, it will probably apply standard terms and conditions to every consignment regarding acceptance and returns, which limits its liability in the event of late or non-delivery, damage to and the return of goods. You should include these terms in your standard terms and conditions.

Be sure to monitor the quality of your contractor's delivery service rather than wait for customer complaints. The contractor's documentation, which should include a delivery log signed by each customer on receipt of goods, enables you to check delivery times against the promised service. Supplement regular inspection of the contractor's records with periodic surveys to test customer satisfaction. The very act of consulting customers will add to your service image. If the contractor's service performance deteriorates and there is no effective response to requests for improvement, do not hesitate to change your contractor.

If your distribution pattern is concentrated in a limited area, the alternative of own transport may be more attractive, particularly when it will be fully utilized. It may make good sense to run one or more vehicles to serve your home territory where there is a density of local customers, and to employ one or more contract delivery services elsewhere.

There are some kinds of business where contract delivery is not a viable alternative. For example if you are a retailer of television, video and hi-fi equipment, installation is an important part of your total service which your customers will expect to be carried out on the spot when the equipment is delivered; by definition, your business is also likely to have a local clientele. Delivery by a contractor and a follow-up visit by your fitter may be cost-effective for you but will damage customer satisfaction. Similarly, if you offer a central heating and plumbing service your business depends on the use of properly equipped vans with supplies of tools and components so your staff can carry out emergency repair jobs. The customer will have no objection to the separate delivery of major items of equipment but will expect the engineer on the job to have at hand everything necessary to complete an installation or repair job.

When you start up, you may be a one-person business requiring a single van, but as this kind of service business grows, the number of vans in permanent use will increase in direct proportion to activity and the number of customers. Quite quickly you will become a fleet manager in your own right.

VEHICLE PROCUREMENT STRATEGIES

The financing alternatives for vehicle procurement – contract hire, finance leasing and contract purchase – are discussed in Chapter 15, 'Asset Management'. Each option has its attractions for the small business. The relative merits in terms of taxation, depreciation charges and capital allowances are discussed there and do not need to be repeated in this chapter. However, for those with funds available to whom none of these financing schemes appeals greatly, it is worth summarizing the arguments for and against outright purchase.

Advantages of outright purchase

- Access to capital allowances.
- The full benefit of residual value.
- Complete control of the vehicle / fleet.
- VAT recoverable when the vehicle is used exclusively for business purposes.

Vehicles purchased outright are, of course, assets that must be registered in the company's balance sheet. However, the maximum writing-down allowance permitted by the Inland Revenue of £3,000 per year per vehicle implies a first-year value of £12,000, based on the maximum rate of depreciation allowed of 25 per cent. Vehicles costing more than £12,000 are treated as individual assets, and a balancing charge is made when the vehicle is sold on – either the remaining depreciation if the selling price is less than the balance sheet written-down value, or a taxable profit if the selling price exceeds the written down value.

Similarly, if the VAT charge when the vehicle was purchased is recovered, VAT must be added to the price when the vehicle is sold on.

Disadvantages of outright purchase

▮ Motor vehicle assets, perhaps backed by borrowing on the balance sheet, may adversely affect gearing ratios and return on asset measures of importance.

▮ Exposure to interest rate fluctuations on borrowings.

▮ The risk that residual values may not meet expectations.

▮ The opportunity (for most cars) to recover 50 per cent of VAT on lease charges.

▮ The inability (for smaller fleets) to benefit from the buying power of the lessor.

▮ If more than several vehicles are involved, the need for operational, administrative and fleet management expertise.

FLEET MANAGEMENT SERVICES

A vehicle fleet of more than just a handful of vehicles imposes legal, administrative and managerial burdens, and demands skills to achieve efficiency and effectiveness of operation that your business probably lacks in-house. Outsourcing some or all of these tasks to fleet management specialists may be a cost-effective solution.

In the case of contract hire and contract purchase agreements, fleet management is very likely to be included. Fleet management can also be the subject of a stand-alone contract to cover the management of user-owned or leased vehicles. Under such a contract, the fleet user reimburses the fleet management company for all costs incurred plus a management fee. For user-owned vehicles VAT is recoverable, and the costs of fleet management are a tax-allowable charge against income.

Among the services commonly included in a fleet management contract are:

▮ sourcing of new vehicles;

▮ the preparation of vehicles to the operator's specifications (eg car phones, corporate livery, specialist racking for vans);

▮ registrations with the Driver and Vehicle Licensing Authority (DVLA, Swansea);

▮ servicing and maintenance;

▮ breakdown replacement;

- accident repairs;
- insurance claims submission and management;
- fuel services (eg the provision of corporate fuel cards);
- settlement of accounts for running costs;
- maximization of residual values and disposal of used vehicles;
- cost monitoring and control routines, covering vehicle utilization, mileage, fuel economy and risk assessment of the fleet and drivers.

Many fleet management added-value services involve information gathering and analysis by the management company. Before signing up, you should ask the company to demonstrate its successful application of IT to reduce operating costs and simplify administration. Whether the fleet management company you select is independent or linked to a finance house, you should arrange for the contract period for fleet management to coincide with that for the hire contract or lease.

Disposal of vehicles

Fleet management schemes require a disposals policy that is compatible with the assumptions made in the original financing. Whether your fleet has been financed by purchase or a financial lease, a successful outcome will depend on maximizing the residual when it is sold.

Residual values can be estimated quite accurately for any model of vehicle of given age and mileage, by reference to *Glass's Guide*, the motor trade's monthly publication, or by reference to a number of Internet Web sites. However, residual values can be volatile as they depend not just on the supply of used vehicles, but on the extent to which the new market is oversupplied and the discount terms available, which may attract private buyers to new rather than used vehicle purchases.

The original financing is based on estimates of residual value, and the fleet management scheme disposals policy is framed accordingly. If these assumptions prove over-optimistic, it may be necessary to intervene and dispose of a vehicle before its due date, to avoid a greater loss later. Alternatively, it may be beneficial to keep the vehicle in service until maintenance costs become excessive or until it is fully depreciated.

Alternative disposal routes

If you are a sole trader or a small fleet operator replacing only a few vehicles at a time, and you seek to purchase replacements outright, negotiating a trade-in against the cost of the replacement may be the most effective course of action. The services of specialist car auctioneers, such as British Car Auctions, are available to operators with larger volumes to dispose of at the same time. Both the trade-in and the auction route carry the advantage that the vehicles are sold 'as seen' and that there is no potential liability towards a subsequent owner.

Extras and accessories

Vehicles can be supplied to almost any factory specification by lessors and hire companies. Of course, factory extras increase the initial vehicle cost and therefore the monthly payments; they also tend to depreciate quickly and may not be reflected in residual values. On the other hand, in the case of used passenger cars, private buyers' demand is usually higher for 'mid-range', if not 'top of the range', models compared with the basic model.

'Extras' fitted to the vehicle, such as car phones, stereos and extra lights, are also likely to affect residual values adversely. Many hire and other financing contracts, where ownership does not pass eventually to the user, impose restrictions on extras or insist that they remain in place when the vehicle is returned. Similarly the respraying of a vehicle and the fitting of advertising decals may be subject to restrictions, and will be taken into account in contract purchase agreements where the user has the right to sell the vehicle back. There may be a financial case, after all, for retaining that anonymous plain white van!

Checklist

▌ Your customers will judge the quality of your firm by your delivery service, as well as the intrinsic value of your products or services.

- If you are supplying goods over a wide area, perhaps nationally, contractor services will probably offer the most efficient delivery.
- Incorporate in your standard terms and conditions those of your contractor relating to acceptance and delivery which limit their liability.
- Monitor you contractor's service by regular inspection of its delivery records, and carry out periodic customer surveys.
- Run your own vehicle(s) where your distribution pattern is concentrated or the success of your business relies on installation and repair services.
- Review the alternative merits of contract hire, finance leasing and contract purchase, in terms of taxation, depreciation charges and capital allowances, against the advantages and disadvantages of outright purchase.
- For more than a handful of vehicles, consider outsourcing fleet management services to a specialist firm.
- The successful outcome of fleet purchase or a financial lease depends on maximizing residual values on disposal. If residual value estimates prove optimistic, you may need to dispose of a vehicle before its due date to avoid later loss, or to retain it until full depreciated or maintenance costs become excessive.
- Both the trade-in and auction routes involve selling the vehicles 'as seen' and avoid potential liability towards a subsequent owner.
- Factory extras increase initial vehicle cost and monthly payments to hire companies; they also depreciate quickly and may not add to residual value. Hire and financing contractors may insist that accessories remain in place on return and restrict respraying or fitting of advertising decals.

10 | Financial and Management Accounting and Controls

It is wise to remember that setting up and running your own business is primarily an opportunity to fulfil your dreams and satisfy your ego. The freedom from large corporate structures and all that they imply is often the impetus that gets businesses off the ground, but it has to be the desire to create something better than already exists, and an urge to improve yourself both personally and financially, that will drive you to succeed.

We point this out because this chapter is all about tying down the guyropes on your dreams. If the number one reason for start-up businesses failing is poor cash management, then the number two reason is probably that better cash management did not allow the managers to achieve the growth they expected. The only way to manage the often contradictory forces of growth and weak cash flow is through carefully implemented controls. This chapter will help guide you through the financial and management accounting options to achieve good control and, hopefully, create sufficient cash to grow your business successfully.

CASH MANAGEMENT

Two sets of people are interested in your cash management – you and your backers (both potential and existing). The latter group will be analysing your accounts with some standardized ratios, so

We've planned the perfect package to help you start up in business

There's a lot to think about when you start up in business - and not just whether you're getting the best banking deal.

That's why we've created a start-up package that not only gives you 12 months' free banking, but also includes real help to get you off to a great start.

- 12 months' free banking
- Free start-up guide
- Free legal & tax helpline
- Free business planning software

If you are thinking of starting a business call us FREE on

 0800 587 0800 quoting reference AH0190
lines are open 8am to midnight, 7 days per week

 www.mybusinessbank.co.uk

Alliance Leicester

Business Banking

All applications are subject to status. Applicants must be 18 or over. Written quotations are available on request. Business users only.

All telephone calls between you and the Alliance & Leicester Group may be recorded/monitored both to make sure that we carry out your instructions correctly and for security and training purposes. Girobank plc. Registered Office: Carlton Park, Narborough, Leicester LE9 5XX. (with effect from 1 June 2002 the postcode will change to LE19 0AL). Company No: 1950000. Registered In England. A subsidiary of Alliance & Leicester plc.

NEW ALLIANCE & LEICESTER GUIDE HELPS GET NEW BUSINESSES OFF TO A GREAT START

There's no denying that starting your own business takes guts, confidence and a great deal of hard work.

But to make a real go of things, you'll need to be absolutely certain your business idea is viable. You'll have to make sure that the family is on your side – and prepared for the inevitable financial hardships in the early months. You'll also need to know your market – and its requirements – inside out. Plus you'll have to tackle such things as drawing up a Business Plan, a Cashflow Forecast and a Profit & Loss Forecast. And all that's before you even think about dealing with tax, National Insurance and VAT, or finding premises and taking on employees.

Thankfully Alliance & Leicester Business Banking have written a free Small Business Start-Up Guide that covers many of the issues you'll face when setting up in business. The guide comes complete with useful templates for the various plans you'll have to complete, as well as innovative interactive business-planning software.

Step by step sections to help make things easy

In ten logical, clearly written sections, the Alliance & Leicester Small Business Start-Up Guide will take you through the many issues you'll need to consider.

One of the major mistakes many business start-ups make, for example, is underestimating just how much income they'll require to cover their existing commitments. Similarly, many hopelessly overestimate the demand for their product or service – or rush headlong into an idea without thinking it through.

Completing the Cashflow Forecast in the Alliance & Leicester Business Start-Up Guide will help you to work out how much money you'll need for your new venture. When estimating your Cashflow, remember that the time period between you having to pay suppliers and actually receiving payment from your customers can vary greatly. So take care at the start not to expand too quickly as you could literally run out of cash.

Identifying your skills

At the end of the day, you're going into business because you wish to exploit a particular skill, ability, talent or trade – and not because you have all the expertise needed to successfully run a business. So take time to think through all the aspects of the business. Identify your skills and those of your associates. Make sure that whatever your chosen business, between you, you have the ability to deal with production processes, management, sales, marketing and the running of the business.

Researching the market

Whatever your idea happens to be, make sure it's feasible. All too often new businesses fail simply because they haven't been properly considered. If it's a special skill that you can offer, check that it will be in sufficient demand. And if your offering is fairly generic, make sure that the marketplace isn't already oversubscribed or that changing market trends could kill demand.

Knowing as much as possible about your market, your customers and competitors is vital. As well a using published material, carry out your own market research amongst potential customers. Ask their opinions. If possible, test-market your products to gauge customer reaction. And check out your competitors, their market share, products, services and pricing strategies. Also think about how you'll promote your company – and how potential customers will reach you.

Pricing your products

Never forget that you're going in to business to make a living. To at least break even, the prices you charge must be sufficient to cover your business and private expenditure. Only after covering these costs can you start to make a profit.

When fixing a price for your goods, you must, as a bare minimum, make enough sales for your gross profit (sales less direct costs) to cover your overheads, the money you need to take from the business (your drawings) and an allowance for the use of your assets (depreciation). This is known as the break-even point.

Finding business premises

It's hardly surprising that many small businesses choose initially to work from home, as this provides an attractive option that's both cheap and convenient. If you decide to work from home, check that you have enough space and are permitted to use the property for business purposes. Also check your insurance arrangements – your domestic insurance policy may not cover your business equipment or activities.

If your proposed venture requires business premises, take time to find the right location and check whether any restrictions apply. Retail premises require good passing trade. A manufacturer may need space – plus access to a skilled workforce. And virtually all businesses require good access and parking.

Funding and selecting business equipment

For most businesses, finding premises is only part of the story. Your venture may require office equipment, furnishings – even plant and machinery. After carefully establishing the equipment you need, ask an accountant to help way up the advantages of buying or leasing.

For your free copy of the Alliance & Leicester Business Banking Small Business Start-Up Guide, call free on 0800 587 0800.

that they can compare your business with the others they may invest in or lend to. Clearly, it is in your best interests to make sure that your business has cash ratios that will be satisfactory to these people. There are a variety of ways that you can arrange your business to achieve this, which are covered in the chapter on asset management. At this stage, however, it is useful to know what the ratios are, and more critically gain a good understanding of how they operate.

The most frequently used, and therefore important, statistic is the current ratio. This compares your current assets against your current liabilities to give a figure that shows how many times the former will cover the latter.

Current ratio = current assets/current liabilities.

The figure is expressed as a ratio, such as 2.6:1. This example means that your current assets are 2.6 times greater than your current liabilities. What does this mean? Not a lot by itself. There is no overall ideal figure you should be trying to achieve. Each industry and sector within an industry will have different sets of ratios. The more risky your business is, the more susceptible to market changes, the greater the first figure should be. In an ideal world where you have little risk and you can project with certainty what is going to happen in the future business cycle, the nearer 1:1 you get the more efficient use of capital you are achieving. Thus we reach the first dilemma: your backers want you to get the highest return with 'their' cash as possible, but without exposing them to an unacceptable level of risk. This is something of an impossible task to achieve consistently to everyone's satisfaction, as different people (and therefore different backers) have different levels of risk aversion.

Your level of risk acceptability is the key here. The first question you must ask yourself when considering your financial controls is what level of risk you are prepared to accept. Given that you are willing to set up on your own in the first place, you are probably not totally risk averse. But does that mean that you are happy to remortgage your house to fund the business? If so, if it all goes wrong, you may lose not only your business but your house as well. Many banks seem to think that this is an acceptable thing to ask someone to do. It may secure their loan but does it mean they are attracting suitably cautious borrowers?

_____

Having worked out what level of risk is acceptable to you and your backers (regretfully this can only be a general awareness of the risk rather than an absolute number), you can now look at how to achieve a level of exposure that fits. There are three main elements to managing your cash: credit control – overseeing the flows of cash out of and cash into the business; stock control – how much cash you have tied up in stock at any one time; and cash management – what you do with any spare cash or indebtedness that you have.

Credit control

Credit control is the management of both your debtors – those who owe you money – and your creditors – those you owe money to. The best situation is where you have only cash sales but all your purchases are on long payment terms. This way you may well be able to sell all your purchases for cash before you have had to pay for them yourself. This is not such an idealistic situation as you may believe. A bakery, for instance, will buy in all its flour, butter and other ingredients from a trade supplier who most likely will give it 30 days payment terms. If the business is managed well, it can have sold all the ingredients as cakes and buns for cash well before the 30 days are up. This may even allow the business time to gain interest on a cash surplus until it has to pay the supplier.

The opposite situation, where all supplies are purchased with cash but sales have to be given on account, is unusual, but sadly arises most often with start-up businesses. If you are selling business to business you will most likely have to offer payment terms to your customers. Your competitors will be doing so, which means you will have to as well. But as a new business you may find that your suppliers are unwilling to give you credit payment terms until you have some track record, often at least six months to a year of trading, to show that you are able to pay. This is an extra burden on any start-up business, but there is little way around it other than ensuring that you have sufficient cash to cover any shortfall.

The most frequent situation is where you have a mixture of trade customers and suppliers on account. There are specific ratios to calculate your exposure to creditors and debtors in any one period, which can be used for comparative purposes. However, at this stage what is important is to have a clear picture of the 'age' of your debtors and their amounts, and a similar view of your creditors. If you know how much is due in and how reliable the debtors are (or are not), and you know how much you have to pay out and how long you have to do so, and that the latter is not more onerous than the former, you will be all right. The trick is how do you do this. The ratios referred to above will give a figure that is useful for benchmarking with others in your industry (if you can find their figures) or against your prior performance; however, the most useful information will be gathered from producing an 'aged debtors schedule' and 'aged creditors schedule' (as in Table 10.1). This information should be easily found in your sales and purchase day books, which are discussed further in the next chapter.

Table 10.1   Aged debtors schedule

Customer	Current	30 days	60 days	Older
Mitchell's & Co Ltd		195.20		
Moen & Sons	80.25			
Pollocks		36.50		
J Reuvid				68.68
D Smith			340.85	
Suarez Bros	176.45			
U-Twist plc			277.43	
Whittakers Ltd	594.77			
Total	**851.47**	**231.70**	**618.28**	**68.68**

Should you start experiencing problems with your credit control, it will be necessary to analyse these schedules to see where you can improve the flows. Do you have any persistently late payers (late payers are more likely to be a problem than bad debtors)? If so, you may be able to persuade them to shorten their payment period. You may even have some customers who are happy to pay cash. It is also worthwhile going through your creditors to see if any will give you better terms. If you understand your two schedules well, this element of cash management will be relatively straightforward.

Stock control

Depending on the type of business you operate, the role of stock control will vary in importance. If you are a service provider, such as a software programmer, you are unlikely to have much stock to control. However, any manufacturer or producer and any retailer will have more to consider. Manufacturers will have three types of stock: raw materials, work in progress and finished products. Every piece of stock you have sitting in your store or warehouse represents tied-up cash. Clearly you need to have stock to sell and raw materials to make your product, but to make your use of working capital (the money required to keep the business running on a daily basis) as efficient as possible, you should minimize the amount of stock without prejudicing your trade.

This is not as simple as it seems. The amount of stock you buy will depend on various factors beyond how much you can afford to buy at one time. Buying in bulk will often be substantially cheaper than buying items in small quantities, because of bulk discounts or because the transport costs are high. Some items may be difficult to source or rare. If you are an antiques dealer, then whether or not you buy an item will have more to do with its value than your immediate cash flow: if you spot a real bargain you will make sure you find the funds to purchase it rather than pass it up. Similarly you will not want to be still holding last season's stock this year if fashions are constantly changing. The factors that affect your stock levels are very varied. You are the best judge of what level of risk you can take with your stock to avoid running out, but be aware that apart from certain peculiar items that gain value with age (wine, for example), most stock is losing you money if the alternative use for its value was cash earning interest in the bank. In technical terms, this is the 'opportunity cost' for holding stock.

Pure cash management

This final element of the cash management control system focuses on either the spare cash you have in the business or your borrowing methods. If your business generates large amounts of surplus cash, even for short periods of time only, then you will be wise to gain some benefit from it. Your normal business account is unlikely to pay you interest on any positive balance; so you should get a business savings account to transfer any temporarily surplus cash into, so that you can earn interest on it.

In the more likely event that your small business is a cash borrower, you should keep an eye on whether your lender is offering you the best rate available. In practice this will not be as easy as it first sounds. Your options for borrowing funds as a small business are quite limited, and often require a sustained relationship with your bank before it will allow you the flexibility to have an extended overdraft. You will probably do your business more harm than good by trying to change your lender at every tweak of its interest rate. That said, if you feel you are materially worse off with your bank than with another lender it is certainly in your interests to point this out to your bank manager or adviser. Lenders often have a certain degree of latitude in these matters, and while they advertise that they will always look after your interests, in practice they are unlikely to be as protective of them as you are. If you do not ask for a better rate, then it is unlikely that you will get one.

COST ANALYSIS

A pound saved is a pound earned, they say; but look at how much a 1 per cent cost saving earns in an increased percentage of profit at the bottom line. (See Table 10.2.) Where cash control analyses your use of cash, cost control analysis focuses on whether or not you are getting the best deal for your purchases. In reality most entrepreneurs will be very aware of their costs. Visualizing cash flows is not an intuitive skill; we have to order our information carefully to be able to build a picture of it. However, we all have a built-in mechanism that alerts us to whether we are getting a good deal or not or, at the very least, gives us a desire to get the best deal available.

How, though, do we know we are getting the best deal available? Like so much in business there is no easy answer to this. If the cheapest option was always clearly available then it would attract 100 per cent of sales; the market is neither that efficient nor that simple. Goods and services differ in quality, ease of acquisition and

Table 10.2 Cost Savings

A 1% saving in costs, in this example, returns a 10% increase in profit.

	Before		After 1% cost saving		Extra performance	
	£	%	£	%	£	%
Sales	10,000	100	10,000	100	–	–
Costs	9,000	90	8,900	89	–100	–1
Profit	1,000	10	1,100	11	+100	+10

specifications, as well as price. The only way to ensure you are not paying over the odds is to keep yourself well informed. Read the trade press, search the Internet, talk to everyone you can in the same industry, from your suppliers to your competitors to the delivery drivers. Do not forget that your own staff will know snippets of information that you do not.

Do not be afraid to talk to your competitors, unless you are selling exactly the same goods to exactly the same people in exactly the same way; there will be enough differences between your businesses to give you each space to make a profit. They will be encountering the same problems as you and will be as eager to learn your thoughts as you will be to learn theirs. In this way, you will build up a good knowledge of your purchasing options and should be able to benchmark your system against others.

Beyond this information-gathering method of cost control you should occasionally analyse your costs more methodically. Theoretically, you can construct a break-even chart having broken down your costs into fixed and variable. This will give you a useful understanding of the mechanics of your business, but it is difficult to do this accurately with a range of products with different costs and prices. A better approach is to work your way through the purchases and wages day books (see next chapter) and evaluate each cost individually, considering whether it gives you the best value available. This way you can create a costing system where you identify each element of your business as a cost object (a particular item that incurs costs) or a cost centre (a particular function that incurs costs).

When you examine each cost object you will see that it may incur costs purely associated with it, such as raw materials, labour, specific machinery and running costs. The object will also have indirect costs, which are those that support the creation of the object, such as premises (where the cost is rent) or insurance. Allocating the direct costs is fairly straightforward. Allocating (or apportioning) the indirect costs is more difficult, requiring your own subjective judgement. A simple method of cost allocation is to work out how much total percentage revenue each product makes, and allocate the indirect costs accordingly. However, this can be misleading, and more sophisticated methods can be used to give more accurate analysis. (For further information on the complexities of cost allocation see *Accounting and Finance for Managers*, Kogan Page 2001.)

PRICING AND ESTIMATING

Having gained a full understanding of your costs, you will need to decide on your pricing strategy. There are a variety of approaches to doing this but, as with so much else in running your own business, there is no magic formula. The most simple methods are cost-plus and cost-times. (See Table 10.3.)

However, these methods do not take account of the market. Your customers do not base their purchase decision on whether or not you cover your costs. Customers choose to purchase on value for

Table 10.3 Cost-Plus and Cost-Times

	Cost of production (incl raw materials)	Cost-plus (cost plus £30)	Cost-plus (cost plus 10%)	Cost-times (two times multiple of cost)
Price	£100	£130	£110	£200
Profit	–	£30	£10	£100

Note: Cost-plus and cost-times are very similar. Cost-plus is in fact the same as cost-times if you are using percentages (cost plus 10% is the same as cost times 1.1). Generally cost-plus, whether you use a fixed amount or a percentage, is used for contracts where the costs are not predictable until you start work, or in public service and internal contracts where maximizing profits is not the objective.

money and price comparison. Therefore, while you clearly have to be able to charge more than your costs, you also have to keep your costs at a competitive and attractive level for the market. The prices of many everyday goods and services are well known to the market, and thus your room to alter pricing is very limited; there is an accepted going rate, which you can undercut but not exceed. If your goods or services are unique or exceptional then your room to alter prices is much greater. Economic theory provides a range of rules and equations to discover your 'price elasticity', which you may be interested to learn more about to build up a good working understanding of your business (see *Financial Management for Small Business*, Kogan Page / *The Sunday Times*, 5th edition, 2001). However, this is by no means absolutely necessary, as you will probably have a fair idea what price level your business can sustain.

To choose your pricing successfully you must know what your sales will be. This is clearly not information that is available before you start to sell. As such you have to estimate what level of sales you expect to achieve. Let's take a simple example of a plumber. He knows that his overheads for any given week are the repayments on his vehicle, his professional indemnity insurance, his advert in the local paper and what he pays his bookkeeper. This totals £100 per week. He expects to have three jobs a day and work five days a week. That is 15 jobs a week. In pricing scenario 1, if he charges himself out at £20 per call out and the first hour, plus £15 per hour thereafter, and each job lasts two hours on average, he can expect £35 per job, or £525 per week. He then deducts his £100 for costs, leaving him with £425 profit for the week. If he has incorrectly estimated his number of jobs or the length of time they take, then his profit looks very different. (See Table 10.4.) In scenario 2, if he only averages two jobs per day of two hours each, then his week's takings fall to £350. In scenario 3, if he still has three jobs a day but only of one hour each, then his takings will have fallen still further, to only £300, leaving him with only £200 after his overheads. In this case he would have to increase his call-out charge to £35 to return to his original takings figure, as in scenario 4. However, the market may not support a 75 per cent increase in call-out charges, in which case his total number of jobs may fall yet again.

Table 10.4   Plumber example

Scenario	1	2	3	4
No of jobs per day	3	2	3	3
Cost per call out	£20.00	£20.00	£20.00	£35.00
Extra hours	15	15	0	0
Takings per day	£105.00	£70.00	£60.00	£105.00
Takings per week	**£525.00**	**£350.00**	**£300.00**	**£525.00**
Costs per week	100	100	100	100
Profit per week	**£425.00**	**£250.00**	**£200.00**	**£425.00**

We see in this example that even where there are few variables that may affect your revenues, the impact of incorrect estimates is large and the effect on your prices therefore critical. Where you are a retailer with many items on sale and the need to attract a sizeable number of customers, the implications of your estimates become ever more important.

A few thoughts ought to be borne in mind when finalizing your pricing:

▮ First, decide whether you are marketing your business on quality or price. If your strategy is price-led then you will need to create volume, and must be clearly cheaper than the equivalent level of competition. If you are quality-led then low prices may send out the wrong impression.

▮ If you are a new business and do not know your correct price level, it is easier to start high and then lower your prices than to start too low and then discover that you need to raise them.

▮ If you believe that your goods or services are of a high quality, do not be afraid of pricing them accordingly.

▮ Make sure you have fully costed all your product or service inputs before finalizing your price.

▮ Do you have any goods or services that you can advertise as 'loss-leaders' to attract customers to your business?

▮ See the checklist at the end of this chapter.

BUDGETING AND CASH FLOW FORECASTS

The three sections above on cash management, cost analysis and pricing, and estimating form the core information that help you to create your budget or cash flow forecast. Essentially, your budget will tell you whether your plans allow you enough working capital actually to run the business, and if so how much you will have to play with. The 'how much you have to play with' element will show you what is available to use for marketing, product development, training and so on.

The budgeting process is often one of iteration, where you can try out different 'what if' levels of investment in your budget model and see the different outcomes. An obvious example of this is if you increase the advertising budget. Does the estimated increase in sales revenue suggest this to be money well spent or not?

For obvious reasons developing your budget on a computer spreadsheet or specialist software (see Chapter 12) allows you more flexibility and complexity in trying out these different scenarios. Some time invested before you start the business (when you are likely to have more time in any case) in building up as sophisticated and accurate a cash flow model as you can will be time well spent. Your backers and the bank will require cash flow forecasts as a first step before being able to consider whether they will help you or not (see Chapter 5, 'Raising Capital').

Table 10.5 shows a cash flow forecast for a business that delivers ready-made meals; it consists of the projected costs and revenues for taking on a new sales manager. At first glance it appears to be a baffling array of figures; however, with the aid of the explanatory notes, it becomes more comprehensible. The final figure of increased profit of £33,510 seems well worth the investment. However, it would not take an investor very long to wonder whether the model was fully costed. The manager's national insurance and pension contributions (if relevant) have not been included. Neither are there any figures to approximate his telephone and travel costs (a salesperson who never calls or visits anyone will not be very effective), or any estimates for extra sales and publicity materials.

Table 10.5

New Sales Manager Cost/Revenue

Month		1	2	3	4	5	6	7	8	9	10	11	12		
Cost of Manager (6)	8500	£708.33	£708.33	£708.33	£708.33	£708.33	£708.33	£708.33	£708.33	£708.33	£708.33	£708.33	£708.33	£8,500.00	
Commission	8.00%	£37.31	£82.98	£133.24	£215.37	£287.78	£340.60	£430.74	£501.28	£555.97	£626.52	£673.55	£740.16	£4,625.49	£13,125.49
Offices															
Extra Orders/mnth (1)	£35.00	5	12	20	35	45	55	70	85	90	105	115	125		
Av Order Size (2)	£29.82														
Ex-VAT		£149.10	£357.84	£596.40	£1,043.70	£1,341.90	£1,640.10	£2,087.40	£2,534.70	£2,683.80	£3,131.10	£3,429.30	£3,727.50	£22,772.84	
GP (3)	83.00%	£123.75	£297.01	£495.01	£866.27	£1,113.78	£1,361.28	£1,732.54	£2,103.80	£2,227.55	£2,598.81	£2,846.32	£3,093.83	£18,859.96	
Private															
Extra Orders/mnth	£17.00	15	40	60	100	135	160	200	230	260	290	310	340		
Av Order Size	£14.48														
Ex-VAT		£217.26	£579.36	£869.04	£1,448.40	£1,955.34	£2,317.44	£2,896.80	£3,331.32	£3,765.84	£4,200.36	£4,490.04	£4,924.56	£30,995.76	
GP	83.00%	£180.33	£480.87	£721.30	£1,202.17	£1,622.93	£1,923.48	£2,404.34	£2,765.00	£3,125.65	£3,486.30	£3,726.73	£4,087.38	£25,726.48	£44,586.44
Wholesale (4)															
Extra Orders/mnth (5)	25.00	4	4	8	8	12	12	16	16	20	20	20	24		
Av Order Size	25.00														
Ex-VAT		£100.00	£100.00	£200.00	£200.00	£300.00	£300.00	£400.00	£400.00	£500.00	£500.00	£500.00	£600.00	£4,100.00	
GP	50.00%	£50.00	£50.00	£100.00	£100.00	£150.00	£150.00	£200.00	£200.00	£250.00	£250.00	£250.00	£300.00	£2,050.00	£46,636.44

'Extra Sales GP' less 'Manager Costs' £33,510.95

(1) These figures represent the extra number of orders the sales manager is projected to add to sales in each month. The numbers are cumulative. That is, month 2's figure includes month 1's figure, and month 3's includes both months 1 and 2's figures and so on. By month 12, we expect to see 125 extra office orders a month, as against month 0. This equates to approximately 6 orders per day (5.68), presuming a 22 working day month.

(2) Average order size is projected on the basis of each office order being for 4 people at just under £8/hd. We currently provide orders to three offices on an irregular basis, and this is a conservative figure on current experience. An average order size of £50 would be closer to our current office order size.

(3) The average gross profit (cost less ingredients) of our own made products is 83%.
   If the orders were to include a high than normal proportion of wine/soft drinks/ice-cream etc (which we sell at a GP of 50%) then the average will clearly fall.

(4) Currently we have one wholesale outlet which orders from us daily, at an average order size of £25+.
   However, this company orders from us every working day. Thus if we were to find another such company the monthly extra orders would be 22 rather than 4. However, on a cautionary basis I have projected that new wholesale orders would only be for the likes of small delis etc, which could expect to take 8 to 10 pies per week.

(5) Wholesale food carries no VAT.

(6) The manager position would in fact be a split between four hours of sales work through the afternoon, and four hours plus in the evening for five days a week, thus making an eight-hour day, 40-hour week. This job would replace the current evening manager position which is currently paid approx £6.5K/ pa. Thus the new position only requires £8.5K extra revenues, although the salary would in fact be £15K/pa.

Thus we see that poorly constructed budgets can be dangerously misleading. It is always desirable to have a third party go over your figures to see if you have overlooked any costs. Another hazard with these models is that they are inevitably built on a series of assumptions. In Table 10.5 the projected increases in sales figures are based on current experience and then reduced on the basis of caution – this is wise. With an entirely new business you may not have 'current experience' to project from, so your assumptions will be based on observations and guesswork. This may be reasonably accurate (or not) for your first week's or month's projections, but a small error can be compounded into a significant one by the twelfth month. It is therefore best to always err on the side of caution with your assumptions – the entrepreneur's natural optimism needs careful controlling at this stage.

VARIANCE ANALYSIS AND MONTHLY ACCOUNTS

Once you have created your budget it is important that you compare it against actual monthly results. This is good practice as it will inform you either that you are or are not meeting your targets. This will have important implications for your spending ability within the business, and you must take action accordingly. It is also important for you to discover why the budget and the actual results have diverged. This process, variance analysis, can be made as sophisticated or as straightforward as you desire. If you are familiar with statistics you may be interested to measure the stochastic volatility, chart its homoscedasticity and run a regression analysis. More simply, you can approach variance analysis as working out where your budget and actual results diverged and then finding a good reason for it.

Do not be disheartened by the fact that your budget figures were not entirely accurate; after all, they will have been based on estimates only. It is possible that the figures do not match because of simple errors in your calculations of either the forecasts or the actual figures – it may be worth checking this quickly. It is also possible that the real figures have changed because of a single one-off occurrence that has affected sales or costs, that could not realistically have been factored in to the budget, such as an 11 September effect on sales, or a flood in the stock room. This would not necessarily imply that the budget forecasts were unreliable. The most likely reason, however, is that your assumptions were inaccurate somewhere, and it is essential that you discover where so that you do not make the same mistake in the next set of budgets.

The most important task when studying the variances is to reset the accounts so that you are measuring like with like. It is easy to think that all your estimates are wrong when in fact only one line has upset the process. So you must identify which are the core variables that have not met expectations and then reset your budget

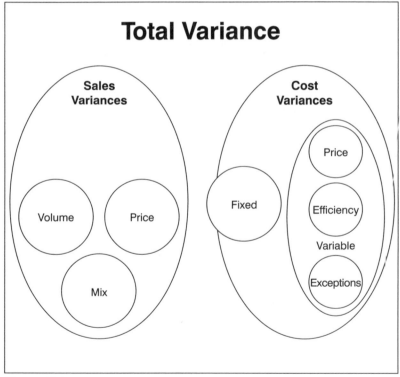

Figure 10.1

accordingly. To help you identify where the changes are, see Figure 10.1.

Checklist

▪ Do you know the ratios currently used in your type of business to measure and/or benchmark performance?

▪ Do you have a system that clearly shows your debtors and creditors and can age them?

▪ How accurately do you know your stock value and levels? Can you improve this accuracy? Can you reduce the levels without affecting your efficiency?

▪ Do you have a business savings account? Are you aware of how much you spend on debt interest and gain in savings interest? Can you do anything to improve this?

▪ How frequently do you analyse your costs? Can you lower the prices from your suppliers, especially from the utility companies?

▪ What method do you use to price your goods? How recently have you considered changing the prices? Do you know what your target market will stand?

▪ Budgeting is an active management tool – do you use it properly?

▪ Have you let someone else check your budgets/forecasts?

▪ Do you compare your budgets against actual monthly results?

▪ Do you analyse where the anomalies have come from and alter future figures in the light of these facts?

11 Bookkeeping and Administrative Systems

THE BASICS

Bookkeeping is one of the banes of the entrepreneur's existence but, as every successful businessperson knows, it is ignored at the business's peril. It is a rare person who sets up his or her own business, with all the hard work and risks that it requires, who also actually has an appetite for the careful and meticulous recording of all the transactions the business makes.

Your tax, your VAT payments and your creditworthiness are assessed on the basis of your bookkeeping figures, and it may seem that all this toil is just for them. But it is worth bearing in mind that while you may think that the hours spent keeping your books up to date is work done for the benefit of the Inland Revenue and Customs and Excise so they can take their share of your profit and VAT, a more positive reason for keeping good accounts is as a management information tool. The standardized manner in which a bookkeeping system operates allows you to monitor your progress, assess your areas of strength and weakness in a measurable financial manner, and gives you a range of figures by which you can benchmark yourself against your competitors or the industry averages. These are vital statistics indeed, and while you may be irritated by the compilation of them, you should be hungry for the results and their implications. In those dark hours late at night when you are having to 'do the books', try to remember that, here anyway, while the bookkeeping journey may be tedious the destination is well worthwhile.

Before we examine the hows and whys of bookkeeping and administrative systems, it may be useful to remind ourselves of what bookkeeping is. Essentially the bookkeeper creates a system that will track every single transaction of the business: all the outgoings – the payments – and all the incomings – the receipts. At first glance this should be very straightforward, but as we shall see, the range and timings of transactions can vary greatly (pre-payments, payments on account, pro-forma invoices, credit and discounts etc) and this instantly makes the tracking of the flow of funds much more complicated.

There are a variety of ways in which the tracking of these flows can be monitored and all will have their advantages and disadvantages. When choosing a system for your business you should endeavour to keep it as simple as possible, but retain the ability to allow the system to grow in sophistication as does your business. While there is no point in creating a system that can happily accommodate 100 people on the payroll when there is just you working for the business, equally there is no advantage in using a system that will not allow you to add a couple of staff when the moment arrives.

All systems should have the capability to record daily takings and split them into different categories; analyse receipts and payments to your bank accounts; record and analyse miscellaneous expenditure; manage your VAT and wages bills; and draw all these figures together to give you a monthly set of accounts and business overview. The system should also form a method for filing all the invoices and receipts. Your first real decision will be whether to use a manual (whether paper or spreadsheet-based) or commercially produced software system. If your business is a beautifully simple one (which all should aim to be if they can), such as a cook who sells his own services, or a translator who sells hers freelance to only a handful of clients, with no premises, no staff, and minimal overheads, then you may well be able to manage with a manual paper-based system. By increasing the complexity of the business you increase the complexity of the system required to monitor it. If you expect to have employees (even occasional casual labour),

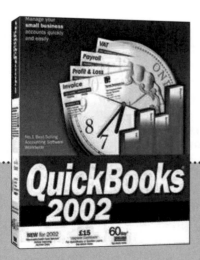

QuickBooks

Although starting your own business is exciting and challenging it can also provide major headaches. Keeping on top of who owes you what and when as well as what you owe is fundamental to business success – especially considering that businesses can fold these days owing as little as £1,500.

Setting up in business means getting to grips with such issues as budgeting, invoicing, profit and loss forecasting, supplier management, payroll as well as managing obligations such as tax and VAT.

But help is at hand. Investing in accounting software such as *QuickBooks* – designed specifically for the SME – is a cost-effective way to put all this important information at your fingertips, ensuring you've more time to spend growing your business.

For many businesses, time is a critical feature. With many business managers working a 12-14 hour day, the provision of readily available information on their business tends to be something they think about at the end of the day. As the business grows, how does the owner manager manage with demands of staffing, payroll, suppliers, and look after his customers at the same time?

For Andrew Blackburn, the solution lay in choosing a software package that met his needs. In March 1997 he set up the Extreme Pizza Company originally as a take-away employing five part time staff. The business has now expanded to two full-time and eight part-time staff.

'Running a small business is a constant juggling act', says Andrew. 'Apart from cooking and hosting the restaurant, I'm also keeping track of orders, stock and overall management. I therefore have very little time to spend on accounts, so I need a software package that is quick, efficient and easy to use'.

Andrew now needs to spend only 30 minutes a day updating his books. He uses *QuickBooks* to log invoices from food and drink and packaging suppliers and to produce instant reports on the best selling products and overall sales analysis.

'Now more of my time and energy is focused on growing my business – not wading through complex and manual accounts'. Recognising the pressures of running a business, many successful managers today are choosing to invest in systems such as *QuickBooks* to free up their time and give them a competitive edge.

premises with all their heating, lighting, insurance costs (whether this is your bedroom or serviced offices), and a range of suppliers and customers, then your system is already a lot more complex than the previous example. A manual system is still perfectly possible for tracking this level of business, but one of the many computer-based systems may be more cost-effective. Be aware that the software packages often also offer useful advice lines, at a price.

Although we have suggested that a commercial software system may be a more flexible and easier option, it is still well worth spending a little time understanding how a manual system operates. This will give you a feel for the figures that either system produces, and therefore put you in a better position to comprehend the options that may be suggested to you. The remainder of this chapter will show you how a manual system works, and will also point out where the computer-based system will differ.

SINGLE ENTRY BOOKKEEPING

At its most basic, you should create a single entry cash book. Take a columned sheet and record every piece of money received (gross receipts) and every cost (payments or disbursements). The periodic totals (whether daily, weekly or monthly) should then be totalled for both receipts and payments; then you have started to create a rudimentary system that shows your cash flow.

Table 11.1 shows such a cash book, with the left-hand four columns showing the receipts and the right-hand four columns the payments, with the periodic totals at the bottom of the page. This enables the reader to better understand the cash flows in terms of both time and amount. A further level of sophistication can be achieved if the 'details' column is broken down further into subcategories such as for the payments analysis: office expenses, travel, marketing, rent and electricity and so on. If each of these are given their own column in the ledger, then a breakdown of where the costs are coming from can easily be seen. While all this can be done on paper, clearly the use of a computer spreadsheet will allow more space and therefore detail to be noted.

Table 11.1 Single-entry bookkeeping example

Receipts				Payments			
Date	Name	Details	Amount £	Date	Name	Details	Amount £
1 May	Balance	Brought forward	540.00				
4 May	Mckays Ltd	Sales	232.33	4 May	Newmans & Co	Stock purchase	478.54
6 May	Jade Bros	Sales	88.50				
				8 May	Oldmans & Co	Stock purchase	98.65
				12 May	Tricity plc	Electricity charges	113.20
14 May	Smith & Co	Refund on returned stock	153.66				
17 May	Jade Bros	Sales	190.45				
				18 May	U-rent Ltd	Tool hire	66.66
20 May	Frasers	Sales	397.55				
				22 May	Roamaround plc	Mobile phones	72.56
31 May	Monthly total		1602.49	31 May	Monthly total		829.61
1 June	Balance	Brought Forward	772.88				

Bank reconciliation

The above system is single entry bookkeeping and has no self-contained mechanism within its structure to enable you to check whether you have made any mistakes or not. The only proof of whether the books have been kept properly is if your end of month cash total matches that on your bank statement.

However, this is quite likely not to be the case, as the vagaries of the banking system and your customers' own banking habits will inevitably mean some cheques do not clear quickly, credit card transactions go awry and invoices raised do not get paid. For this reason, you must make a bank reconciliation where you check off against each month's bank statement the cheques you have written against those that have cleared, and also those you have paid in that are cleared. As time-consuming and tedious as this checking process may be, it is crucial if you are to retain any control over your cash. Once you start losing sight of which payments and which receipts have actually been cashed, you will also lose sight of your real cash position.

DOUBLE ENTRY BOOKKEEPING

If what you read below is too mind-achingly complicated, tedious or both, then after discussion with your accountant it may be simpler to stick to single entry and let the accountant transfer your simple records to double entry software to prepare the accounts. This clearly will not work for every business, and it will take your accountant longer to prepare the accounts and therefore be more costly, but it may be better than countless hours spent getting the double entry system wrong and then having to have your accountant sort it out. Do not despair over the bookkeeping.

A more complex but more effective bookkeeping system is the double entry system. This is the system that all accountants and professional bookkeepers use. This balances every flow of cash with an equal value of goods or service. Thus if you have a telephone expense of £100 you have a balancing cash credit of £100. Immediately we have encountered the bookkeeping jargon problem of credits and debits. All is not what it seems at first with these expressions. Think of the bank as a third party between you and your suppliers and customers. The credit and debit expressions apply to your relationship with the bank. You sell some widgets and give the proceeds to the bank. The bank now owes you that money, so it is a debit. You buy something with money in your bank account. The bank pays out the money, you now have credit with the bank, so it is a credit.

While these descriptions are often confusing to interpret, the following always holds true: debits go in the left-hand column and credits always on the right. A useful rule to keep you straight is to consider all transactions as 'from–to'. Return to the telephone expense example above. The money to pay the bill comes 'from' cash and goes 'to' the telephone. 'From' is credit, so credit the cash account; 'to' is debit, so debit the telephone account.

In order to record both the entries for every transaction you need to have a 'set of books'. These will take the form of 'day books' or 'journals' and ledgers.

Day books or journals

Day books or journals are where every transaction is entered in date order. In most businesses you will have separate journals for the different types of transactions you encounter. You will have a general journal that will record all transactions in date order, and also area specific journals that will include a cash book, sales book (for non-cash sales, ie those on account or credit) and purchases. Every book must have at least five columns: date, account, reference, debit and credit column. You can have more columns to give greater detail should you wish. It is a good idea to separate your VAT amounts, if applicable, when they are first entered in the day books. See Table 11.2.

Each purchase entry should have an additional internal reference, not so much for the accounting part of the bookkeeping, as from the filing and administration aspect. All your payments are likely to have an associated invoice with a number; however, you should create a new reference for each transaction that identifies where and when it was filed for your purposes. Both the debit and credit side of the entry will carry the reference. This enables you to check your entries against the original paperwork should you need to later.

The day books will build up a mass of transactions that will enable you to analyse your cash position accurately and also gain a picture of how the cash flows operate within the business generally. However, the amount of information on any page will obscure any detailed analysis of who you are paying and who is paying you. To gain this information the information gathered in the journals needs to be re-presented as a ledger.

Table 11.2 Day books

Sales Day Book

Date	Detail	Inv #	Total	VAT	Net Sales	Amt Pd	Date Pd	Chq/cash
02/03	G Goddard	223	44.66	6.65	38.01	44.66	06/04	Chq
02/03	D Fisher	224	145.76	21.71	124.05	145.76	01/04	Chq
05/03	S Pate	225	111.33	16.58	94.75	111.33	03/04	Chq
07/03	K McLeod	226	287.55	42.83	244.72	287.55	13/04	Chq
			589.30	87.77	501.53	589.30		

Purchases Day Book

Date Pd	Detail	External Ref #	Internal Ref #	Total	VAT	Stock	Power	Telephone	Motor dxps	Date
04/05	Newmans	3325	5/1	478.54	71.27	407.27				02/06
08/05	Oldmans	4137	5/2	98.65	14.69	83.96				02/06
12/05	Tricity	2013	5/3	113.20	16.86		96.34			02/06
22/05	Roamaround	1536	5/4	72.56	10.81			61.75		15/06
23/05	Franks Wheels	2042	5/5	310.00	46.17				263.83	15/06
				1072.95	159.80	491.23	96.34	61.75	263.83	

These two are clearly quite similar. The purchases day book records all supplies for goods and services bought on credit terms. Analyse each invoice according to the type of expense and remember when payment of the invoice is recorded in the cash book, the total amount must be entered in the 'creditors' column.

Ledgers

Ledgers are the same information we have noted in the journals but listed differently. You copy the entries from the journals but into account-specific ledgers, so all the telephone entries go into a telephone ledger and all the widget sales into a widget ledger. Thus you can get a picture of exactly how much you spend on different areas of the business and how your sales of different products are performing.

The copying of the different entries from the journals to the ledgers is called 'posting'. As with journals, there will be a general or 'nominal ledger' and specific ledgers for each of the major accounts.

COMPUTERIZED ACCOUNTS

As should be clear by now, bookkeeping involves careful filing and data entry. Double entry bookkeeping provides a safer and more detailed analysis of the current state of your business's affairs, but it involves far more entries and cross-referencing. It is precisely this time-consuming data management that computers can eradicate. If your business accounts are at all complex, it would be wise to consider using such software. Discuss with your accountant what is available and would best suit both your needs and your accountant's.

OTHER ADMINISTRATIVE ISSUES

Invoicing and credit control

Invoicing is clearly a critical part of the bookkeeping paperwork. It is the source of all your sales and credit information, and has the advantage of being quick and simple to do. If you manage your invoices efficiently you should always be able to construct the debit side of your day books and ledgers correctly. Not only will your invoices record information of your sales, they also record your VAT and your creditors.

Your invoices should give the following information: your business name, address, telephone number, and perhaps a Web page or e-mail address as well. Also include your VAT registration number (if you have one) and, if you are a limited company, your company registration number. This can all be printed on the invoice. Each separate invoice will have a reference number, unique to it, and the purchaser's name and address. You may also need to note down a delivery address if this is different from the invoicing address. Finally the invoice will need the date (of sale, if different from delivery) and the items purchased, with their net price, the total including VAT, and the VAT payable. (See Figure 11.1.)

Each invoice ought to have a minimum of two but possibly three copies: one for the customer, one for the cash or sales day book, and a third for the customer ledger. If you are using a computerized system you will only need to print out the customer copy and one copy for yourself. If your hard drive is large enough to record all your sales without occasionally having to clear it out, you may not have to produce any hard copy for yourself, so long as you make sure you back up all your files regularly.

With this information you can fill in your sales day book (for non-cash sales) and keep track of your customers' payments. You will also manage your VAT accounts from this information. Each month you should total up the different columns in the sales day book and see that the subsidiary columns (if you have split sales into different columns for analysis purposes), plus the VAT, balance your total gross revenue for that period.

At the end of each month you should see which of your customers have not paid their invoices. You should have made clear your standard payment terms – usually 30 days – either on the invoice or in discussion with them. If you have not received payment by this time then you will need to chase them up. Two golden rules with credit control are, one, do not be embarrassed about chasing debt. It is why you are in business, and the customers must expect to pay for what they have bought. Two, the softly, softly approach will work much better than an aggressive one. Your customers most probably have not paid because they have other priorities; a gentle reminder will put you back near the top of their list. If they have difficulty paying, an aggressive

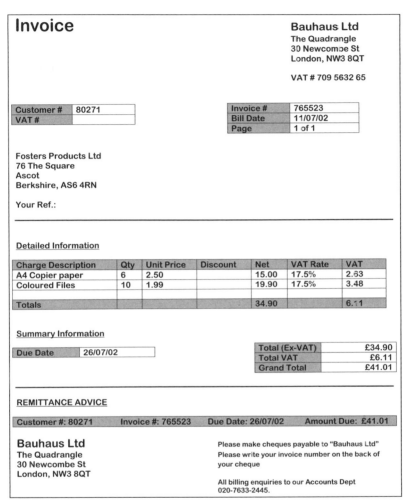

Invoice

Bauhaus Ltd
The Quadrangle
30 Newcombe St
London, NW3 8QT

VAT # 709 5632 65

Customer #	80271
VAT #	

Invoice #	765523
Bill Date	11/07/02
Page	1 of 1

Fosters Products Ltd
76 The Square
Ascot
Berkshire, AS6 4RN

Your Ref.:

Detailed Information

Charge Description	Qty	Unit Price	Discount	Net	VAT Rate	VAT
A4 Copier paper	6	2.50		15.00	17.5%	2.63
Coloured Files	10	1.99		19.90	17.5%	3.48
Totals				34.90		6.11

Summary Information

Due Date	26/07/02

Total (Ex-VAT)	£34.90
Total VAT	£6.11
Grand Total	£41.01

REMITTANCE ADVICE

Customer #: 80271	Invoice #: 765523	Due Date: 26/07/02	Amount Due: £41.01

Bauhaus Ltd
The Quadrangle
30 Newcombe St
London, NW3 8QT

Please make cheques payable to "Bauhaus Ltd"
Please write your invoice number on the back of
your cheque

All billing enquiries to our Accounts Dept
020-7633-2445.

Figure 11.1 Sample invoice

approach is no more and probably less likely to work than a friendly one. If you create a rapport with their accounts department you are in a better position than if they immediately go on the defensive when they hear from you. If they are being wilfully unhelpful the Small Business Service and Small Claims Courts are able to help you – but this should be a last resort. A good timetable to go by for credit chasing is as follows:

Issue of invoice → Statement of account two to three weeks later → a gentle telephone reminder after another two to three weeks to the accounts department (at this point you can try to find out if there is any problem brewing) → a polite letter indicating that three months have now passed since the invoice was issued, and prompt settlement is now required.

Only after this has failed is it worth considering legal action. But it is worth weighing the amount outstanding against the time, effort and expense of reclaiming it.

If customers habitually pay late (often large companies claim their settlement departments take two to three months to pay out), then you should discuss this with them if it causes you difficulty. If you are worried about any customers, then you should also suspend their credit facilities, with a clear explanation why you are doing so. Discounts for prompt payments can help to speed the process up, and the lost revenue is often more than made up by reduced credit-chasing expenditure. Just be sure that the discounts are noted in the day books correctly.

Employee-related administration

As soon as you take on staff, even occasional casual labour, you face two separate sets of extra administration. First, there is the legal requirement to pay national insurance and income tax for them and also offer a Stakeholder Pension scheme, if you have over five employees. Second, you will need another set of day books and ledgers to account for all employee-related expenditure.

To deal with the bookkeeping side first, you will need to record all transactions related to your employees. (See Table 11.3.) Primarily, this will be each week or month, with a line against the employee's name showing his or her gross pay, the income tax due on it, the employee's contribution for national insurance due and thus the net pay for the period. You will also have to note the employer's contribution for national insurance.

You may also have to enter any other deductions or contributions you have made to the employee's pay. Sick pay, maternity pay, cash advances, discounts on purchases, private health care schemes, pension contributions and so on must all be accounted for.

Table 11.3 Wages book

June entry for A Harris, paid fortnightly.

Date	Name	Code	Gross Pay	E'ees NI contb.[1]	Tax	Net Pay	E'ers NI contb.[2]
07/06	A Harris	461L	811.21	63.32	130.80	617.09	74.72
21/06	A Harris	461L	753.20	57.52	116.72	578.96	67.87
			1564.41	120.84	247.52	1196.05	142.59

1 *Employee's National Insurance contribution*
2 *Employer's National Insurance contribution*

The cheques, cash or direct transfer from your bank to employees' accounts to pay your staff will all need to be noted in the cash book or petty cash book, as will the national insurance and PAYE contributions you send to the Inland Revenue. These amounts must all balance your entries for the period in your wages book. As with the other elements of bookkeeping, the ability to keep your records up to date and in order is critical to avoid future problems. If you are using a computerized system for your bookkeeping, then it may be wise to also use a payroll software package to make your life easier, or alternatively use a local payroll services firm. The latter, as a third party, can also be useful in taking the heat out of any query between employee and employer over pay issues.

Your employees will require payslips with their pay each pay period. These can easily be acquired from office stationers; they will allow you to show their current pay broken down into basic pay, overtime, statutory sick or maternity pay; the total amount; the pay so far this tax year and the deductions outlined above.

The government requires you to keep certain statutory information about your employees. Each employee must have his or her own confidential file containing at least the following:

- full name;
- address;
- date of birth;
- national insurance number;
- date of starting work;
- salary;
- position held;

▌ date of leaving (if relevant);
▌ record of absences;
▌ record of injuries sustained at work or illnesses (in some occupations as part of health and safety records).

You should also keep all other relevant information such as job applications, references, contract of employment, letter of employment outlining the employee's pay, hours, job title and so on, notes of any disciplinary action or discussions, and similar information.

The Department of Work and Pensions can provide you with a great deal of information relating to your obligations, rights and requirements as an employer. The Small Business Service is also worth contacting for any specific small business changes in practice. Note that it is a legal requirement to keep all your books for six years, even if you have ceased trading, after which they can be destroyed.

In summary, bookkeeping is an essential chore for any business. However, if you approach it as a management information tool which also provides the tax and company registration authorities with the information they want, then perhaps you can persuade yourself of the need for regular application to keeping it up to date. There is no doubt that 'little and often' is the best way to maintain any bookkeeping system. The best system for your business is probably best decided in a discussion between you and your accountant. Bear in mind that there is a wide range of computer software that can help save you time – but that you also need to understand how the system works so you will know if the figures do not look right.

Checklist

▌ Have you decided what you want your administrative system for: VAT records, corporation tax and accounting purposes, invoicing, credit control, other management information gathering purposes?
▌ Have you discovered whether you can manage without a computer-based system?

■ Have you spoken with your accountant/tax adviser to make sure your systems meet his or her needs as well?
■ Do you file invoices immediately they arrive?
■ Do your business's invoices clearly state your terms?
■ Do you issue invoices promptly on delivery?
■ Do you issue statements promptly each month?
■ Do you have a credit chasing timetable, and do you follow it?
■ Do you know your statutory obligations as an employer?
■ Do you keep proper records on all your employees?

12 IT and Management Communications

Chris Hutber

INTRODUCTION

The world of information technology (IT) seems to be getting ever more complex. The good news is that as more powerful technology comes within the reach of businesses of all sizes, so the opportunities for using IT to manage your business more effectively are increasing all the time.

The availability of high-speed connections to the Internet, for example, has meant that online wide area networking has come within the budgets of small companies with more than one location. Only two or three years ago, such private networks were the preserve of big corporations with big budgets: now with the advent of virtual private networking (a secure way of transferring data over the Internet), any geographically spread business can enjoy the benefits of linking all of its computer systems together.

PLATFORM CHOICE

With so much choice and new technology, where does one begin? The personal computer (PC) running MS Windows has become the standard for computer systems for small and medium-sized businesses. Some businesses in design and the media may prefer the

Apple Mac, but using the alternative as the prevalent platform for your business could seriously restrict the availability of business software.

Even if you are a design guru, with the smartest Mac-based systems in the trendiest part of town, chances are that as you grow, your company will need PCs to run, for example, its accounting systems.

APPLICATIONS

Microsoft dominates the office application market probably above anything else. Even if you go for a Macintosh and its inbuilt operating system, you probably need a very good reason for using any products other than Word and Excel for your office applications. A cut-down version of MS Office, Microsoft Works, exists, and is often bundled with new PCs. But after a couple of months' use, you are bound to find that within the 10 per cent of Excel that you will ever use is the one vital thing not included in MS Works. So go for the full product: you should be able to get it at a good price bundled with a new PC.

Shareware word processing and spreadsheet software is available for downloading from the Internet, but unless you have a political objection to making Mr Gates even richer, I would not recommend it. Most job applicants will have experience of using Microsoft applications, and the brand has become the de facto standard for business. Certainly avoid paying £99 for a bundle of software you have never heard of: there is a very good reason it's cheap. In fact, often PC manufacturers will make more money on these 'afterthoughts' than they will on their advertised hardware price.

FORECASTING SOFTWARE

Even before a business has started trading, forecasting software may provide a useful tool. When you input predicted sales, costs, overheads and other variables, specialist forecasting software can enable you to produce the figures for detailed business plans. Once

Chrysalis TV

CISCO SYSTEMS

®

EMPOWERING THE
INTERNET GENERATION℠

The Company

Chrysalis Television Limited, part of the Chrysalis Group, is a growing TV production company. The sport it now covers includes Formula 1, World Rally Motor Racing and Italian Football. It has also diversified from sport to include series, such as the *"Top 10"* music series for Channel 4.

The Challenge

"Many people spend much of their time out of the office, be it on location or in editing suites," says Matt Abraham's, IT Manager. *"They may be away for whole days or weeks at a time. For example, with the Formula 1 contract there is a different location for each event so our employees are constantly travelling around the world."*

"At any one time, the company may have between 25 and 40 employees out of the office who need to access the office remotely and with whom we need to communicate on a constant basis. For this reason, we needed to provide our employees with some form of contact with our network," adds Matt.

The Solution

The initiative to provide remote access was taken by the IT Director of the Chrysalis Group.

The first step, which was taken three years ago, was to add remote access to email. A hotmail type service has been made available which can be accessed from any computer in most countries around the world. The company uses GroupWise bolt on web access. It uses dedicated client and web based Citrix servers for file access and a Cisco 1603 router. It also uses laptops which can be connected to land lines or a mobile phone with GSM cards.

The Rewards

Prior to the installation of new technology communication was difficult: There was a lot of phoning and faxing which was much more costly.

The benefits have been in efficiency, speed, time and reliability.

Matt says: *"Nobody wants to go back to the old ways of communicating by sending faxes and phoning people from remote areas. Without this technology, life would be much more of a chore for the people on location. Now they can be part of our network without having to be here. A lot of their work can be done on location, without having to make notes and type them up when they get back to the office. This saves duplication."*

The Future
Over the next twelve months the company plans to make remote access to files available to its staff. The company is looking into the possibilities of using Ipaks; Windows CE based palm top computers and blue tooth mobile phones for remote access. This technology is very portable and provides full office suite applications for mobile workers.

"The potential for using other Internet technology is huge for us," says Matt. *"We are looking to use more IP telephony and to provide more remote access so that employees can have full network access."*

Conclusion
Technologies enabling employees of Chrysalis Television to be mobile and work remotely have been key to the successful running of this company, where so much work is done on location.

Cisco Systems Limited
10 New Square Park
Bedfont Lakes
Feltham
Middlesex TW14 8HA
Tel: +44 (0)208 824 1000
Fax: +44 (0)208 824 1001

Chat Moderators

CISCO SYSTEMS

®

EMPOWERING THE
INTERNET GENERATION℠

The Company

The company started in 2000, moderating chat
rooms and forums for a children's Internet company. Its principle
responsibility was keeping the chat rooms and forums safe, specifically to
screen out violent or sexual imagery and to monitor potentially unsafe
conversation.

Recently, the company has widened its field of operation to provide
monitoring for commercial sites where the potential for brand libel is
wide, and moderators for special web events such as celebrity interviews
and management seminars. They now employ 36 people.

It is the only UK company to specialise in this service; other software
houses operate it as a sideline. Clients of Chat Moderators include Pop
Idol, Sony, BBC, Government Departments, Liverpool Football club,
Friends Reunited, EMI, and BT.

The Challenge

The use of remote access was critical for the initial setting up of the
company and to minimise start-up costs. *"We started the business in our
bedroom and with limited funds so minimising costs was one of our key objectives,"*
explains Neil Blackburn, Co-founder and Director of Chat Moderators.
*"Office space in central London is so expensive that having employees offsite is a
major cost advantage for us,"* adds Neil. The flexible nature of both the
company employment contracts and the clients means that staff don't have
to travel to an office.

The company's workforce are mainly part time with 60% only working
20 hours or less a week. *"Our employees are mainly graduates and professionals
with families and other commitments, for them being mobile and working remotely
is essential,"* explains Neil. With the average commute from Greater
London into the company's office timed at over 1.5 hours, mobile
working has also greatly increased employee productivity, whilst saving
transport costs and other overheads.

The Solution

The company provides all employees with 24/7 Internet Access with
ISP's using Cisco products. Using a number of ISP's (including Spitfire,

Pipex and BT), the IT department is able to set up instant links to client companies which enables the moderators to monitor chats from their own portal.

The company is fully interactive, utilising E-mail, Elearning, and MSN Chat for conferencing and its own Intranet.

The Rewards

"All of our employees work remotely at some point, on average 80% of our workforce are working from home or remotely, which is a huge cost saving for us," comments Neil.

Saving office space, hardware costs, travel expense and time are the main benefits. As research has proved software filters to be inconsistent at chat room regulation, human monitoring remains the most secure option. Enabling mobile working ensures that employees can be fully productive but also able to combine employment with other interests. This leads to a high degree of job satisfaction.

The Future

With interactivity increasing, greater expansion is likely for the role of chat moderators. In addition to the security screening, monitors are well placed to prevent libel, promote brands and provide instant market research.

With transport efficiency problems and costs impacting negatively on part time workers, remote access solutions are ideal for this type of specialist business.

Conclusion

Starting from the bedroom of one of the co-founders, Chat Moderators has successfully used remote access to grow and expand its client base whilst keeping operating costs at a minimum.

For Chat Moderators, an interactive service product and mobile working practices have combined successfully to create synergy.

Cisco Systems Limited
10 New Square Park
Bedfont Lakes, Feltham
Middlesex TW14 8HA
Tel: +44 (0)208 824 1000
Fax: +44 (0)208 824 1001

mastered, this type of software is far quicker than a spreadsheet to manipulate, particularly for 'what-if type' scenarios.

Once your company is up and running you will be able to produce quick and accurate forecasting at the touch of a button, including Profit & Loss and Cash flow statements, enabling you to make key decisions about your business.

The output should of course be capable of being integrated into word processing and spreadsheet applications for smart document production. The availability of a link to your chosen accounting solution will mean that rekeying opening financial data will be unnecessary; there will be one less thing to take up your time. Such software will cost hundreds, but not thousands of pounds.

ACCOUNTS AND BUSINESS MANAGEMENT SOFTWARE

At the entry level, accounting software tends to come as an integrated package with financials, order processing and stock control bundled together. The better packages have a basic form of contact management included. This will be useful for both sales prospecting and credit control.

Generally, such entry-level software should be user-installable. Check if training courses are available. Beware though: at this level, if you want your supplier or accountant to handle the implementation, as you will probably be spending more on the services than on the software itself. For a single user system expect to pay anything between £99 and £1,000. For multi-user you can expect to pay anything up to about £2,000. At this level, though, most users can get up and running with a basic understanding of computing and accounting principles.

As your business becomes larger and your requirements more sophisticated, then accounts software tends to become modular, allowing you to pick and choose the areas of business management that you want to encompass within the system. Modules will certainly include the nominal ledger, sales ledger and purchase ledgers, with others such as cashbook, stock and order processing available. Some systems have project costing and manufacturing modules too.

Make sure you see as many demonstrations of the software as you need to be convinced that it is right for you. Companies selling business management software should be as keen as you are to ensure that the software meets your requirements. Don't assume that because lots of other people are using the software, or because companies you recognize are using it, the system will do what you are expecting it to do. Focus on the sharp end of your business. If rapid delivery is important, then focus on order processing. If monitoring the profitability of projects is paramount, start with the part of the system that provides this.

At the modular level of business management software you will undoubtedly need professional support. Moreover, this is probably the point at which you will need to turn to a company that specializes in implementing accounting systems, rather than your accountant. For modular systems you should be budgeting anything from £5,000 to £20,000 including implementation.

CUSTOMER RELATIONSHIP MANAGEMENT (CRM)

We mentioned that entry-level accounting systems often provide a degree of contact management. Such packages can also be purchased separately. As a general rule, the more you pay, the more functionality and flexibility you get. Once again, the basic solutions (starting at £99) will tend to run largely out of the box, but as requirements become more complicated, so the price of the software and the cost of professional implementation will rise significantly.

Customer relationship management (CRM) is the acronym for this type of solution. The last few years have seen countless cases of failed CRM implementations. The difficulty is that with modern software the potential for automation of the sales process is phenomenal. For this reason, people undertaking CRM projects have a tendency to set themselves objectives that are unachievable. The secret is to go for quick wins. Define the essential processes and work out the best way of automating them. You can always come back for the 'nice to haves' at a later stage.

Integration here is the key. Being able to automatically generate mail-shots and e-mail shots should be taken as read. As the business grows, will a mobile sales force be able to read and update customer information while on the move? Can the system integrate with your business systems to allow you to provide quotations and convert them into orders without the need for any rekeying? Is there a version of the software that runs on hand-held devices? Can you then have a detailed order history for customers so that you can market suitably to them in the future?

INTERNET CONNECTIVITY

The Internet age has brought, above all, the availability of inexpensive bandwidth to smaller businesses. Bandwidth is how much data traffic can flow within a set period of time. This has meant that not only is communication with customers, suppliers and banks more immediate than ever before, but using broadband connections, a business can have online connections to remote sites and offices in a cost-effective manner. If nothing else, this means that an owner-manager should be able to select systems in such a way that he or she can keep an eye on day to day activity from home, the motorway service station, the airport or even the ski slope.

If it is available in your area, go for ADSL. Check at www.btopenworld.com/broadband to find out availability for your exchange. ADSL provides relatively high bandwidth for a low monthly charge. If you are running the type of business that requires a leased line with guaranteed bandwidth availability, you probably should not be relying on the contents of this chapter.

If you are having any sort of network installed, check with whoever is installing it that you are ordering the correct ADSL configuration. Do *not* rely on BT for this advice!

E-MAIL

Having your own domain name is very important to provide a professional image. For example, your mail should come to joe.bloggs@yourcompany.co.uk. Save free e-mail services such as

Hotmail for personal use. Use a product at least as powerful as Outlook Express to ensure that the e-mails you send and receive are properly spell-checked and archived.

Unlike a letter, an e-mail is something that, once written, is nearly always sent immediately, and is very rarely retractable. Never send an e-mail when you are angry. In fact, never even type an e-mail when you are angry. You cannot park outside the postbox and bribe the postal operative to give you your letter back if you regret sending it. If an e-mail is very important, draft it in a word processor and copy and paste it into your e-mail package once you have perfected it. That way you are less likely to lose it from not saving it, or to send it incomplete.

Remember that with an e-mail, even if you are skilled in the art of smilies (codes like ;-) to indicate winking or irony), you can never be sure what sort of mood the person you are sending to will be in when he or she opens it. Individual personnel or disciplinary matters are nearly always better dealt with face to face. You can always confirm the outcome by e-mail.

THE WORLD WIDE WEB

Your Web site

Having a Web presence is also important for any business. Again, having a domain name properly registered is important (www.yourcompany.co.uk). It will make your business seem so much more professional than using an extension of an Internet Service Provider's.

Web sites can be put together very simply and cost-effectively. Bear in mind that in the business world, people want to be informed rather than entertained. Make sure that your telephone number is easy to find on your Web site. There are certain industries (eg design, media) where dazzling customers with clever graphics is important. But as a rule, people will be put off by unnecessary animation and cleverness, if they are just trying to find the basic details about your company. There are few experiences more frustrating than going to a Web site you remember to find a company's phone number that you don't, only to be met with a 'contact us' page that has contact by e-mail (or worse, form-submission) only. Even organizations like Easyrentacar, that rely on the low costs associated with not having many customer services staff on the end of the line, have their phone numbers clearly placed on their Web sites.

If you are going to have a news section on your site, make sure that it really does contain news. Bear in mind that many sites are updated every minute of every day. Yours doesn't need to be, but why let it outdate itself if you don't plan to update it religiously?

Make sure that your company e-mail and Web site details are on all of your printed literature: letterheads, business cards and so on.

Web site submission

Search engines such as Google, AltaVista and Yahoo! are used to search the Web for sites. We find Google best for looking for business information. They give details of sites that fit the criteria provided by the search words given. There are packages and even companies that charge money for submitting your site to the major search engines. This is a service that is probably not necessary for a small business. Submitting your site to the major search engines can be done once, visiting them. If you submit at Yahoo!, AltaVista and Google once, their indexing mechanism will automatically revisit your site and keep their records up to date. Multiple submissions can actually be counter-productive: the search engines may treat them as spam (junk communications) and remove your site from their listings.

Useful sites

www.yell.com   completely free and quicker than the directory enquiries services at:

www.bt.com   another telephone directory service: private numbers too

www.royalmail.com   postcode finder

www.multimap.com   maps and directions

www.rac.com and **www.theaa.com**   traffic information

www.systransoft.com   translation site

www.companies-house.gov.uk   company info

www.businesslink.org   advice and guidance for small businesses
www.reed.co.uk   free recruitment site

Procurement

The Internet is a great medium for comparing prices. Most stationery and supplies companies have Web sites where you can buy products online, usually more cost-effectively than in physical retail outlets. Moreover, sites such as acequote.com allow you to invite quotes and responses for products and services. Acequote.com is one that operates for IT.

Currently e-procurement, where corporations make major cost savings by automating their buying departments, is mostly about maximizing economies of scale in large businesses, and is not generally used in the SME sector.

HARDWARE AND NETWORKING

When you select PC hardware, brand will not be overly important. You will pay slightly more for the comfort of knowing that your chosen manufacturer will probably be around for years to come, but the main reason why personal computing has become so accessible is because nearly all of the components are interchangeable. Dell, for example, can choose the cheapest supplier for each component to ensure a very cost-effective product. As your business grows, it makes sense to standardize on a particular manufacturer. In the meantime, go for as powerful a machine as you can afford from a supplier you trust, even if that means a local firm building computers in a garage.

Ensure you have a fast, reliable means of backing up all of your data (and applications). Even then, ensure you have as much support as you think you need. PCs usually come with a hardware warranty. This means that if, for example, your hard disk fails, the manufacturer will replace it for you. But what about reloading the applications? This will usually cost extra. Many small businesses will have the IT equivalent of an odd-job man, paid by the hour to deal with minor issues. Businesses with one or two PCs should consider a basic computer insurance policy. Premiums include cover for the reinstatement of data, providing proper back-ups have been performed.

Once the business has grown, and a mission-critical network is in place, then it will probably be better to consider having a professional support agreement from a services company in place. Make sure you know what will be the result of any eventuality; for example, are on-site call-outs included in the price?

PRINTING

For a small business, one of the all-in-one copier, fax and scanning devices available today might be the answer. But for printing items that are sent outside the business, a laser-quality printer is essential. Laser printed invoices, cheques and payslips all portray professionalism. When choosing a printer, select a major, branded manufacturer: it is essential that toner and spares are readily available.

SECURITY

Virus attacks have been well publicized over the last year or so. Install professional anti-virus software and make sure you keep it updated. Anti-virus software is sold on a subscription basis, and once you have purchased a subscription (usually for one to three years) you will be able to keep it updated either via the Internet or by a disk sent out by the vendor. If you have a network, make sure you have protection for the desktops, the server and the e-mail gateway.

If you have a permanent connection to the Internet (including ADSL) you must have a firewall. A firewall will prevent unauthorized users (hackers) from accessing your system. Don't necessarily go for the one your ISP tries to sell you. Buying elsewhere can bring savings.

NETWORKS

If you think you are on a network then you probably are. A local area network is where two or more computers are linked together in the same building. At its most basic level, just the drives are shared using the Windows operating system. You have to be careful about who is logged in and whose PC is switched on, and, although since the advent of Windows 2000 networks have greatly improved, generally they are not terribly reliable.

As a general rule, typically up to four users would use a peer-to-peer network. This is where there is no dedicated server. If you have more than three users, you should seriously consider a dedicated server: that is, a machine that is kept switched on constantly and only 'serves' the other (client) computers. The server does not have to be a fantastically expensive machine, providing you are taking proper, regular back-ups. Ask yourself the question, how long could my business survive without its computer systems? If the answer is more than one working day, then having someone on hand who can restore your applications and data in the event of a disaster is probably more important that spending several thousand pounds on the most resilient server available.

MOBILE COMPUTING

All sorts of devices from Personal Digital Assistants (PDAs) to mobile phones can now be connected and/or synchronized to your office computer systems. PDAs began life as personal organizers, with suites of applications such as word processors and diaries to make life easier. Today they offer Internet connectivity, as well as a vast array of hardware and software choices.

At the entry level PDAs will physically connect to your PC for synchronization. Many have infra-red connections to mobile phones. At the top end, wireless technology allows them to be updated constantly. There are a number of standards vying for market domination. On the basis that marketers win platform wars, and with the vast amounts of money behind it, Bluetooth will probably emerge as the dominant standard.

Entry-level PDAs start at around £100, going up to £500 for top of the range Bluetooth models.

SUPPLIER CHOICE

In this complex world it is tempting to turn to your dentist's whiz-kid nephew for advice. He may well know a thing or two about PC systems, but would you follow this approach for tax planning advice? There should be a choice of local professional suppliers who will be pleased to provide you with advice, albeit with the hope that you will be buying from them. Your local Business Link will have an IT adviser who will be able to provide impartial advice and very cost-effective consultancy. Whether you take independent advice or not, be sure to ask to speak to reference customers of your selected supplier.

The smaller your business is, the more local your supplier can be, and the lower the costs associated with the services it provides should be. If you just need a single PC and you can't find a local sole-trader IT specialist you can rely on, then PC World is as good as anyone. Why pay a regional business to business half-day call-out rate (£300+) to do a job that PC World will do for £14.99 if you take your equipment to them?

For more complex systems, always get at least two quotes. Ask your preferred supplier if it is happy for you to get mission-critical software and services from it and shop around for the hardware: enlightened IT services providers will see hardware items as commodities, and should be happy to point you in the right direction. You may of course see safety in the idea of having a single point of supply for everything: it will avoid the possibility of anyone ducking responsibility. Some companies offer an 'open book invoicing' service for customers who really want them to provide everything. They simply provide the hardware at their actual cost plus 10 per cent. This may even be less than the best possible price at the time of quotation: hardware pricing will often creep down between you checking the prices and the supplier providing the equipment!

CONCLUSION

Having computer systems connected to the Internet is as standard for a small business as having a telephone was 20 years ago. With quality, branded, accounting software available for less that £100, there is really no excuse for not using it. For anything beyond that, investing in IT should follow the same basic rules as investing in any other aspect of your business. Define your requirements, investigate the options available for meeting them, and decide whether their likely benefits justify the cost.

Checklist

■ Choose your platform on performance and software usage as well as cost.

■ Beware that cost-cut applications may end up being more troublesome than they are worth.

■ Forecasting software can, over time, be a worthwhile investment.

■ Appropriate accounting software depends on your business size. Simple entry-level software should suit most start-ups. Larger organizations may require modular packages.

■ Make sure that your software really does what you require – ask for a demonstration.

■ Your customer relationship management software should be adaptable and easily accessible, so it can grow with your needs.

■ Acquire a business domain name and e-mail address, for simplicity and professional image.

■ Never send an e-mail when you are angry – you cannot 'unsend' it!

■ Keep your Web site simple – and make sure that a phone number is clearly available.

■ If you have a 'news' section on your Web site, keep it up to date.

- When purchasing hardware, brand is less critical than power.
- Make sure all your data is backed up – as frequently as possible.
- Keep your anti-virus software updated.
- Permanent Internet connections should have 'firewalls' in place.

13 | **Taxation**

Paul Waite

TAX PLANNING

Tax planning should form an integral part of the overall plan of every business. In order to plan effectively it is necessary to take advantage of every possibility the law allows for reducing the burden of taxation. Efficiently organizing a business's tax affairs helps to reduce your reliance on external finance and to maximize the company's existing resources.

There are two golden rules in tax planning: pay only the minimum amount of tax due, and pay tax on the latest date permissible. Simple as the strategy may sound, carrying it out is one of the most complex challenges in the life of a company, starting even before the business comes into existence. It begins with the decision what kind of organization to create in the first place, in order to realize the best tax position for the owner(s). Basically, the decision is whether to operate as an incorporated or unincorporated business: that is, as a private limited company or as a sole trader/partnership.

Sustained changes in company legislation by Chancellor Gordon Brown have made operating as a limited company an increasingly favourable option. Indeed, the government seems to be doing everything possible to encourage businesses to trade as limited companies.

Historically a decision whether or not to incorporate depended largely upon one of two factors: the owners' attitude to risk, and whether or not business profits were such that an unincorporated business would create substantial higher-rate income tax liabilities for the sole trader/partners. Individuals pay tax at the higher rate of 40 per cent. Following the increase in employees' national insurance in the recent budget, the higher tax rate is in reality 41 per cent from next year. The highest rate of company tax is now 30 per cent, although marginal tax rates can reach 32.5 per cent. Companies with a profit below £300,000 pay tax at a rate of 20 per cent, and profits up to £10,000 attract a zero per cent corporation tax rate.

In the current climate there are few disadvantages in deciding to trade as a limited company. In the following sections the nature of the major taxes that relate to businesses is considered. In the final section of the chapter we return to the topic of tax planning for close company shareholders.

INCOME TAX

Each individual is responsible for tax on his/her own income. Companies pay corporation tax instead of income tax. Income tax is charged broadly on the income of UK residents, whether it arises in the UK or abroad, subject to certain deductions for individuals who are not ordinarily resident or domiciled in the UK.

The tax year runs from 6 April in one year to 5 April in the next. Tax is charged on income at the following rates:

- a starting rate of 10 per cent;
- the basic rate of 22 per cent;
- the higher rate of 40 per cent.

The most common sources of income tax are earnings from employment, and interest from banks or building societies. Tax on employment earnings is collected through the Pay As You Earn (PAYE) scheme, at whichever rate the earnings are taxable. Individuals trading as sole traders or through partnerships also pay income tax, usually under Schedule D Case 1, on the income

HOW TO PREPARE A SUCCESSFUL BUSINESS PLAN

There are many issues with which you should familiarise yourself before embarking in business on your own. In this article, we address the issue of preparing a successful business plan.

The Business Plan – What exactly is it and what is it not?

A business plan is the encapsulation of the short-term financial goals of a business covering the previous twelve months in some detail and the next two to three years in summary format. It is based on the medium to long term strategy of the proprietors and management.

A business plan is not:
• just an annotated profit and loss account;
• a fairy tale scenario of good news with better and better news to come.
It should be a coherent balanced discussion on the realistic goals and needs of the business for the planning period, addressing both the good and bad news.

What are its uses?

Apart from concentrating the minds of management on the strengths and weaknesses and opportunities and threats facing the business, there are two main areas.

1. Communicating a clear path of development

There are a number of benefits to be derived from a business planning exercise. Firstly there is an increase in management commitment, which is built up during the preparation of the business plan. Often a team spirit and an uplift in morale is generated, as the direction of the business in the future becomes clear.

An abridged version of the business plan can also be used to inform employees of business goals and help them understand the needs of the business and where they fit in.

It can also help to retain and win new business. Many of your customers will vet their suppliers and you can keep, or improve your status, by giving them an indication of your direction (this also applies to finance houses and credit brokers, who are also keenly interested in where you see yourself going). Similarly, you can use an abridged version to build confidence in potential customers and clients. Use it to demonstrate the professional way you run your business.

2. Financial Uses (Raising finance or maintaining existing facilities)

In any 'start up' situation, a business plan will certainly be required if your are looking for external financing.

When it comes to the expansion of your business, it can provide comfort to financiers when increasing or renewing facilities. Financiers believe it essential for management to have clear plans. One word of warning here – if the increase in finance is required because you have pressure on working capital, it is often a sign that you may well be overtrading. You should therefore tackle any credit control problems in your presentation.

What makes a successful Business Plan?

A Business Plan should be aimed at specific groups – not all audiences want the same message.

For example, a bank is concerned with the cash flow generating capability of the business. Their concern is to ensure that you are able to repay any loan. They would also need to examine profitability to cover interest payments and be satisfied with their security, not just the quantity but the quality – which could include the business' uncharged plant and machinery, other fixed assets etc, and its current trade debtors. Sometimes this may extend to the Directors' own assets and personal guarantees.

On the other hand, a Venture Capital Provider will be interested in growth and profit profiles and exit routes to dispose of his investment in the longer term. In this case you might state your intention to sell out to another trade competitor, or even a management buy back of the venture capital at a later date.

A business plan should take the form of a written explanation of:
- Your business' activities
- Its future prospects
- Its strengths and opportunities
- Its weaknesses and threats, and how they are managed.

You should concentrate on facts not fiction and provide supporting evidence wherever you can.

As far as other evidence is concerned, usually the most sensitive and difficult area is the Sales Forecast. It is very important to outline the process of generation with evidence, perhaps you have:
- some forward contracts?
- enquiries from potential clients?
- an historic rate of conversion of enquiries into firm orders?
- extracts of market surveys to verify trends in the industry?

The Business Plan should be prepared by you but reviewed by an external person – preferably an accountant to ensure the numbers 'make sense'.

Most financiers evaluate the strengths of management. They are concerned about track record in managing the business and employees. They are looking for demonstrable skills and whatever qualifications you may have. Therefore the business plan must reflect your views of your own business.

In conclusion
- Ensure that your business plan is to the point
- That it is actually based on facts
- Have supporting evidence available wherever possible
- Make sure your forecasts are realistic

Kingston Smith produce a free guide to 'Starting Your Own Business', for a copy contact:
Paul Samrah, Partner
Kingston Smith Chartered Accountants
Surrey House
36-44 High Street
Redhill
Surrey
RH1 1RH

Telephone: 01737 779000
email: psamrah@kingstonsmith.co.uk
www.kingstonsmith.co.uk

Chartered Accountants

derived from their businesses, after deduction of allowable expenses incurred in the running of the business.

Taxable income may be reduced by certain allowances. The personal allowance and blind person's allowance are deducted from income, and save tax at the individual's highest tax rate. Current personal allowance rates are set out in the checklist at the end of this chapter.

From 2001/02 single parents, married couples and unmarried couples living together as husband and wife, who have one or more children under 16 living with them, have been able to claim a children's tax credit, £5,290 at the 10 per cent rate in the current tax year ending 5 April 2003.

Under self-assessment, half-yearly payments of income tax and Class 4 national insurance contributions for the self-employed are made on 31 January and 31 July, based on the previous year's figures, with any balancing adjustment shown in the tax return and payable or repayable on the following 31 January.

NATIONAL INSURANCE CONTRIBUTIONS

The population as a whole can be placed into one of two groups.

Employed earners group

Class 1 contributions account for over 96 per cent of the National Insurance Fund's contribution income. Up until April 2000, Class 1A contributions were charged only on the provision by employers of cars and fuel for private use. Class 1As have been extended after that date to most taxable benefits in kind. From 6 April 2000, employer national insurance contributions are charged on all taxable benefits in kind. This is achieved by way of an extension to the existing Class 1A structure rather than the creation of any new charge.

Self-employed earners group

A self-employed person pays both Class 2 and Class 4 contributions. Class 2 contributions are payable at a flat weekly rate and entitle the contributor to incapacity benefit, basic retirement pension, widow's benefit and maternity allowance. Class 4 contributions are payable at a fixed percentage on profits chargeable to income tax under Schedule D, Class I or II which fall between specified upper and lower limits. They carry no entitlement to benefits of any kind.

Class 2 contributions

If an individual becomes self-employed, he or she must notify the Inland Revenue within three months. He or she must also make arrangements to pay Class 2 contributions, unless he/she is not liable to pay.

Class 4 contributions

If someone has more than one self-employment, all the profits are added together when calculating his or her Class 4 liability. In general, profits are calculated for Class 4 contributions in the same way as for income tax, but certain special rules apply.

Self-employed and employed in the same year

If an individual is both self-employed and an employee, he or she will be liable to pay Class 1, 2 and 4 contributions, and if he or she has more than one employment, he/she will be liable to Class 1 contributions in each employment. However, there are two separate maximum figures above which contributions will be refunded. If you expect that your contributions will exceed the maximum, you should apply to defer payment of Class 4, 2 or 1 contributions (in that order) as appropriate.

CORPORATION TAX

Since 1 April 1964, companies have been liable to corporation tax on their 'profits', defined as net income after deduction of allowable business expenses and chargeable gains in each financial year. Corporation tax is charged on profits of 'financial years'; which run from 1 April, so the 'financial year 2002' means the year from 1 April 2002.

The profits of a company are calculated by reference to its accounting periods. The reduced rates of corporation tax that apply to 'small' companies are defined by reference to their profits in an accounting period.

Any company that is resident in the UK is liable to pay corporation tax in respect of all its 'profits', wherever they arise. A non-resident company that carries on a trade in the UK through a branch or agency is liable to corporation tax on the income and gains of the branch or agency. Members of a group of companies are each dealt with independently, but there are a number of special provisions relating to the taxation of such members.

CAPITAL GAINS TAX

Background

Capital gains tax (CGT) commenced on 6 April 1965. It relates to chargeable gains in a 'year of assessment' accruing to individuals, personal representatives and trustees. The year of assessment is a year ending 5 April.

An allowance, known as the indexation allowance, was introduced by the Finance Act 1982 with the intention of adjusting for the effects of inflation. In the Finance Act 1998, the original base date for indexation of 6 April 1965 was replaced by 31 March 1982. All assets held at this date are revalued to their open market value at that date.

For CGT purposes, indexation allowance was frozen at its April 1998 level by the Finance Act 1998. Assets acquired after 31 March 1998 do not attract indexation allowance at all. For disposals after 5 April 1998, the allowance is replaced by a taper relief whereby a chargeable gain is progressively reduced according to the length of time the asset has been held, with more generous reductions for business assets (as defined) than for other assets. A business asset now needs to be held for two years for full taper relief to apply, leaving an effective rate of 10 per cent.

Individuals' liability to pay tax

Usually a person is liable to pay capital gains tax in respect of chargeable gains accruing to him/her in a year of assessment. Transfers between spouses living together are made on a 'no gain, no loss' basis; this can create opportunities for married couples to reduce their overall capital gains. In broad terms the rates of tax for capital gains are the same as those under income tax for individuals; they are detailed in the checklist at the end of the chapter.

Companies' liability to pay tax

Capital gains made by companies within the scope of corporation tax are not chargeable to capital gains tax; they are taxed in the same way as their other profits and at the same rate. The changes relating to indexation allowance and taper relief do not apply for the purposes of corporation tax on chargeable gains.

CAPITAL ALLOWANCES

In preparing their accounts, businesses will make a provision for the depreciation of assets, matching the cost of an asset with the income stream it is able to generate over its useful economic life. This provision is not allowable for tax purposes, but a substitute is allowed, known as 'capital allowance'. Capital allowances apply in respect of :

- industrial buildings;
- plant and machinery;
- agricultural buildings.

In each case the total allowances are given as a deduction in arriving at the profits to be charged to tax under income tax or corporation tax.

Industrial buildings

Industrial buildings allowance (IBA) is given in respect of buildings used for productive manufacturing, processing and some other specified trades. The annual allowance available is 4 per cent of the costs of construction (excluding land) and is based on original construction cost only.

Plant and machinery

Plant and machinery are not defined in law, and the term has been subject to close scrutiny in the courts in a number of cases over the years.

First year allowance

A special first year allowance is available on plant purchased. The allowance is 40 per cent of the cost of the plant, and is available for all small and medium-sized businesses.

Writing-down allowances

Where a pool of plant and machinery is in existence, the writing-down allowance is calculated as 25 per cent of the value of the pool, as follows, having regard to disposals.

Computer equipment

From 1 April 2000, small businesses have been able to claim 100 per cent first year capital allowances on computer equipment. This covers computers, software and Internet-enabled mobile phones.

Balancing adjustments

Where a pool is in existence there will only be a balancing adjustment either when the business ceases or when the disposal proceeds in any year exceed the written-down value of the pool.

Capital allowances are an essential part of tax planning, and are given regardless of the length of time the asset is owned in an accounting period.

RELIEF FOR TRADING LOSSES

Companies may incur losses in their trades, in the course of letting property, in relation to investment income if expenses exceed the income, and in their capital transactions.

Reliefs available

Trading losses of companies are calculated in the same way as trading profits. The following alternatives are available for obtaining relief for such losses:

- set-off against current profits from other sources;
- carry-back against earlier profits from all sources;
- carry-forward against future trading profits;
- group relief.

Partnership losses

Relief for partnership trading losses may be claimed by each partner quite independently of the others. Thus, one partner may decide to carry forward his/her share of the loss, another to set it against income of the same tax year, another to carry back against the income of the previous three tax years of being a partner and so on. The carry-back loss rules for the first four years of a new trade only apply to a new partner, not to the continuing partners.

VALUE ADDED TAX (VAT)

Definitions

VAT is a sales tax levied by businesses. All goods and services that are VAT rated are called 'taxable supplies'. VAT must be charged on taxable supplies from the date the business first needs to be registered. The value of these supplies is called 'taxable turnover'.

There are also 'exempt supplies', which are business supplies that have no VAT charged on them at the standard or zero rate.

Exempt supplies do not form part of the taxable turnover. If the only services supplied are exempt supplies, the business cannot normally be registered for VAT. If the business is registered for VAT and has some exempt supplies, it may not be able to get all of its input tax back. Some examples of exempt supplies are: insurance, leasing, letting land and buildings.

VAT compliance

If a business's 'taxable turnover' goes over a certain limit, it becomes a 'taxable person' and must then register for VAT by completing Form VAT 1. From 25 April 2002 the VAT registration threshold was raised to £55,000. Therefore, registration must take place if at the end of any month the total value of taxable supplies made in the past 12 month or less is more than £55,000, or if at any time the value of taxable supplies is expected to be more than £55,000 in 30 days alone.

If a business is registered or needs to be registered, VAT must be charged and accounted for whenever there is a supply of any standard or reduced rate supplies. These supplies are called 'outputs' and the tax charged is called 'output tax'. If the customer is registered for VAT and the supplies are for its business, then they are 'inputs' in its VAT accounts.

If only zero-rated goods are supplied (but exceed the registration threshold) a business may not register for VAT, but must inform Customs & Excise of the liability to be registered and apply to be 'exempt from registration'.

Cash accounting

Provided that turnover is below an annual limit of £600,000, a taxable person may, subject to conditions, account for and pay VAT on the basis of cash and other considerations paid and received. The main advantages of the scheme are automatic bad debt relief and the deferral of the time for the payment of VAT where extended credit is given.

Bad debt relief

If a customer fails to pay, VAT may be reclaimed on any debt which is more than six months old and has been written off in the business's accounts.

TAX PLANNING FOR CLOSE COMPANY SHAREHOLDERS

All businesses should have a tax strategy, which will involve considering:

- the interaction of income against corporate taxes;
- commercial considerations, such as the need to demonstrate a high level of profit to satisfy the company's lenders;
- availability of cash flow;
- the age and extent of the company's fixed asset base;
- what is likely to happen in the future – tax planning has to be proactive;
- when to time expenditure to best advantage;
- if applicable, how to plan expenditure to avoid the company paying tax at high marginal rates;
- the most appropriate corporate structure if the owners have more than one business interest;
- what is the optimal remuneration strategy.

The majority of close companies are small companies, and vice versa. A 'close company' is defined as a company under the control of five or fewer shareholders, or any number of shareholders who are also directors of the company: that is, it is controlled by director shareholders.

As we noted at the beginning of this chapter, UK corporation tax rates are highly favourable at the moment, and if they practise good tax planning, it is possible for companies to have an effective rate of tax well below the normal companies rate of 20 per cent.

Remuneration strategy

Personal remuneration options include:

- salary;
- dividends;
- bonuses;
- benefits such as car and private health insurance;
- pension funding;
- maximizing wives' allowances.

A dividend strategy can be highly effective, as basic rate taxpayers can receive dividends right up to the higher tax rate starting point effectively free from taxation. Dividends also have the advantage of being exempt from national insurance (both employees' and employers').

From a tax viewpoint, shares should be held equally by a husband and wife unless the wife receives substantial income from an external source. Roughly £70,000 can then be received without paying any income tax or national insurance – an attractive proposition.

However, it is important to ensure that business taper relief is not compromised. Companies that are bound by IR35 legislation should not implement such a strategy as, upon investigation, the Inland Revenue will substitute for the dividend wages taxed under PAYE. If you are in any doubt, you should contact your professional adviser.

The downsides to dividends are:

- they do not represent a deduction from profits assessable to corporation tax;
- they do not make a contribution towards earnings necessary to maintain the basic national insurance levels;
- they do not represent earnings for pension funding purposes;
- external parties such as mortgage lenders prefer salaries, regarding them as a more permanent form of income;
- while dividends can be waived, if there is a dividend policy all shareholders will receive the same amount per share. This can be a problem if there are passive shareholders, or there are large imbalances in shareholding.

In most cases it is advisable for the owner-manager to receive a salary. Salaries represent allowable deductions against taxable profits, and while pensions are hardly the flavour of the month at present, everyone should make some provision. Pension funding cannot take place in the absence of a salary.

Bonuses are excellent for planning purposes and can create good management incentives. The Inland Revenue allows bonuses to be paid up to nine months after the financial year end, making it possible, certainly in the first year, to get tax relief effectively one year early on normal salary. The principle can be applied to all employees. On a cautionary note, particularly for companies with financial year ends after 5 July, the Inland Revenue may disallow a bonus paid within nine months if it falls within a new tax year.

Benefits tend to create a state of well-being but, as discussed further in Chapter 14, 'Employment and Human Relations', they have been highly targeted by the Inland Revenue.

The taxation treatment of the car benefit is now arguably the most unfair in operation, and if you intend to award yourself the use of a company car, you should research the matter fully with your tax adviser.

Company planning: minimizing corporation tax

Any business with serious aspirations should draw up an annual capital expenditure budget. Interest rates are highly attractive at present, so buying assets on finance is a good option. Remember that capital allowances at 40 per cent can be claimed for the whole year even if the asset was purchased on the final day of the accounting year, so timing is highly relevant. However, the Inland Revenue will disqualify the expenditure if the asset was not 'brought into use' by the end of the year.

If applicable, expenditure on information and communications technology (ICT) and research and development attracts even better tax breaks. If profits are high, try to plan other expenditure so that, where possible, it is brought forward into the applicable financial year.

Of course, reality may be rather different and may impose its own agenda. Tax planning should never prevail over other commercial considerations, particularly if cash is a scarce resource. Some regard also has to be given to the likely profit in the next financial year.

Corporate structure

If more than one company is under common control, then the rates are divided by the number of such companies. To ascertain whether there is common control, one needs to look at the fewest individuals who can control a company. For tax purposes, this is deemed to be more than 50 per cent. It may well be worth having companies under common control in a conventional group environment, since tax losses can be transferred between companies as can assets. If there is no need for a group environment, subject to the demands of corporate and inheritance taxes you should seriously consider arranging the corporate structure so that each company can be run separately on its own merits.

TAX RATES

Table 13.1   Tax rates

Main income tax relief	2002/03	2001/02
Allowed at top rate of tax		
Personal Allowance	£4,615	£4,535
Personal Allowance (65–74)	£6,100	£5,990
Personal Allowance (75+)	£6,370	£6,260
Blind Person's Allowance	£1,480	£1,450
Allowed Only at 10%		
Children's tax credit	£5,290	£5,200
Children's tax credit – baby rate	£10,490	0
Married Couple's Allowance (65–74)	£5,465	£5,365
Married Couple's Allowance (75+)	£5,535	£5,435
Income limit for age related allowances	£17,900	£17,600
Important limits		
Individual Savings Account annual limit	£7,000	£7,000
Rent a room exemption	£4,250	£4,250
Enterprise Investment Scheme annual limit*	£150,000	£150,000
Venture Capital Trust annual limit*	£100,000	£100,000

* relief restricted to 20%

Income tax rates and bands

Lower rate on first	£1,920	£1,880
Basic rate on next	£27,980	£27,520
Higher rate at taxable income over	£29,900	£29,400
Tax rates unchanged		

	D	I	O
Rates differ for dividends/interest/other	D	I	O
Starting rate	10%	10%	10%
Basic rate	10%	20%	22%
Higher rate	32.50%	40%	40%

Dividends taxed as highest part of
income, then interest
Discretionary trust rate (25% on dividends) 34%

Car Benefit Assesment 2002/03

Charge based on a percentage of the initial list price of the car, including accessories, delivery charges and VAT. The percentage depends on the CO_2 emissions rating of the car, and whether the engine runs on petrol or diesel.

Ratings	Petrol	Diesel
0–165g/km	15%	18%
Over 165g/km	+ 1% for each extra 5g/km	
Maximum	35%	35%

Special rules apply to older cars that do not have a CO_2 rating.
Company vans are charged at £500 (£350 where 4 years or older)
Employee contributions for private use are deducted from the taxable figure.

Car Fuel Benefit	2002/03 (2001/02)	2002/03 (2001/02)
Up to 14000cc	£2,240 (£1,930)	£2,850 (£2,460)
1401–2000cc	£2,850 (£2,460)	£2,850 (£2,460)
Over 2000cc	£4,200 (£3,620)	£4,200 (£3,620)

Tax Free Mileage Allowance

	Up to 4,000 miles 2002/03 (2001/02)	Up to 4,000 miles 2002/03 (2001/02)
Cars up to 1500cc	40p (40p)	25p (25p)
Cars 1501–2000cc	40p (45p)	25p (25p)
Cars over 2000cc	40p (63p)	25p (36p)
Motorcycles	24p (24p)	24p (24p)
Bicycles	20p (12p)	20p (12p)
Business passengers	5p (0p)	5p (0p)

Fuel-only allowances for company cars

	Petrol 2002/03 & 2001/02	Diesel 2002/02 & 2001/02
Up to 1400cc	10p	9p
1401–2000cc	12p	9p
Over 2000cc	14p	12p

Capital Gains Tax

Annual exempt amount 2002/03: individuals £7,700, trustees £3,850.
Relief given for effect of inflation for periods of ownership up to April 1998. Tapering relief given for periods of ownership after 6 April 1998 (with one year added for ownership on 17 March 1998 in the case of non-business assets):

Disposal after 5 April 2002 owned for	% of gain charged	
	Business asset	Non-business asset
0–1 year	100%	100%
1–2 years	50%	100%
2–3 years	25%	100%
3–4 years	25%	95%
4–5 years	25%	90%
5–6 years	25%	85%

Taper increases at 5% p.a for non-business assets up to a maximum of 10 years (40% relief)
Retirement relief for disposals 6 April 2002–5 April 2003: max relief is 100% of first £50,000 plus 50% of balance of gain up to £200,000.
Relief is abolished after 5 April 2003.
Net gains after all reliefs and annual exempt amount are taxed at marginal income tax rates for interest income (ie 10%, 20%, 40%).

Corporation Tax

	Year to 31.03.2003	31.03.2002
Main rate	30%	30%
Profits above	£1.5m	£1.5m
Small companies rate	19%	20%
Profits between	£50,000–£300,000	£50,000–£300,000
Starting rate	0%	10%
Profits below	£10,000	£10,000
Small/large marginal band	£300,000–£1.5 million	£300,000–£1.5 million
Fraction (effective rate)	11/400 (32.75%)	1/40 (32.5%)
Starting/small marginal band	£10,000–£50,000	£10,000–£50,000
Fraction (effective rate)	19/400 (23.75%)	1/40 (22.5%)

National Insurance Contributions
Class 1 (employees)

	Within SERPS	Contracted Out	
		Salary related	Money purchase
Employee contributions:			
– on earnings between £89.01 and £585 pw	10.00%	8.40%	8.40%
Employer contributions:			
– on earnings between £89.01 and £585 pw	11.80%	8.30%	10.80%
– on earnings above £585 pw	11.80%	11.80%	11.80%

Employer contributions (at 11.8%) are due on most benefits in kind and on tax paid on an employee's behalf under a PAYE settlement.

Class 2 (Self-employed)
Flat rate per week	£2.00
Small earnings exception; profits per annum	£4,205

Class 3 (Voluntary)
Flat rate per week	£6.85

Class 4 (Self-employed)
On profits £4,615–£30,420 (Max £1,806.35)	7.00%

Personal Pensions (PPPs) and Retirement Annuity Premiums (RAPs)

Max contributions	% of net relevant earnings	
Age at beginning of year	RAPs %	PPPs %
35 or less	17.5	17.5
36–45	17.5	20
46–50	17.5	25
51–55	20	30
56–60	22.5	35
61 and over	27.5	40

Maximum net relevant earnings for 2002/03 PPPs: £97,200.
No limit for RAPs. People with no net relevant earnings can pay contributions of £3,600 gross in 2002/03, except for some members of occupational pension schemes.

Inheritance Tax

Charges on or after 6 April 2002	Rates %	Charges between 6 April 2001 and 5 April 2002
0–£250,000	Nil	0–£242,000
Above £250,000	40%	Above £242,000

Lifetime chargeable transfers at half the death rate, ie 20%.

Business property relief of 100% for all shareholdings in qualifying unquoted trading companies and for most unincorporated trading businesses; agricultural property relief at 100% for qualifying holdings of agricultural land.

Annual exemption for lifetime gifts £3,000.

Small gifts: annual amount per donee £250.

Reduced tax charge on transfers within seven years of death

Years before death	Percentage of death rates
0–3	100%
3–4	80%
4–5	60%
5–6	40%
6–7	20%
Over 7	Nil

Value Added Tax

Standard rate (7/47 of VAT-inclusive price	17.50%
Registration level from 25 April 2002	£55,000 per annum
Deregistration level from 25 April 2002	£53,000 per annum

Main Capital Allowances   Allowance %

Plant and machinery:

First year allowance for small or medium businesses	*40
Writing-down allowance (6% on some long-life assets)	25
Computers for small businesses	**100
Cars (max £3,000 pa)	25
Industrial buildings writing-down allowance	4

*100% if assets to be used in Northern Ireland

**For three years from 1 April 2000

Success

"Don't compromise your prospects"

We are experts in proactively helping start up and growing businesses throughout Wessex

We can help in all stages of the business process

- Business Plans   Raising Finance
- Tax Planning   Business & Financial Planning
- Proactive Advice   Full Range of Services

Aspen Waite Chartered Accountants

"MORE THAN JUST ACCOUNTANTS"

Rubis House, 15 Friarn Street,
Bridgwater, Somerset, TA6 3LH
Tel: 01278 445151 Fax: 01278 445152
e-mail: enquiries@aspen-waite.co.uk

INITIAL CONSULTATION FREE OF CHARGE OR PHONE FOR A FRIENDLY CHAT

14 Employment and Human Relations

From the moment that you move on from being a self-employed sole trader and employ your first member of staff, your business becomes subject to employment and discrimination law. The main provisions of employment law apply equally to businesses of any size, private or public companies, although some requirements become more onerous when you employ five or more people. Therefore, this chapter begins with a briefing on employment rules and regulations before moving on to the practical business issues involved in engaging staff and other relevant aspects of human relations.

EMPLOYMENT LAW

The law focuses on the rights of employees, most of which apply from the date of first employment and are extended according to length of service. Generally, the size of the employer's business is irrelevant. Discrimination law has made employee administration more complex, particularly in the recruitment and appointment of workers. Employment regulations change quite frequently, and it is incumbent on you to keep yourself informed and to ensure that your business complies in the recruitment and administration of staff and in the termination of employment. Comprehensive guidance is given in Barry Cushway's *The Employer's Handbook* (2000), Kogan Page, of which revised editions are published every year or so.

Some recent legislation refers to 'workers' rather than 'employees': for example the Working Time Regulations, with the intention that it should also apply to other employment relationships, such as agency workers on assignment. In this chapter, therefore, we shall use the word 'employee' to refer to all members of staff whom you may engage to work for your business.

Employee rights from date of engagement

- Equal pay.
- National minimum wage.
- Itemized pay statement.
- Statutory sick pay.
- Maximum 48 hours work per week (except by choice) and 4 weeks annual holiday.
- Non-discrimination on grounds of sex, race or disability.
- Non-discrimination because of trade union membership or non-membership.
- Ordinary maternity leave (18 weeks).
- Time off work with pay for ante-natal care.
- Time off work to care for dependants.
- Time off work with pay for safety representatives.
- Time off work with or without pay for trade union duties.
- Time off work with pay for employee representatives.
- Non-dismissal or disadvantage because of pregnancy, parental or maternity leave.
- Non-dismissal or disadvantage for asserting legal rights, whistle-blowing or taking action on health and safety matters.
- Consultation about proposed redundancies.
- Minimum period of notice.
- Application for arrears of pay, holiday pay, notice etc from Secretary of State on insolvency of employer.

Employee rights after one month's employment

- Written statement of employment particulars.
- Medical suspension pay.
- Guaranteed payments (short-time working).

Employee rights after 26 weeks' employment

▌ Statutory maternity pay (SMP).

Employee rights after two years' employment

▌ Redundancy pay.
▌ Time off work with pay to look for work or training if under redundancy notice.
▌ Application for redundancy pay on insolvency of employer from Secretary of State.

The main proposals of the new Employment Bill of 7 November 2001 are the introduction of paternity and adoption leave; changes to the law relating to maternity leave; changes to employment tribunal procedures; and the use of statutory procedures in employment disputes.

ADDITIONAL EMPLOYMENT REGULATIONS THAT APPLY ACCORDING TO NUMBER OF EMPLOYEES

No. of employees	Additional rules
Five or more	Safety policy
	Safety committee, if requested
	Consultation on health and safety
	Stakeholder pensions
	No exemption from providing suitable employment for a woman returning from maternity leave
15 or more	The Disability Discrimination Act 1995
20 or more	Disciplinary rules and procedures
21 or more	Recognition of a trade union mandatory where a majority votes in favour

Even from these lists of rules and regulations it is clear that the administration of employees becomes a time-consuming element in running your business as it expands. But compliance with the detailed provisions of employment law is not enough. Maintaining best practice in human relations to ensure that your employees are properly motivated, do their best in working for the business, and stay with you, requires additional attention and your personal input.

DISCRIMINATION LAW

Direct discrimination is usually apparent, and arises where one or more persons are treated less favourably because of their sex, race, marital status or disablement. The most common form of discrimination, which is provided for in the Equal Pay Act, is where men and women are not paid the same wage or salary for performing the same work – invariably to the disadvantage of the woman. There have been some recent well-publicized cases in big companies, mostly in the financial services industry, but the legal process for achieving redress is long-winded and may even involve recourse to the European Court of Justice. This form of discrimination is less common in small service businesses, where job functions are usually not shared and there is less 'comparability'.

However, there are three other forms of discrimination to which specific laws apply:

Sex discrimination	Sex Discrimination Acts 1975 and 1986
Race discrimination	Race Relations Act 1976
Disablement discrimination	Disability Discrimination Act 1995

You will be most vulnerable to offending against any of these Acts when recruiting staff. You must take care to avoid indirect as well as direct discrimination, starting with the job profile that you develop for recruitment purposes. The following are just a few of the more common examples of indirect discrimination in job specifications:

▌ specifying a higher level of spoken and written English than the job demands;

▌ excluding candidates from a location where the ethnic population is high;

▌ requirements on height and weight that clearly discriminate against women;

▌ age and experience requirements for professional positions that effectively rule out women returning to work after bringing up families.

Avoid any questions that might be construed as discriminatory on grounds of sex, race or disability, implying that factors other than ability to do the job may be taken into account, such as, 'Are you planning any children in the near future?', 'Would you want to take long holidays in your country?' or 'Will you have to take more time off for hospital visits?' The only exception to the rules on sex or race discrimination is when there is a 'genuine occupational qualification' (GOQ).

Sex discrimination GOQs

▌ Where the essential nature of the job calls for a man (or woman) for reasons of physiology.

▌ Where considerations of decency or privacy require the job to be held by a man (or woman).

▌ The jobholder has to live in premises provided by the employer who cannot reasonably provide facilities for both sexes.

▌ Where the job is in a single-sex establishment for persons requiring special care, supervision or attention.

▌ Where personal services to individuals provided by the jobholder can be provided most effectively by a man (or woman).

▌ Where the job involves work outside the UK in a country whose laws or customs are such that the job can only be done effectively by a man (or woman).

Race discrimination GOQs

▌ Jobs in the performing arts or as an artist's or photographic model, where a person of a specific racial group is required for reasons of authenticity.

■ Jobs in restaurants or similar places where a person of a specific racial group is required for reasons of authenticity.

■ Where personal services to individuals promoting their welfare can only be provided by a job-holder of the same racial group.

Disablement discrimination

In the future it is likely that the Disability Discrimination Act 1995 will be extended to cover all companies, even those employing less than 15 people. When you are considering applications from a disabled person, this entails considering what adjustments can reasonably be made to the job or workplace to enable the applicant to meet the job requirements.

OTHER ISSUES INVOLVING EMPLOYMENT OR DISCRIMINATION LAW

■ Part-time workers: any employee who does not work as many hours as your full-time employees is classified as a part-time worker. The general rule is that part-time employees should be treated no less favourably than full-time employees, that is, they should receive the same pay and benefits on a pro rata basis.

■ Employment of offenders: an offender does not need to give the employer details of any past offence for which he or she is considered to be rehabilitated. Nor may the employer take any such offences in account.

■ Employment of children: children under 14 may be employed only on 'light work'; hours of work for children under and aged 15 are legally restricted; you may not employ any child during school hours or for more than two hours on a school day or Sunday. You may not employ any child under 13.

■ Employment of overseas nationals: all EU nationals have the right to work in the UK. Other nationals will generally need a work permit.

▊   Asylum and Immigration Act 1996: it is a criminal offence to employ persons aged 16 and over without a NI number or alternative evidence of entitlement to work in the UK.

▊   Dealing with absence: produce a policy with clear written guidelines for reporting absences, notification in the event of sickness, frequent lateness, persistent unauthorized absences and pay during absence.

▊   Personnel records: maintain personnel records and a personal file for each employee within the provisions of the Data Protection Act 1998.

▊   Mergers and takeovers: if you are thinking of acquiring the whole or part of another business or if your company is the target of a takeover or merger, be aware of the Transfer of Undertakings (Protection of Employment) Regulations 1981 (TUPE) and its likely impact.

▊   Dealing with grievances: you are legally obliged to draw up grievance procedures in writing to be made known to all employees; allow for the employee to be accompanied by a fellow employee or trade union representative, if desired, when holding a hearing.

▊   Claims to employment tribunals: when employment is terminated, a written compromise agreement signed by the employee will prevent him or her from making a later claim to an employment tribunal. In the event of a claim, be sure to take professional advice; do not attempt to handle the proceedings in court yourself.

RECRUITING STAFF

Deciding whether to recruit and defining the job

When starting up your own business you will aim to keep staff recruitment to a minimum, both to avoid incurring fixed overhead expense wherever possible and to avoid some of the administrative burden that the legal requirements entail. Options which may avoid or defer permanent staff engagements include:

_____

∎ subcontracting certain activities;
∎ the use of part-time casual workers on a job or function basis, such as double-glazing installations or bookkeeping;
∎ sales agents paid on a commission basis;
∎ temporary staff.

However, as your business takes off you will probably require permanent staff to help you handle the workload and to develop the business further. Exceptions include those providing personal services as a consultant, skilled expert or as a sole trader, where partnership or joint venture models may be more appropriate to your business expansion.

The first step in deciding what staff to recruit is an objective, critical assessment of your own capabilities. Self-assessment is always a difficult exercise, and it may be helpful to ask members of your family or business friends to offer their opinions. If you have started your business working from home, your family will certainly have formed a view of your strengths and weaknesses which they will be pleased to express – although you may not be entirely comfortable with their evaluation! However, the object of the exercise is to identify the personal skills and expertise which your business lacks and which a new recruit should have, to complement your strengths.

For example, if you are a good business developer – and in starting your own business you will have demonstrated your entrepreneurial outlook – but you are poor at managing your own time and in delivering your service or product to schedule, then you need someone who is strong in customer relations and in supporting you, to create the time for you to provide the technical input or expertise that a project needs.

Operating a small business means that all members of staff need to have multi-function capabilities, and will probably have to take responsibility for or carry out tasks that they find tedious, or would otherwise prefer not to perform. As owner of the business, you are not excluded from this requirement, and your staff will expect you to lead by example. Moreover, there are some functions for which you and you only should retain responsibility: in particular, the control of cash flow as well as human relations. However tiresome and time-consuming you may find the accounting function, and although the basic bookkeeping may be delegated without risk, you must engage yourself in financial planning and control of the cash flow. As we have emphasized already in Chapter 10, more young businesses founder from lack of cash flow, through over-trading or failure to match expenditure revenue, than for any other reason.

There is no legal requirement for a full job description or a person specification, but both are useful for recruitment, and in determining training needs later. Therefore, you should input all these considerations into the job specification that you draw up before starting to recruit.

The recruitment process

The four main methods of recruiting externally are by:

- word of mouth;
- local or national advertising;
- recruitment agencies;
- selection consultants or executive search firms ('headhunters').

In the early stages of start-up and growth, only the first three are relevant.

The first method includes the recruitment of staff from among your own acquaintances, possibly from the company which you worked for previously or from a customer or supplier of your previous employer. You are trying to build a small team of multi-skilled people who are prepared to put in long hours and much effort, and are dedicated to the success of the business you have set up. Therefore, personal relationship skills will be at a premium, and it is important that all members of the team are able to work interactively and harmoniously. Someone you have worked with before, or whose work is familiar to you and whom you respect, will probably be more attractive than an unknown candidate. Again, someone who is unknown to you but recommended by a business acquaintance whose judgement you trust may be a better bet than an unknown candidate from an advertisement.

If there are no word of mouth candidates or you prefer to advertise, the most suitable media will probably be the employment pages of the local press, or the trade press of the industry or profession in which your business operates. Alternatively, you might choose to advertise through a recruitment agency for a specialist skill set or more senior position, although this will also involve agency fees.

In designing the advertisement, the basic details to be included are:

- job title;
- location;
- brief description of the key responsibilities and duties;
- qualifications, skills and experience required;
- salary and main benefits;
- how the application should be made.

Advertisements often omit information about salary for various reasons, such as not wishing to alert other staff, uncertainty about the rate for the job, hope that the hiring can be made cheaply, or even genuine flexibility. Generally, it is a mistake not to indicate salary range; lack of detail usually reduces the number of applicants.

Application and interview

When recruiting you will have to decide whether or not to use a standard application form or alternatively to ask candidates to submit a CV. When setting up your business you are less likely to be hiring senior staff, so an application form is more appropriate. You can design your application form to provide all the basic information you need, so that it can be used as a template for interviews. If you are advertising and expect a large number of responses, a structured application form will make it easier to compare applicants, and the information can be transferred readily to a database.

Interviewing face to face is a skilled activity in which most of us are unlikely to excel without considerable experience. However, when you start to interview selected applicants for jobs in your fledgling business you will probably have the experience of being interviewed yourself and have a fair idea of the techniques that do and don't work. The following are among the important points to bear in mind when interviewing others:

I   Make sure that enough time is set aside for each interview, that the location is suitable, away from outside noise, and that the interview is free from interruptions.

I   Read all application forms or CVs and prepare questions in advance of interviews.

I   Avoid any questions that might appear to be discriminatory on grounds of sex, race or disability (for example, 'Do you intend to have (more) children in the near future?' may be an important issue for you as you are seeking continuity from the staff you engage, but you must not ask the question).

I   Be sure to ask many open-ended questions that demand more than a 'Yes' or 'No' answer, such as:
   –   What interests you about this job?
   –   Describe your present job.
   –   Why did you leave your last job?
   –   What do you consider to be your main strengths?
   –   Looking back over your career, what would you have done differently?
   –   What have been the biggest problems in your current (or last) job?
   –   What contribution can you make to this company?

I   Remember that the interviewee should do most of the talking. Listen carefully to the answers, try to read between the lines, and do not hesitate to probe where there is lack of clarity.

I   Keep notes and, in the absence of a photograph, write a short pen-portrait of each candidate. You may find it helpful to prepare an assessment form as a scorecard, where the candidates' ability to satisfy the key attributes for the job can be rated on a three- or five-point scale.

I   At the end of the interview, invite the candidate to ask any questions he or she has about the job or the company, and explain what will happen next and when he/she can expect to hear the outcome.

I   Tell the candidate how to claim for any travel expenses in attending the interview.

Making the job offer

Don't keep the candidates you have interviewed waiting too long for a decision. Once you have made your selection, the first step is to be in touch with the successful candidate, conduct any final negotiation on salary or other terms, and write a job offer.

If you have not already taken references, you may wish to make the offer conditional upon satisfactory references, or on passing a medical examination if you decide that is appropriate.

Delay writing to other interviewed but unsuccessful candidates until you have a clear acceptance from your preferred choice, but you should then write to each of them, avoiding any detailed explanation of the reasons for rejection. You may be prepared to offer a verbal explanation if you think that will help the candidate in any subsequent application, but be careful not to suggest any covert discrimination in your choice.

As a minimum the job offer should contain:

- the title of the job;
- conditions of the offer (eg references, medical examination);
- definition of any probationary period;
- job location;
- details of wage or salary, payment intervals and annual review date;
- any significant benefits;
- hours of work;
- holiday entitlement;
- the starting date;
- to whom the new employee should report;
- further action (eg acceptance procedure).

The job offer forms a part of the contract of employment with an employee, so it is important to make sure that the terms of the offer have been accepted. For this reason, it is normal to send the appointee a second copy of the job offer with a statement of acceptance at the end of the copy letter, to be signed and returned to you.

CONTRACTS OF EMPLOYMENT

You may have noticed from the first section of this chapter on employment law that there is no legal requirement to give an employee a detailed written contract of employment, and many employers do not go further than the minimum legal obligation to provide a written statement of employment particulars after one month's employment. However, you should be aware that the absence of a written contract does not necessarily mean that no contract exists. Terms implied by the parties' conduct or agreed verbally denote a contract, even if there is nothing in writing.

The statement of principal terms and conditions of employment must include all the matters listed in the job offer contents above plus:

- details of any previous employment that may count as continuous employment;
- details of overtime and overtime rates of pay;
- entitlement to and method of calculation of outstanding holiday pay on termination of employment.

In addition, the following further information must be given to the employee but may be provided in separate documents:

- duration of contract, if temporary or fixed-term;
- notice required to terminate contract by both parties;
- details of any collective agreements affecting terms and conditions (unlikely for start-up businesses);
- sickness or injury terms, including any sick pay premiums – if none, say so;
- pension and pension schemes (whether a contracting-out certificate is in force);
- disciplinary rules and procedures, including identification of someone to whom the employee can turn for help in sorting out work-related problems (probably yourself);
- special rules for those working abroad for more than one month.

It may be that you do not feel the need for a more extensive written contract, in which case this 'principal statement', as it is commonly called, including the job offer and other additional terms, may form all of the employee's written contract and could be used as primary evidence of the nature of the relationship in the event of court or tribunal proceedings. However, the principal statement does not have contractual force unless it is signed formally as a contract by both parties. The provisions of a document given to an employee, even if receipt is acknowledged, are not conclusive.

Therefore, to remove uncertainty the simplest expedient is to convert the principal statement into a contract of employment by arranging for two copies of the statement to be signed by the employee and yourself as employer.

Updating employment contracts

It is important to update contracts to encompass new legislation. Recent examples are stakeholder pension legislation and the Working Time Regulation 1998. The new Employment Act which became law in 2002 imposes further penalties on employers who do not conform to minimum requirements. An employee with no principal statement who is claiming unfair dismissal will be awarded an extra four weeks pay for this failure.

The new law further provides a statutory grievance procedure where no grievance procedure is specified in an employment relationship. Failure by either party to use the statutory procedure risks a scaling up or down of any compensation award.

TERMINATION OF EMPLOYMENT

The key to terminating employment in a small organization without incurring the risk of employment tribunal claims is to define and put in place a clear set of disciplinary procedures that follow the recommendations of ACAS. Essentially, the procedures should:

- be in writing;
- provide for swift execution;
- indicate the disciplinary actions that might be taken and under whose authority;
- give individuals the right to be informed of the complaint against them and to state their case before decisions are taken;

▌ ensure that each case is carefully investigated;
▌ give individuals the right to be accompanied by a work colleague or a representative;
▌ ensure that no employee is dismissed for a first breach of discipline, unless it is gross misconduct;
▌ give an explanation to the individual for any penalty imposed;
▌ provide for the right of appeal.

However small your organization, you would be unwise to short-circuit these requirements, since employment tribunals always take into account whether the ACAS recommendations have been followed.

For your business, a simple statement of procedure should define:

1. objective;
2. stage 1: informal warning;
3. stage 2: formal warning;
4. stage 3: suspension or dismissal;
5. appeal.

A distinction is made in law between misdemeanour and gross misconduct. Misdemeanour covers issues such as poor performance, bad timekeeping and attendance, or inappropriate attitudes. For these you cannot dismiss without a warning, and dismissal requires notice. Gross misconduct covers issues such as theft or fraud, refusal to obey a reasonable instruction, fighting, causing a severe safety hazard, or breach of confidentiality code. For this you can dismiss instantly without a warning, and no notice is required.

Claims to an employment tribunal can be made on contractual grounds, in the event that you dismiss a member of staff in breach of the terms (or implied terms) of the employment contract, or on general considerations – broadly referred to as 'natural justice'. To avoid or defend successfully the latter category of claim, you must focus on ensuring that your management actions are seen as fair, considered and consistent, not abrupt and arbitrary.

Automatically unfair reasons for dismissal include any breach of basic employee rights under the law as already listed in the first section of this chapter, including dismissals related to:

- race, sex or disability discrimination;
- trade union activity or activities as a redundancy or pension representative;
- maternity;
- taking action on health and safety grounds;
- a shop worker's or betting worker's refusal to work on a Sunday.

Finally, there is the category of 'constructive dismissal', where no dismissal is carried out by the employer, but employees consider that they cannot continue in employment. Grounds for such a claim could involve:

- being downgraded or moved to a lower-status job;
- having a major benefit removed without due reason;
- being a victim of sexual harassment;
- being bullied continually;
- being humiliated in front of peers.

In the business that you have set up and are running there should be no instances of claims for constructive dismissal. If there are, the fault is likely to be your own, and any occurrence would indicate that your objective of building a well-integrated and mutually supportive team has failed.

However, following the rules and the simple guidelines set out above will not guarantee that you achieve your team-building objectives. The more positive elements of staff management are reviewed in the remaining sections of this chapter.

EMPLOYEE BENEFITS AND INCENTIVES

Since you are the owner or part-owner of a young, growing business, the range of benefits you may consider offering your employees is likely to be limited. Where statutory benefits are provided (eg sick pay, maternity leave and holidays) there is not a strong case for providing additions to the statutory minimum. Benefits that are granted to only one or two employees are likely to be divisive in a small company with only a handful of employees, unless there is a logic for them in attracting key members of staff.

For example, relocation expenses or a season ticket loan might be a necessary incentive to recruit someone from outside the area where the company is located.

Some benefits, such as childcare facilities, sports and social facilities or subsidised meals, are clearly unavailable to companies that are too small to provide more than a 'no frills' working environment. The major benefits of pension, car and medical insurance all have tax implications for the employee, and are expensive additions to overheads. In particular, the company car environment has changed irrevocably, with taxation charges on company car drivers being set both against the car's price and linked to carbon dioxide emissions. It is now common for a car allowance to be paid, instead of a car being provided to employees who need the use of a car for the effective performance of their jobs, and cars are used less than formerly as a recognition of status.

If the business you have set up is heavily reliant on a small group of trusted employees, each of whom makes an individual contribution to its operations, then it may be a worthwhile expense to provide group membership of a medical insurance scheme. In the event of serious illness or the need for surgery you will ensure that the employee gains access to quality care and attention quickly and that absence from the job is reduced to a minimum. You might consider adding death in service life assurance benefits in recognition for the long hours and dedication you will expect from your staff.

Pensions

The private pensions environment is in disarray at present, and it would be foolish to think about introducing a company pension scheme for your young business until government legislation or guidelines for a new breed of regulated pensions have been established. Whatever the outcome, it seems likely that the traditional final salary scheme, with defined benefits based on length of service and final salary, will pass into history.

Stakeholder pensions

In the meantime, if you have five or more employees you are obliged to arrange access to a stakeholder pension scheme for all those who earn more than the national insurance lower earnings limit. The law does not require that you set up a scheme, only that you contact a commercial provider and pass the details to your employees. Introducing a scheme involves: choosing one or more registered stakeholder pension schemes; discussing the scheme(s) with qualifying employees; formally choosing a scheme and giving contact details of the provider to your employees; arranging to deduct contributions from the pay of those employees who choose to contribute through you; and sending any employer and employee contributions to the pension scheme provider within the set time limits. Details on stakeholder pension schemes are available from the Occupational Pensions Regulatory Authority (tel: 012733 627600) or on its Web site (www.opra.gov.uk).

Incentives

While you are in the early stages of building up your business you may be unwilling to commit yourself to any form of formal profit-sharing scheme whereby the employees are awarded a proportion of net profits, perhaps above a predetermined level or in proportion to salaries. However, cash incentives, although subject to income tax deductions, are probably the most effective form of incentive.

The traditional Christmas or year-end bonus has the merit of putting cash into employees' hands at a time of high family expenditure, but has the disadvantage through repetition of becoming a benefit expected 'as of right' and therefore an element of basic remuneration. Regular salary reviews are preferable, since increases may be performance-related and therefore the incentive rewards are directed to those who are contributing most to the business.

Share ownership schemes

Share ownership schemes are now encouraged by the government and subject to quite generous tax relief. Their motivational value has been proven in many cases, not least in those companies that are heading for flotation or an ultimate trade sale when the added value can be realized. Employees who own shares in an organization tend to show a higher level of commitment and are more likely to have an interest in the company's performance and development. Option schemes can provide that employees lose their rights to subscribe for shares if they leave the organization, thereby encouraging staff retention.

There are two types of approved scheme for which tax relief has been granted: the Enterprise Management Scheme (EMI) and the All-Employee Share Ownership Plan (AESOP). The EMI permits a company to grant share options to up to 15 of its key staff members, up to a maximum value of £100,000 per employee and for a period of up to 10 years. No tax is payable when the option is granted or exercised. Capital gains tax applies on disposal, but tapering relief can reduce the tax charge to 10 per cent.

AESOP regulations are more complex but provide flexibility through three alternative schemes:

1. Up to £3,000 of free shares can be awarded to eligible employees each tax year free of income tax and national insurance. The awards can be linked to individual or team performance.
2. Employees can buy partnership shares up to £1,500 per annum out of pre-tax salary.
3. An employer can gift up to two matching shares pro rata to each partnership share purchased by an employee, up to a value of £3,000 per annum.

The employer can differentiate between employees when awarding AESOP benefits according to grade, length of service or hours worked, provided that it applies consistently the rules which it lays down.

Again, you should not feel under any pressure to rush into any form of share ownership until your business has 'bedded down' into a mature organization and the shape of its development becomes predictable. However, timing is important; from your employees' point of view, particularly those purchasing shares under an AESOP, the company's shares should still have a relatively low value when the scheme is adopted so that the prospects for capital appreciation are really attractive.

Understandably, you may feel tempted to grant options under an EMI to the 'faithful few' who were essential to the company's success in its early days and on whose loyalty and dedication you depend, but it may be difficult to grant them on the basis that the options lapse if they leave the company, without signalling that you expect them not to stay. Of course, the uncomfortable truth, which you can address only partly through training, is that some of the key staff who started out with you may be unable to grow with the company. As the business grows, enhanced skills and capabilities will be required and management roles will become more demanding. Some of your original team will probably not make the transition. When that happens and you have to recruit experienced management with track records, you may need to offer share options to attract the best, and might regret earlier acts of gratitude.

HUMAN RELATIONS

For smaller companies, 'human relations' may seem no more than a fancy title for personnel management, the staff administration function covering most of the matters referred to in the employment sections of this chapter. As your business grows you may be able to delegate most of this administrative detail but it will be some time before you will want or be able to afford a full-time Human Relations (HR) manager focused on career development and training, staff communication and assessment, human resource planning and other HR disciplines. Until that time you will retain the responsibility for what, in a bygone age, used to be called 'man management'.

However, there are lessons to be learnt from HR best practice which you can apply with advantage from the earliest phases of your business development:

- **Communication:** make a point of communicating freely with your staff, both informally on a daily basis and through monthly staff meetings. Install a bulletin board. Be sure to keep them informed of major events – the arrival of a big order or the loss of a major customer (the bad news as well as the good). Their livelihood depends on the success of the business and they have the right to know when it is doing well or badly. Of course, you are not going to make an announcement when the bank manager tells you to reduce the overdraft, but you can give them a general indication each month of how the business is doing. Failures and successes in customer relations and past due product or service deliveries can be reported too.

- **Training:** you want your staff to improve their skills and competencies to support the growth of the business. It is up to you to identify where they are deficient and where their particular aptitudes lie. Encourage them, and pay for them, to enrol on courses that you select with them and that don't take them away from the day job too much. Day release schemes and evening classes will be available locally in a multitude of skills. Help them to gain qualifications. Today, distance learning is available in most management disciplines, both through study guides and online. This is cost-effective education, both in minimizing loss of work time and in the use of content and a delivery method that can be used again by other staff members. Reward attainments with increased responsibility or, where appropriate, promotion.
- **Performance reviews:** all staff are entitled to an annual review. Use this review as an opportunity to assess performance against pre-established objectives. Involve each staff member in procedures for past performance assessment and in setting attainment targets for the following period. Use performance reviews as a basis for the merit element in salary increases.
- **Standards of practice:** however small your organization, it is big enough to adopt best practice standards in business ethics, customer care, supplier and staff relations and corporate governance. Articulate your standards simply in a mission statement and a company code of practice to which all staff are required to conform.

So long as your business remains under your personal management and control, the driving force will reside in your leadership. This means that your behaviour must at all times embody the company's code of practice, and you will be judged by your treatment of and relationships with all who work for you. In many ways the responsibility is awesome, and goes way beyond the exercise of human relations skills. You will be regarded as the barometer of the company's condition; your staff will tolerate some degree of personal idiosyncrasy, but their confidence, enthusiasm, optimism and calmness in crisis will be a reflection of yours.

It would be encouraging to look forward to an easier time when your business has grown, you are supported by a competent management team, and your primary role is to manage them rather than the workforce individually. That time may well come, but your human relations role will be no less demanding. Managing more remotely through departmental heads requires a further set of people skills which may be outside your experience. And your staff will continue to consult the barometer on the wall.

Employer's checklist

- Most employee rights run from the date of engagement. Others accrue with length of service. Be conversant with basic employment law.
- Discrimination law applies to sex, race and disability discrimination. The only exception to the rules on sex or race discrimination is a 'genuine occupational qualification' (GOQ).
- Part-time employees should be treated no less favourably than full-time employees. Be aware of special rules governing employment of offenders, children and overseas nationals.
- Draw up grievance procedures, and guidelines for notification and treatment of absences, to be made known to all employees.
- Take professional advice in court proceedings arising from employment tribunal claims. When you terminate employment, a written compromise agreement signed by the employee will prevent a later claim.
- In the early stages of your business keep staff recruitment to a minimum. When advertising for a position, state basic details including a salary indicator.
- Use a standard application form when you expect a heavy advertisement response. When interviewing be

sure to ask many open-ended questions demanding more than a 'Yes' or 'No' answer.

■ A job offer forms part of the contract of employment. Include most of the employment particulars (principal statement) required by law for all employees after one month's service. Require the employee to sign a copy of the job offer.

■ Have the complete principal statement signed formally as a contract by both parties. An additional, more formal contract is not usually necessary.

■ Minimize the risk of employment tribunal claims by putting in place and observing disciplinary procedures that follow ACAS recommendations.

■ Keep benefits to a minimum in the early stages (maybe medical and death in service insurance). Limit pension activity to statutory introduction of stakeholder pensions.

■ Profit-related incentives are preferable to bonuses which can become taken for granted benefits. Delay option schemes and share ownership plans until your business matures and the future shape of your company becomes clearer.

15 Asset Management

Your business's assets are worth careful attention for a variety of reasons – all of them important. A business can be valued on a number of criteria: turnover, profit, future growth and assets. If at some point you expect to sell the business, the value of the assets will clearly be part of the equation. In the more immediate term your assets represent your ability to operate – take away any one part of your machinery, your transport, your premises or your personnel and you will be severely compromised. It is therefore critical that all are maintained and retained. Finally, your assets have a current value which has to be paid for. The way in which you choose to do this will mean that you have more or less cash available for other purposes. Your choice of asset financing has implications for your whole business.

FINDING THE RIGHT PREMISES

Your choice of premises is likely to have an effect on your business for a significant period of time. It is therefore wise to make the right decision. As with all asset selection there are two parts to the process. First you must identify your requirements, and second you then must find the 'best fit' from what is available that meets those requirements. The first part is relatively simple, the second much less so as it requires those elusive business elements, luck and timing, as much as skill and judgement.

Perhaps the first question to ask yourself is, 'Do I need premises?' Maybe a mobile phone, laptop computer and a PO box will be enough. Presuming that you do need premises, you must decide how important location is. If you are a retail or distribution based business it is likely to be three times critical. If you are manufacturing something, space may be a higher priority. How much room for growth do you require? What specialist services will you use (eg broadband access, three-phase electricity, suitable storage for chemicals)? What transport access do you need both for customers (public transport facilities?) and suppliers (large lorries/forklifts?). What storage facilities do you need? Only you can know what your business processes require. Work your way through all the different parts of the business and list all their requirements in terms of space, remembering height as well as area, power and services needs, and transport and location requirements.

You will also need to identify your budget for the premises; we discuss the financing options below in more detail. Once you are furnished with all the above information, you are in a good position to start looking for your premises. This is where you are likely to need third-party assistance. Contact either a local chartered surveyor or a commercial estate agent. They should have a good knowledge of the current market and be able to tell you whether your requirement list is achievable and affordable or not. The property market is far from perfect, so you should trawl for as much information as possible. Other sources are the local press, Internet property search sites, trade magazines, local authority business assistance units and other business agencies. You will be well served by driving around and seeing what is on offer with advertising boards. As ever, the more people you talk to, the better informed you will become.

Working from home

An increasing number of people are now working from home. It is no longer seen as an unusual way of working. However, it is a *different* way of working, and if you are thinking of doing it there are a number of issues to consider.

Be aware that there are probably more downside factors to working at home than benefits, but the benefits are likely to outweigh the downside factors. The clear benefits of working from home are reduced start-up costs and overheads (which can be critical for your cash flow when setting up a business) and increased flexibility in organizing your working time, including the elimination of any commuting time. There may also be 'lifestyle benefits', such as enabling you to continue looking after your children or any dependants.

The downside factors are numerous. While none of them individually need be an absolute problem, cumulatively you may find them stressful. Most of the problems are related to separating your working and non-working life. However, we should mention there are tax implications from working from home (you can lose some of your principal residence capital gains exemption) and possibly some planning restrictions as well. Space is often the first issue to be noticed. Most people find that they need a dedicated space, whether it be a room or a desk area, that is their 'office'. If you find yourself having to use the same area for non-work activities it may become confusing and then irritating. Your business will inevitably accumulate papers and files that will need to be stored and yet be accessible; you must have space for these as well.

When your office is also your home you will have to consider what to do if you need to have a meeting with a client or colleague. Ushering clients past the pram and over the dog bowl is not very professional. If space is limited this becomes even more of a problem. It may be wise to meet at a hotel or have access to a serviced office or similar short-term facility.

The ability to stop working is often compromised at home. Sooner or later you will leave your office each day and go home. If your office is also your home there is always the temptation to check your e-mails before you go to bed, answer the business telephone at 10 pm or just nip into the office on a Sunday afternoon. Occasionally the opportunity to do this is a real bonus, but it can become routine to the detriment of the rest of your and your family's life.

The final series of problems to consider is less tangible but no less important. Working from home means working alone, usually. At first you may revel in the freedom that this offers. Over time, however, you may begin to feel cut off and isolated. The paradox is that as the Internet makes working from home much easier, it can also increase the feeling of isolation. With the vast majority of your communication being made by concise e-mail messages, you may spend days without actually speaking to anyone! This is a problem that you should manage actively; try to arrange lunch-time meetings with colleagues or other home-workers. It can revitalize and invigorate you and your work. For more detail on this topic see *Kogan Page's* publication *Your Home Office.*

Buying or leasing

If your business owns its own property it frees itself from the uncertainties of rent increases, potential lease termination and, if you have an unhelpful landlord, the possibility of poor maintenance, constant interference, inflexible approach to changing needs of the business and so on. That said, most of these complaints should not arise if you have a good relationship with your landlord and a well-worded lease agreement. What you will definitely acquire with owning your own premises is an increased cash requirement before you even start trading.

Commercial mortgages are difficult to obtain for start-up businesses with no track record, and you certainly will not get the same attractive rates and high percentage of purchase price loans that residential buyers are currently offered. Your mortgage repayments may be fixed for a short period, but they are essentially at the mercy of the world capital markets, and where the Bank of England (or possibly the European Central Bank, if the UK decides to join the euro during the period of your mortgage term) chooses to set interest rates.

The main reason for purchasing your own business premises will be as an alternative business investment to your start-up business. If you believe the property will increase in value then it may be worth considering. However, you must make a clear distinction between your property investment and your business one. They are separate businesses. Historically, although perhaps not currently, the return from a successful business will be greater than

Mortgages For The Self Employed

Going It Alone?

The good news is that mortgages for self-employed borrowers are now more competitive than ever.

Ingrid Hendrickson Mortgage Manager at The Chorley & District Building Society offers some help and advice on mortgages for the self-employed and takes a look at the Buy- To- Let market.

There was a time not too long ago when being self-employed and getting a mortgage was not a particularly attractive proposition, both for the lender and the self-employed applicant. There was simply too much of a risk.

The conventional mortgage application did not match the circumstances of the self-employed applicant. On the one hand, there are employed customers with a regular income supported by a guaranteed income confirmed by the presentation of a series of wage slips and an employers reference, on the other hand, there are the self-employed with variable incomes and fluctuating cash flows.

Today however, self-employment has grown considerably and represents around 11% of the working population, a sizeable niche in marketing terms, which mortgage lenders can no longer ignore. Now mortgage products have been more tailored to meet the needs of the self-employed.

While proof of income remains a tricky area, building societies' like The Chorley for example will insist on seeing audited accounts from the last three years, or two years with a one year projection.

Fine if you are up and running as a business, but not so promising if you are just about to set sail.

So what about the potential 'go it alone' candidate, can a self-employed mortgage be feasible? Yes, but this is very much the domain of the High St lenders, it all depends on the circumstances and every case needs to be looked at on an individual basis.

However you must have a whiter than white credit history, if a favourable response is to be forthcoming from a lender, all of whom will have access to your credit rating.

Buy To Let

The 'buy-to-let' market has been very active recently, fuelled by the lower mortgage rates, strong property price increases and the fact that lenders are now prepared to offer a mortgage at a more competitive rate.

This is certainly an area that requires careful consideration and as with any investment there are risks involved in buying to let, such as,allowing for periods when the property is empty.

What happens if the mortgage rate rises? Is the rental income sufficient to pay the mortgage? Can you negotiate the income you require? Will you manage the property or would you be better to utilise the services of a Letting Agent. Are you aware of the tax and insurance implications?

You will also need to be aware of your legal responsibilities as a landlord, these include-

- carrying out repairs
- ensuring the safety of gas and electric appliances
- and ensuring that the furniture and furnishings meet fire safety requirements

An offer of a buy to let mortgage will only be made on the condition that certain criteria has been met. In the case of The Chorley & District Building Society you would need provide the following:

- Set-up fees
- An administration fee of £200 is required on submission of the application form.
- In all cases interest rate will be charged at 1% above the Society's Standard Variable Rate. However, the Society may make additional schemes available from time to time.
- Rental income must be 120% or more of the mortgage repayment.
- Full status is always sought; the Society does not accept previous defaulters.
- Maximum LTV 70%.
- A 6 months Shorthold Tenancy agreement is a mandatory requirement. Maximum term for a Shorthold tenancy agreement is 12 months.

There are a number of exclusions which are worth noting:
- Housing Associations or company let cannot be parties to the tenancy agreement.
- Multiple Tenancy Agreements are not acceptable on one property.
- The Society does not lend for properties which are to be rented to DSS claimants, students or divided into bedsits.

Lending criteria may vary from lender to lender

Generally speaking becoming a landlord is a lot more complex than ever before, you need to undertake your research, find out what potential tenants are looking for, in terms of location, affordability and furnishings, fixtures and fittings. This is a long term investment with lots of strings attached.

from successful property investment, although the former's risks are usually higher as well. You may find that it is more tax-efficient for you to own the premises personally and rent it to the business, or to set up a separate company to purchase the business. In this way you remove the mortgage debt from your balance sheet. These issues are best discussed with your tax adviser, with regard to the specifics of your situation.

The most usual way for a business to acquire its premises is through leasehold. In this way you do not need to find any capital to fund your premises; you just ensure that the business creates enough cash to pay the rent. The rent can be fixed for fixed periods of time, with rent reviews which can be subject to impartial third-party arbitrations should you think them unreasonable.

The law (Landlord & Tenant Act 1954 and amendments) operates reasonably strongly in the commercial tenant's favour. You have the right to renew your lease at the end of the term, with a few exceptions if you have exhibited unreasonable behaviour as a tenant, or the landlord requires the premises for its own purposes or wishes to redevelop them. The tenancy agreement is critical, and will require you to employ a good property lawyer to advise you. The landlord may well try to restrict you as much as possible in terms of landlord obligations and tenant rights. You cannot read the small print of tenancy agreements closely enough. Ensure that you have as much flexibility in the agreement as possible, with break clauses, options on changes of use, minimal maintenance responsibilities for yourself, control over any service charges and, if possible, the right to assign the lease. Your property adviser should be able to guide you through the minutiae of the agreement and help you to secure reasonable terms.

Finally, before signing any agreement double check that you fully understand how much you have to pay, not only in rent but also the other charges and the deposit, and that you will certainly be able to afford all these costs. Your business will benefit from a good working relationship with your landlord, and ensuring that your rent is paid on time can only help this. In return, it is likely that you will receive a more sympathetic ear if anything goes wrong with the premises in the future.

LOCAL AUTHORITY ISSUES, PLANNING AND BUSINESS RATES

The start-up process of your business will be affected by the approach your local authority has to encouraging and fostering your type of business. Most local authorities have a unit designed to help small businesses. How effective it is will depend on the individual authority. At the very least you should contact your local authority and discuss with the business development or support unit what help they have available for you. This is likely to range from straightforward business advice to financing help. Your premises may be located in an area that attracts special assistance or loans. The local authority should also be able to guide you through any planning issues that you may encounter.

Planning issues can cover a wide range of different problems, and it is wise to contact the planning department at your local council to find out what planning or business registration your business may require. Clearly, you must check that your premises have the relevant planning permission for you to carry out your business there. See Table 15.1. Also many businesses need to register with the local authority, such as those in the catering or building trades. Many of these registrations are mere formalities, but they are also requirements, and in the event of an accident or problem, the fact that you have followed the correct procedures always helps your case.

The other role of your local authority is less benevolent; to levy business rates. Business rates are generally paid by the occupier of non-domestic properties. This means the owner-occupier or lease-holder. Some non-domestic properties are exempt from rates, such as agricultural land and buildings. If you think you may be exempt, check with your local valuations office. Your home may be eligible for business rates if you work from there; again you can ask the local Valuation Office for clarification for your specific circumstances.

The bill you pay for your property depends on the rateable value that the Valuation Office has assigned to it. These values are set every five years; the next valuation will occur in 2005. You can challenge the rateable value for your property if you believe it is unreasonable, but you should take advice from a solicitor or chartered

Table 15.1   Planning use classes

Use Class	Use	Whether change permitted
A1 **Shops**	Sale of goods and cold food, retail warehouses, hairdressers, travel and ticket agencies, post offices, domestic hire shops, funeral directors, dry cleaners	No change of use without permission, except to A1 plus single flat
A2 **Financial and professional services**	Professional (excluding health and medical services) and financial services (banks and building societies); other services appropriate in a shopping area where the services are provided principally to visiting members of the public	Change to A1 permitted only if there is a ground floor display window
A3 **Food and drink**	Sale of food and drink for consumption on premises, eg in restaurants, pubs, cafes and wine bars; shops for sale of hot food to be taken away	Change to A1 or A2 permitted
Sui generis	Shops selling or displaying motor vehicles for sale Launderettes, taxi businesses, car hire businesses, filling stations, scrapyards	Change to A1 permitted No change of use permitted
B1 **Business**	**a** Offices other than financial and professional services providing for the visiting members of the public **b** Research and development **c** Other industrial processes appropriate in a residential area	Change to B8 (only up to 235 m² of floor space) permitted
B2 **General industrial**	General industry, not within B1	Change to B1 or B8 (only up to 235 m² of floor space)
B8 **Storage or distribution**	Storage or distribution centres	Change to B1 (only up to 235 m² of floor space) permitted

Sui generis	Work registerable under Alkali etc, Works Regulation Act	No change of use permitted
C1 Hotels	Hotels, boarding and guest houses, provided that care is not provided	No change of use permitted
C2 Residential institutions	Residential accommodation for provision of care (eg old age homes); residential schools and colleges and training centres; hospitals and nursing homes	No change of use permitted
C3 Dwelling-houses	Dwellinghouses for individuals, families and up to six individuals living as a single household	Subdivision of dwellinghouses into two or more dwelling houses not permitted
Sui generis	Hostels	No change of use permitted
D1 Non-residential institutions	Clinics, health centres, crèches, day nurseries, day centres, consulting rooms (not attached to doctor's house); museums, libraries, art galleries, public and exhibition halls; non-residential schools, colleges and other educational centres; public worship or religious instruction	No change of use permitted
D2 Assembly and leisure	Cinemas, dance and concert halls; swimming pools, skating rinks, gymnasiums; other indoor and outdoor sports and leisure uses, bingo halls, casinos	No change of use permitted
Sui generis	Theatres, amusement arcades and centres, fun fairs	No change of use permitted

surveyor before pursuing this. The local authority only levies the charge; it is central government that sets the 'multiplier' by which your actual bill is calculated. In 2001/2 the multiplier was 43p for every pound of rateable value. So if your premises have a rateable value of £1,000, your rates bill will be £430 for this year. The multiplier is reset every year, but cannot increase by more than the rate of inflation. You may benefit from transitional or other relief; you can find out more details on transitional relief from your local authority or Valuation Office.

PURCHASE OF PLANT, MACHINERY AND VEHICLES

The purchase of large pieces of hardware, whether it is manufacturing machinery, office equipment or vehicles, will be potentially your single largest capital outlay. There are various ways you can finance the use of these capital assets – and with today's sophisticated financial industry vying for your business, it is wise to familiarize yourself with the various options.

Many large pieces of equipment will be offered with various financing packages. However, it is wise to check whether these are the best deals available. It may well be that you can do better by paying the vendor the full cash amount and borrowing the money from elsewhere, either your bank or a specialist financing firm.

The most sophisticated series of options is to be found in the vehicle sector, but you may well find that financing companies will offer you similar deals on other types of capital equipment.

The most popular type of financing is **contract hire**. Typically this will be arranged directly with a company that provides both the equipment and the financing. The arrangement will be based on a fixed term contract, of say 24 to 60 months, from which a fixed monthly rental will be calculated. At the end of the term the hire company takes back the equipment. The principal financial advantages of this are that:

■ you do not need to find a large amount of cash to purchase the equipment at the outset, when you have limited borrowing opportunities;

The power to support your business

npower is the largest electricity and second largest gas supplier in the UK - supplying over 7 million customers every day. npower business services supports over 380'000 small to medium sized enterprises, with over 50 years' experience it makes us a leading specialist to SMEs.

To find out how npower can support your business call

0845 120 1451

When phoning please quote ref no: Z1502

What would a 20% reduction in energy costs be worth to you?

Most businesses quite rightly focus attention on producing goods or providing services to satisfy their customers' requirements. After all, that is where the profit comes from to maintain and grow the business. Sometimes, so much attention is paid to this primary objective that other, less obvious, ways of improving efficiency are overlooked.

Energy is one commodity that every business uses in one form or another. It's used to convert raw materials into finished goods, for transport, storage, and for general well being through lighting and space heating systems. Although energy usage is not always high on the list of priorities, it can add to (or detract from) the overall profitability of the business.

Using less energy saves money, which is the primary reason most businesses try to cut down. But there are environmental benefits too, as any reduction in energy use is matched by a similar reduction in greenhouse gases, principally carbon dioxide, which contribute to global warming. Savings made now are ongoing into the future, so the sooner you start, the more you save.

Many energy saving solutions can be implemented without cost and others can be achieved at low cost, often recovering the initial outlay within 2 years.

Listed below are a few ideas of how you could save energy:

Lighting:

- Switch off unwanted lights over meal breaks and save up to 6% on your lighting bill
- Replace standard incandescent bulbs with long life, low energy, compact fluorescent lamps and save about 80% on energy and increase lamp life about 8 times
- Replacing standard 1" fluorescent tubes with 1" tubes will produce energy savings of about 7%. (Not suitable in every case)

Heating:

- Turn down your space heating by 1°C and save up to 10% on your heating bill
- Have your boiler serviced regularly and expect fuel savings of up to 10% or more. This will also safeguard against carbon monoxide poisoning
- Replace the programmer on your boiler with a modern optimised controller and make energy savings of about 25%

- If you are too hot, don't open windows and doors simply turn the heating down

Insulation:

- Apply draught proof strip to external doors and windows to eliminate draughts
- Have at least 150mm (6") of lagging in roof spaces. Where you have less, add more over the top of what you already have
- Insulate hot water pipes and central heating pipes

Equipment:

- Screen savers don't save energy. It's better to turn off monitors, which will save the screen and save energy. If possible, turn off computers too
- Buy computers, printers and copiers that are Energy Star compliant (or to a similar standard)
- Encourage staff to switch off unwanted equipment when they leave
- Scrutinise your energy bills to look for abnormal consumption, which could be an indication of equipment left on or thermostats that have been tampered with
- If you have separate systems for air-conditioning and space heating, make sure one isn't trying to cool down a space that the other is trying to heat up or vice versa

Simple energy saving tips can be obtained from the npower small business energy efficiency help line. Simply call **0845 0704019** and quote your npower customer reference number.

For more specific energy efficiency advice, you may find a site energy survey s useful. This will identify in more detail where energy can be saved in your business. In money terms you will see savings on the prime fuel cost (and maybe capacity charges too), Climate Change Levy charges and VAT.

For small businesses, an energy appraisal might be most appropriate, whereas larger businesses may benefit from a more comprehensive energy study.

For more information on how your business can make the most out of energy efficiency, please visit the business section on npower.com.

The UK Government and other sources suggest that businesses in general could save up to 20% of their energy use. As a final thought, **what would a 20% reduction in energy costs be worth to you?**

▪   you can budget your costs accurately over an extended period;

▪   the money saved from not having to make an outright purchase can be used effectively elsewhere;

▪   the equipment, as it is not owned by the company (just rented), is 'off-balance sheet', which improves the key ratios mentioned at the outset of this chapter;

▪   as such you do not have to depreciate the assets;

▪   VAT efficiency;

▪   rentals can be offset against corporation tax, as a legitimate expense.

Often contract hire companies will also offer you maintenance and repair contracts, which can provide a reduction in your administrative costs and peace of mind. These contracts should be analysed closely for value, as they are often the area where the hire companies make their profit.

Another common method of financing is **finance leasing**. This is similar to contract hire with the same advantages, but has one key difference. At the term outset a future value is calculated for the equipment at the end of the term. This value must be paid at the end of the contract, and is known as the 'balloon payment'. Effectively your company is taking on the risk of either purchasing the equipment for its use, or selling the equipment to someone else at the end of the contract. Because you are taking the risk in agreeing to dispose of the equipment at a fixed price in the future, the finance company will offer you much cheaper monthly payments for the duration of the contract, as it knows you must pay the balloon payment at the end. The added advantage with finance leasing is:

▪   lower instalment payments;

▪   opportunity to purchase known equipment at low fixed price;

▪   if you do purchase equipment, your depreciation exposure will be reduced because of its lower price;

▪   possibility that you may be able to sell on the equipment at higher price than agreed 'balloon payment', thereby further improving your cash flow (conversely, the balloon payment may be larger than the equipment's actual residual value).

A third option is **lease purchase**. If you know that you want to continue owning the equipment at the end of the contract term, this may be a suitable option. Structurally it is similar to the two finance options already discussed, in that you avoid the initial capital outlay and instead pay in fixed instalments over the contract term. With lease purchase you are deemed, for accounting purposes but not legal ones, to have full ownership of the equipment from day one of the contract; as such, it is less VAT efficient as you must pay all the VAT up-front or add it to your instalments. It is therefore more costly than the previous options, but can be a useful tool for non-VAT registered businesses.

The traditional finance method is **hire purchase**. Typically you will pay a lump-sum down-payment at the outset of the contract and then fixed equal instalments over the rest of the fixed term. It is somewhat like finance leasing in reverse. However, unlike with finance leasing you do not get the tax advantages or the off-balance sheet advantages as, for tax purposes, you own the equipment from the outset.

Companies that already have a significant amount of capital tied up in vehicles and equipment can often set up a **sale and leaseback** contract with a finance company. This allows them to sell their vehicle fleet, for example, to the finance company and so remove the depreciating asset from the balance sheet while gaining a cash injection, and then lease them back with all the advantages of contract hire.

For the sole trader or small partnership there are some newer financing options specifically designed for the car market. These are similar to the options above but available to private individuals. Personal contract purchase is where the future estimated value of the vehicle is deducted from the initial cost, and the remaining amount is spread across the term as instalment payments plus interest. Usually at the end of the term you can either pay the 'balloon payment' and keep the car, or just return the car. This allows you access to the same buying power as fleet car companies, and also the budgeting opportunities of financing deals.

Vehicle taxation

Specific tax rules apply to cars and vans, and they are therefore treated differently from other capital equipment. Because of the lack of clarity in recording private and business usage of vehicles, Customs and Excise have special rates of VAT that allow them to compensate. It is best to speak to your tax adviser to discover exactly what you may and may not reclaim.

Similarly, the tax benefits for company cars have become less generous and more complex in recent years. The government no longer determines company car taxation on mileage and vehicle age, as it claimed this method encouraged more driving in older vehicles which was not environmentally friendly. Now it bases the tax charge on a percentage of the car's price, graduated according to the level of the car's carbon dioxide (CO_2) emissions. The charge builds up from 15 per cent of the car's price, for cars emitting 165 grams per kilometre (g/km) CO_2, in 1 per cent steps for every additional 5 g/km over 165 g/km. The maximum charge is 35 per cent of the car's price.

INSURANCE

A classic economic definition for profit is the reward for taking risk. On the basis that you are in business to make a profit, you will therefore be taking a risk. The size and effect of the risks you take should be closely related to the profit you can expect to make. There is no point in taking large risks if you are only going to make small profits. Not all risks are financial; some are physical, some ethical. But in business most risks have a financial element – even the physical and ethical ones. If your employee is injured in the course of their work you may well be liable to pay compensation. If your products are discovered to be polluting, then adverse publicity may affect your sales.

Insurance provides a simple way of reducing large downside risks to manageable levels. For most businesses specialist insurance will not be necessary. General insurance can be relatively cheaply and easily obtained to cover most commercial liabilities.

There are a few legal insurance requirements that you must comply with:

■ Employers liability: as soon as you employ someone the law requires you to have employers liability insurance, of a minimum of £10 million.

■ Public liability: the law requires you to have liability insurance to cover any damages payable arising from bodily injury, illness or damage to property incurred during the course of your work.

■ Product liability: the legal requirement to be able to compensate in the event of your product being defective and so causing injury.

Beyond these statutory insurance requirements, a risk-aware business will probably want to cover itself against a range of other potential risks. Commercial insurance is usually split into three categories: liabilities, property and buildings, and business assets and equipment. The latter two are fairly self-explanatory, but your other liability insurance can cover a wide range of alternatives.

In addition to the legal liabilities above, you may also want to consider professional indemnity insurance (against damages caused by your giving poor or negligent advice); key man cover (in a small firm the loss of one key person either temporarily or permanently can cause major disruption to your provision of services); business interruption (damage to plant or supplies can cause your business to temporarily cease production); transit cover (protection for goods in transit); credit insurance (insurance for bad debts); director's and officer's liability (covers due diligence and fiducial duty); and computer cover (insures against accidental damage, theft, breakdown, etc).

Insurance should not be a significant proportion of your costs unless you are undertaking a particularly hazardous project. Specialist insurance is available for almost any event imaginable – at a cost. For any trade overseas you will need to consider a further range of risks, from export guarantees (for payments) to political risks and exchange rate risks.

With your basic insurance requirements most commercial insurance companies will be available to offer you a standard package to cover your legal and essential liabilities. For more specialist cover you will need to contact a broker who can arrange cover for you. As with all such business contracts, it will pay to ask friends and business contacts who they recommend for price, efficiency and reliability.

RISK MITIGATION

Many insurance policies will require you to take some action to mitigate any risk before they will cover you. At its most basic, you will be required to fit good locks on your doors and windows to be eligible for business equipment insurance. For other liabilities you will also find statutory health and safety requirements that must be complied with. The laws covering these requirements are often only evident once a problem has arisen. Your duty as business owner or manager is usually to ensure that all reasonable precautions have been taken to prevent foreseeable accidents or damages, whether this is with office equipment (ie that electric sockets are not overloaded, and machinery is regularly serviced), food hygiene (that due care has been taken to avoid contamination etc) or on building sites (that correct safety procedures have been followed) or whatever area of business you operate within.

The principle to adhere to is that you are able to prove that you have followed such procedures, and not just state that you have. This inevitably requires a 'paper trail' where inspections are noted down, instruction on procedures is written down and issued to all relevant personnel, and occasional testing of this knowledge is carried out. There is clearly a fine balance between taking these actions so that they can prove you have fulfilled your 'due diligence' and their obstructing the efficient performance of your business. A friendly discussion with the local authority officer in charge of such issues may help to clarify your particular situation.

Checklist

- Do you need separate premises?
- If not, can you work from home effectively?
- If working from home:
  - Do you need a separate phone line, broadband Internet access, etc?
  - Do you need planning permission?
  - Do you know whether there are any Capital Gains tax implications of working from your home?
  - Have you discussed implications with other house-holders?
  - Have you considered whether you will feel isolated?
  - Do you have other home-workers to discuss work issues with?
- If seeking premises:
  - How much space do you need?
  - Does this allow for all your equipment dimensions?
  - Does this allow you room for growth?
  - Do you require any planning permission?
  - Is location important to you and your customers?
- Purchase or lease: remember that purchasing your premises is essentially a separate business proposition.
- Lease contract:
  - Get professional advice.
  - Negotiate your terms: at the outset you have your best chance to get the lease you want.
  - Ask about: rent-free periods, break clauses, assignment rights, and rent review terms.
  - Make sure you understand the fundamentals: what upkeep and charges you are responsible for; who pays the insurance; and what your arbitration rights are.
- Asset financing: familiarize yourself with all the options, such as:
  - contract hire;
  - finance leasing;

- lease purchase;
- hire purchase;
- personal contract purchase.
∎ Insurance: double check you have all your legal obligations in place:
    - public liability;
    - product liability;
    - employer's liability.
∎ Think through your other insurance risks:
    - building and plant;
    - stock;
    - professional indemnity;
    - key man cover;
    - business interruption;
    - credit insurance;
    - transit insurance and so on.
∎ Risk mitigation: have you thought through a crisis management plan?

npower®
business services

Part Four:

Managing for Growth

16 Entering Export Markets

MARKET RESEARCH

The initial decision to examine a specific export market will necessarily be based on incomplete information. You may be drawn to a particular market by its size, its rate of growth, your knowledge of the local competition or of the experience of your competitors in entering that market. Perhaps you have limited experience of the market through sourcing supplies for your business from there, attending a trade show in the country or meeting a visiting delegation. Through any of these activities, you may have gained a first order which indicates that market prices are favourable. Perhaps your inclination to enter this particular export market is no more than a perceived affinity with that country and its people.

Whatever the thought process or chain of circumstances that has persuaded you to consider a specific market, your first serious step is market research in at least the equivalent depth to the desk research you would carry out into any new niche market at home. The scope of the research will be wider, to include the legal and regulatory environment, the distribution chain and channels to market, and terms of business, as well as the current and potential market for your product or service, pricing structures, competitor activity and local promotional practices. In developed export markets, particularly those of Western Europe and the EU accession states of Central and Eastern Europe, there are many sources of information for you to tap into, from Internet Web sites and published statistics, to chambers of commerce, trade associations, inward investment agencies and the commercial officers at the local British Embassy.

Good starting points are the Trade Partners UK country desks at the Department of Trade and Industry and the London offices of the joint chambers of commerce between individual foreign countries and the UK, such as the German-British Chamber of Commerce and Industry. From these sources and the further sources located in the market itself, you should be able to develop a 'long list' of potential customers to form the nucleus for a pilot marketing campaign.

Commissioning field research at this stage of your investigation is probably not a cost-effective exercise. It is more important for you or your marketing manager to gain personal exposure to the market. Attendance at relevant trade and industry exhibitions can be a valuable experience provided that you use your time wisely. Some continental trade shows are so large that it is easy to become overwhelmed by the number of exhibitors and to be distracted from visiting the few stands that are most relevant to your business. A good way to avoid such confusion is to collect a copy of the catalogue on arrival before visiting the exhibition, to shortlist the most promising exhibitors' stands and to plan the optimum route between them.

Visiting potential customers on their stands at exhibitions is unlikely to yield immediate orders for your products or services – after all, their objective is to market their own products at the shows where they exhibit. However, in some industries, such as automotive, it is common for original equipment manufacturers (OEMs) to set up buying offices with the express purpose of meeting prospective new suppliers. From your point of view, this is better than 'cold calling' and may serve as a first step in the long process required to establish your company as a qualified supplier to the OEM. In any event, your attendance at trade shows should help you to firm up on a more refined 'short list' of potential customers for a direct sales approach.

SALES DEVELOPMENT

Hopefully, your follow-up campaign of direct approaches to identified potential customers will yield a handful of first orders, and their service will provide you with a learning curve in the management of export logistics with the minimum of financial risk. Export logistics, documentation and the financing of exports are complex subjects requiring great attention to detail, and later sections of this chapter offer an introduction. Although they are not strictly a part of the marketing and sales function, logistics and export finance are an important element in most export customer relationships and may impact the terms of business significantly. Problems in these areas may be the deciding factor in deciding whether or not to open a new account or service a particular order.

It is also time for you to decide how you are going to develop your business in the market you are now opening up, and foster the sales relationships you are establishing with new customers. For the easily accessible markets of Western Europe you may be able to service your customers and develop new business by normal electronic and written communication, supplemented by visits from your export manager or yourself at regular intervals. The personal contact is as crucial in these markets as those that are further afield or less developed, including the United States, which are difficult to manage from the home office, not least because the cost of visiting them regularly is high in terms of both travel costs and senior management time. If you want your business to develop from more than a trickle of sporadic orders, you will require representation. By now, you should have acquired sufficient market knowledge to make a reasoned judgement as to the kind of intermediary your business needs. Basically, the choice is between the appointment of one or more sales agents or, alternatively, distributors.

Sales agents

Working as an independent contractor on commission, the foreign sales agent's task is to gain orders for his principal's goods and convey them to the principal. Normally, the exporter retains responsibility for delivering the product to the customer, which it may delegate to the company's forwarding agent.

The agent is not normally restricted to selling one company's goods, but is restricted either to a well-defined geographic territory, or sometimes a specific market sector within a geographical area – such as the retail trade or mail order houses – for consumer products.

Typically, the agent's characteristics and role can be defined as:

▌ A company or firm or sole trader, usually a local national, having some experience in the product area.

▌ Responsibility for:
  – research;
  – promotion;
  – selling;
  – order getting;
  – customer care;
  – problem solving, etc.

▌ In some cases, additional responsibility for:
  – calling orders off the forwarding agent's local warehouse;
  – confirming delivery schedules;
  – debt collection.

▌ The agent receives commission from the company on sales in its territory, usually between 5 per cent and 10 per cent, based on the exporter's ex-works price and payable only after customer payment in full.

▌ Usually, the agent does not have any responsibility to commit the principal contractually beyond accepting an order.

The benefits of an agent are the ability to start up quickly and the low cost to the exporter. The disadvantages are uncertainty about the strength of the agent's commitment, lack of control over the agent's commercial actions, and the cost penalties of termination in many countries (particularly under EU law).

Distributors

In contrast to the sales agent, the foreign distributor acts as a principal, buying and selling manufactured product for its own account and on its own terms. In effect the distributor is the exporter's direct customer, although not the end-user. Delivery to the territory is made through the distributor, which manages the local customer relationship directly.

Distributors are usually incorporated, and their characteristics and role are definable as:

▌ Purchases goods from the manufacturer and resells into the territory, sometimes as a sole distributor, at a profit.

▌ Makes its profit by marking up the discounted price at which it purchases goods from the exporter to the agreed market price.

▌ Performs all the agent's tasks plus:
  – stocking goods and spare parts;
  – pre- and after-sales service;
  – sales administration;
  – local deliveries;
  – installation;
  – credit control and debtor collection.

▌ Distributors' discounts vary from one product sector to another (industrial goods provide for 15 per cent to 25 per cent mark-ups; consumer goods for mark-ups of 50 per cent or more).

▌ Higher distributors' margins also reflect the additional services they perform compared with agents, and their greater financial risk.

The advantages of exporting through a distributor are that it may be restricted from selling competitors' products under the terms of the distribution agreement, and its activities are easier to monitor than those of the sales agent. The distributor is usually a better channel to market than the agent for technically complex finished product requiring after-sales service and repair facilities.

Selecting sales agents and distributors

You should never appoint an intermediary without developing a clear specification of the role to be filled, and then checking thoroughly that the appointee has the necessary attributes to perform the role. For some national markets with strong regional characteristics, it may be sensible to appoint more than one distributor with clearly defined territories, or a single distributor with several supporting agents. Generally, when one or more agents are appointed for a territory serviced by an exporter's sole distributor, the latter's selling responsibilities are diminished accordingly, and the distributor's margin is reduced by the amount of the agent's commission.

In making your selection of individual distributors and agents, the following criteria are key:

- **Compatibility versus competition:** Familiarity with the same kind of product, bringing market knowledge and customer contacts, is an advantage, but appointing a sales agent or distributor already selling competitors' product would be a mistake, and replacing an existing competitor has its perils. Appointing an agent who is already selling complementary but non-competing products successfully may be a good solution, provided that the complementary products are not inferior in quality to your own.
- **Commercial capability:** Look for market knowledge, marketing skills and promotional expertise allied to administrative capability and, for distributors, logistical capability against warehousing and transport facilities.
- **Technical capability:** Assess technical qualifications of management and staff, and in-house training activity in new products.
- **Financial status:** Perform normal credit reference routines and reviews of trading history, balance sheets and capital adequacy where audited accounts are available.

Through your screening process based on these criteria you will aim to arrive at a short-list of three or four candidates from which you can make the final selection. Final selection should be carried out by making a personal visit to each candidate's place of business; only at this stage should you allow subjective judgement to influence the decision.

However confident you may be in your final choice, be sure to grant only a trial period of representation (typically 12 months). Although the initial engagement is provisional, it should always be the subject of a full written agreement, not just for your company's protection but also to clarify, without ambiguity, for both parties exactly what is being agreed. The agreement should define all of the following:

- products;
- territories;
- duration of the agreement and provisions for termination;*
- quantitative definition of minimum performance levels;
- commission rates / discounts;
- credit and payment terms;
- the principal's duties and responsibilities;
- use of copyright and ownership of IPR;
- limits of the agent / distributor's authority;
- product and commercial liabilities to customers;
- indemnities and / or compensation on termination;*
- law governing the contract (jurisdiction);*
- provisions for dispute resolution.

* for territories within the Single Market, compliance with EU Law is mandatory.

EXPORT LOGISTICS

Until your export trade becomes substantial you will not want to consider staffing an export department within your business, with the additional fixed cost which it would involve. Fortunately, the evolutionary changes of the information age have bred new logistics solutions, and the outsourcing of logistics management to specialist freight forwarders has now become an attractive option for many companies, both large and small. Even the administrative activities of arranging transportation, managing shipping and forwarding agents, arranging insurance, export documentation, customs clearance, and the payment of freight and other charges can be safely outsourced to the freight forwarder, as well as the physical functions of packing and labelling, warehousing and inventory management. Electronic (EDI) technology is already in common use in the freight industry, and freight forwarders can provide cargo tracking facilities online both for the client and the forwarder.

Freight forwarders take the form of:

- Local companies that deal with clients in their immediate areas, or operate at sea ports or airports concentrated on particular types of traffic.

▌ National companies with offices in the major ports and airports and in the largest industrial conurbations throughout the country. They often have overseas agents or correspondents in the markets which they service commonly.

▌ International companies with their own offices overseas and offering worldwide services.

All freight forwarders provide one or more of the following services:

▌ road and rail distribution;
▌ maritime intermodal services;
▌ airfreight consolidation and forwarding;
▌ trade facilitation, customs brooking and consultancy;
▌ logistics and supply chain management.

In selecting a freight forwarder for your export market, make sure that its range of services extend to the cheapest, quickest and safest routing and the best modes of transport. For example, if you are serving Asian markets you will require your freight forwarder to provide consolidation and groupage services – the ability to group together consignments from several exporters and present them to a shipping company or airline as a single large consignment. In this way, you will be able to benefit from a more competitive tariff for your small consignments.

International transport documentation

There are three basic types of international transport document:

▌ documents of carriage, including the airwaybill, bill of lading and consignment note;
▌ documents for Customs and other regulatory bodies;
▌ commercial documents.

Bill of lading

The bill of lading is the central document of carriage for ocean shipment. It is a receipt for goods shipped, a document of title and evidence of the freight contract. Possession of a valid negotiable bill of lading constitutes effective legal control of the goods.

Airway bill

The primary document for the carriage of goods by air. It serves as the contract between the shipper and the carrier, as a receipt of goods for shipment, a form of invoicing, and a document for the import, export and transit requirements of Customs.

Road consignment note

The CMR Convention, a set of legal articles that form the contract between the carrier and shipper, governs the international carriage of goods by road.

Regulatory documents

International transport also requires regulatory documents, such as those for the declaration of goods to Customs authorities, import and export licensing, and the movement of dangerous goods.

Commercial documents

The commercial documents in a specific transaction will depend upon the nature of the consignment and methods of payment, and are likely to include invoices, insurance certificates, letters of credit and shipping instructions. Commercial contracts are usually phrased in 'Incoterms', the set of international rules for the most commonly used terms in foreign trade, produced and published by the International Chamber of Commerce (ICC), originally in 1936 and revised in 2000.

FINANCING EXPORTS

Before engaging in any export market it is important, at the outset, to understand how the differences between international and domestic trade can affect the exporter financially. The key consideration is to minimize any funding gap generated by the company's export activity to a level that can be accommodated comfortably within the company's financing arrangements.

The following factors may have an effect:

▌ Transit times in the carriage of goods and documents are almost certainly longer.

▌ Different time zones, working week cycles, holiday periods and languages may impact communications and payment schedules.

▌ Political risk, customs and excise routines and local laws and business practices may cause problems to the payment mechanism or delays in the settlement of insurance or other claims.

▌ Debt recovery procedures differ, and will be costly and time-consuming to pursue from afar.

Methods of settlement

The following methods of settlement are all in current use and present differing degrees of risk for the seller:

Advance payment

The payment for goods in full before they are received, possibly when the order is placed, is the optimum method for the exporter, although some form of retention until the goods are received and checked is normal. However, except for mail order sales to consumers, it is unlikely that trade or industry customers in developed markets, especially the EU, will agree to advance payment. In undeveloped or risky markets advance payment may be the only safe basis for doing business if a customer is unable to offer documentary credits.

Open account

Under open account conditions the exporter despatches both the goods and documents directly to the importer. The importer receives the goods, and in due course remits payment to the exporter according to the terms agreed between the parties. This procedure is common in the EU between supplier and customer, but in terms of risk it is at the other extreme to advance payment. You will be well advised to limit open account sales to importers of established high standing, or those with whom you have traded satisfactorily for a time.

Documentary collections

The normal alternative to open account, where an exporter wishes to secure payment from lesser known importers, is to make use of the banking system to obtain payment or acceptance of a bill of exchange. Documentary collection procedures, subscribed to by almost all banks in the commercial world and national chambers of commerce, are covered by the International Chamber of Commerce (ICC) Uniform Rules for Collection which came into force in January 1996.

Under these procedures, an exporter normally hands the shipping and other appropriate documents to its bank, after shipping the goods, with instructions that they be transmitted to the buyer's bank and be released against payment by the importer or against acceptance of drafts drawn on the importer. All instructions must be full, clear and precise. Before shipment the exporter should ensure that the importer possesses an import licence that is valid for a period sufficient for the goods to be cleared at their destination, allowing for any potential delay. The exporter should also confirm that current exchange control authorization has been granted to the importer, where applicable, enabling payment to be made immediately or at maturity of the usance drafts, in the currency of collection and as instructed.

There are two main categories of documentary collections – documents against acceptance (D/A) and documents against payment (D/P). D/A is an insecure procedure unless the documents including documents of title (eg full sets of bills of lading) are retained by the bank until such time as the drafts have been accepted by the importer, and the collecting bank adds its 'per aval' endorsement to the acceptance.

We would recommend that you adopt the D/P procedure under which the relevant documents are released to the importer against payment. Assuming that full sets of documents of title are included in the collection, control of the goods is retained until payment is obtained and the seller is in a comparatively secure situation.

There is still the risk, as under D/A, that the goods are not taken up by the buyer, which can be mitigated by asking the collecting bank to store and insure them with a view to returning them to the seller (unless they are perishable) or to finding another buyer, perhaps at auction.

Documentary credits

There are four main types of documentary credit:

▪ **Revocable credits,** where the buyer's commitment can be withdrawn. They are rarely used and best avoided.

▪ **Irrevocable credits, unconfirmed.** The buyer is committed to pay and the seller has the undertaking of the issuing bank, but not the confirmation of a local bank. The risk to the seller lies in the standing of the issuing bank and in the country risk. You may mitigate the risk by demanding that the confirmation of an acceptable bank be added to the credit.

▪ **Irrevocable credits, confirmed.** The seller is assured of payment and the buyer, through the banking system which gives evidence that the goods have been shipped, is assured of receiving shipping documents. However, absolute clarity is essential in the terms of the credit and the specific documentation. You should scrutinize the credit on receipt and seek any necessary clarification or amendments immediately.

▪ **Revolving credit.** If you export regularly to a given customer as a pattern of trade emerges, you will find a revolving credit helpful to your cash flow. Revolving credits are reinstated automatically if they are stated as being 'revolving' according to the written terms and conditions. They may take one of two forms – those that revolve automatically and those that revolve periodically. Your bank will advise you on the detailed mechanisms.

Finance alternatives

In relation to the four methods of settlement there are a series of different finance alternatives for exporters, of which the following are the more common.

Bank overdraft

In cases where a manufacturer or trader agrees with its buyer to accept a documentary credit but cannot finance the manufacture or purchase of the goods covered by the documentary credit, a bank may be persuaded to provide the necessary pre-shipment finance in the form of a short-term bridging loan or overdraft facility to cover the period in question. The arrangements may provide for the bank to have control over the goods as soon as they are manufactured or bought, until such time as they are shipped and the proceeds received from the incoming letter of credit.

Bill finance

Finance can be obtained in the form of an advance, with recourse to the drawer, in respect of bills of exchange sent through the banking system on either D/A or D/P documentary collection. Progress is traceable through the banking system and the advance is liquidated on receipt of proceeds from the collecting bank. Of course, your bank will be more inclined to finance bills sent on D/P.

Forfaiting

Forfaiting is defined as the purchase, without recourse to any previous holder, of debt instruments due to mature at a future date which arise from the provision of goods and services. Most forfaiting transactions tend to relate to commodity trade and the sale of capital goods.

Export factoring

Available from specialist international factoring companies, many of which are owned by banks, export factoring allows the exporter to hand copies of all its invoices drawn on overseas buyers to the factoring company which purchases the debts, often without recourse. Responsibility for credit control, debt collection and foreign exchange risk may be taken on by the factoring company under a variety of schemes offered. As your exports grow, you may find that factoring is the most efficient way of closing the gap in funding your trade.

Currency fluctuation

Any account of trade finance alternatives is incomplete without reference to currency fluctuations and the complex topic of currency management. Foreign trade in any currency other than the trader's own gives rise to the possibility that the rate of exchange of the foreign currency may fluctuate against the trader's own currency, resulting in either an unexpected loss or unrealizable profit.

This concern persuades many exporters and importers to insist on trading in their own currency only, which very often results in a loss of orders or less advantageous prices than trade in the counterpart's currency or a neutral currency, typically the US dollar, the Swiss franc or, of course, the euro. The currency exposure may be redressed by 'hedging' – the purchase or sale of a currency matching the trade contract in amount, currency and value date. If you are exporting to Eurozone members, there is now no practical alternative to quoting, invoicing and accepting payment in euros.

Checklist

- Before committing to an export market, carry out desk research in depth from all available published sources, trade associations and government agencies.
- Attend trade shows to give yourself market exposure. Plan carefully in advance to make best use of your time and help develop short lists of potential customers.
- Use the servicing of your first orders as a learning curve in export logistics and the financial management of exports.

▌ Decide how you are going to develop your export business and on the appointment of intermediaries.

▌ The sales agent is an independent contractor working on commission to gain orders for its principal's goods. The foreign distributor acts as a principal, buying and selling manufactured product at a profit for its own account.

▌ In selecting individual distributors and agents, apply key criteria to screen but make final decisions face to face at their places of business.

▌ Be sure to grant only a trial period of representation, which should be in the form of a full written agreement.

▌ When appointing agents and distributors in the Single Market, make sure that agreements comply with EU law.

▌ Consider outsourcing your export logistics to a specialist freight forwarder whose services extend to the cheapest, quickest and safest routing and modes of transport for your export markets.

▌ Plan to minimize any funding gap generated by export activity so that it can be accommodated within the company's financing arrangements.

▌ Avoid accepting orders on open account except from well-established trade accounts with good payment records. Insist on confirmed irrevocable credits where possible, or documentary collections against payment.

▌ As your exports grow, consider the use of revolving credits and factoring.

17 Financial and Management Issues

If you have a business – you have a problem. It does not matter what size the business is, there will always be issues to deal with. Even if everything is proceeding to plan, you will have to be looking ahead to prepare the business for future challenges.

This chapter looks at the main elements of 'the next stage' in your business's development. Before we look at the three main obstacles that will need to be dealt with when you try to grow the business, there is a vital question to address. Do you want to grow the business? For some, being your own boss, making decisions in a small group without responsibility for many tens of employees, avoiding large amounts of debt and not diluting the ownership of the business may be very attractive. If you are earning a decent amount and no longer struggling to get the business from one day to the next, you may already have reached a happy and sustainable level. If so, read the rest of this chapter and enjoy knowing that there are plenty of stresses and strains out there that you will not be putting yourself through!

However, for many entrepreneurs, building the business is 'what it is all about'. If this is your position, then the same old mantra laid out elsewhere in this guide will be needed again. Identify your objectives; create a plan and timescale to get there. Unless you know where you want to go, no plan is going to be of any use.

Identifying why you want to grow your business is important, because your answer will impact the manner in which you grow it. If you are looking to keep the business in the long term and wish to manage a medium-sized business of your own, then keeping 100 per cent control of the ownership may be a high priority. If you are looking to grow the company quickly to a size where it will be attractive to a potential purchaser, then you will have a different set of priorities and timescales.

Having identified why you wish to grow the business, you will create the plan to carry this out. At this stage, you will need to identify whether your growth strategy will be an organic or acquisitive one. Organic growth is when the expansion is created internally, the increases in turnover are achieved by furthering your current product range, or perhaps widening your sales area. The alternative to this approach is to buy other companies that will give your business greater depth or breadth immediately. Clearly both choices have their pros and cons.

Whatever the direction you intend to take your business, having decided to grow it, you will encounter the same three basic sets of problems. The way you tackle these problems will differ depending on your ultimate objectives, but the problems will be the same: financial problems, predominantly cash flow and secondary funding; process problems, creating systems that work efficiently for larger and more diverse organizations; and personnel problems: the larger the organization, the more people are needed.

FINANCIAL PROBLEMS

Cash flow

As we noted in Part Three, cash flow is the most notorious slayer of small businesses. Some businesses are very cash generative when they work well; pubs, for example, can take a lot of cash up-front and pay their suppliers later. Most businesses are not so lucky. If you are not only trying to pay your current bills but also expand your advertising, pay for some research into a new product or market, or most probably pay the interest instalments on the new piece of equipment you require to expand production or distribution, then you may find your cash situation very much stretched.

The problem scenario

If you are following the organic growth strategy, managing your cash flow will be critical to your success. It will require you to cost out all your expansion requirements very carefully against a timeline of expected sales increases. You are unlikely to be able to run all your growth projects simultaneously on current cash flow, and this may lead to problems with implementing your strategy. You will need to prioritize which elements are required first. It is not worth spending large sums on an advertising campaign if you do not have the capacity to manufacture or distribute product to meet the increased demand. However, you may not be able to pay for the new equipment if you have not increased sales, which will require extra marketing expenditure.

The solutions

The solution to your requirement for increased working capital is that you will have to either borrow it or buy it (sell a share of your business in return for the money). The decision which course you follow will be dependant on the answer to the question posed above, what you are growing your business for, and also on the amount of extra cash you require.

If your extra working capital requirements are not vastly greater than your current situation, that is if, say, your monthly expenses are currently £10,000 per month and your new requirements increase this to £15,000 per month and not £40,000 per month, then your bank will probably be able to help you. If the new situation is a multiple of your current situation, that is the £40,000 per month scenario, then your bank may be less obliging, and a number of alternative solutions present themselves.

Whatever your new need, the providers of the extra cash will require to see a fully costed business plan for the project. The more detail and accuracy of your plan, the more weight it will carry. You will probably also need to produce the figures with a number of different sales scenarios. This will show how the repayment amounts can be met with expected sales, and lower than expected sales. If you are selling some of your business to fund the expansion, a set of better than expected sales figures will whet the appetite of the investors.

Bank provision

Your bank will be the simplest way of accessing your extra cash needs. It can either loan you a lump sum that you repay in predetermined instalments, or extend your overdraft facility. The lump sum loan will probably be less expensive than the overdraft, but you may find that you do not really need a single large sum to accommodate your cash flow requirements, but rather, occasional short-term funds. In this case, the overdraft facility may well be more cost-effective. You will have to determine which is the best for your particular situation.

If you have managed to establish a good, communicative relationship with your bank manager or adviser, and have produced a well-constructed business plan, your bank ought to be sympathetic to your plans. If you cannot persuade your bank to either loan you the money or provide an extended overdraft facility, or you are unhappy with the terms it offers you, you should speak to other small business banks. Often a particular bank may have a computer model that for whatever reason has a problem with an aspect of your business plan. Another bank's model may be constructed in such a way that your plan is acceptable to it, or its own internal targets may be more open to business lending at that moment. It is always worth asking around, especially if you already have a good business plan to present to the manager.

From the other side it may be that your plan is flawed, and that the bank manager is unhappy with it. If the manager is unwilling to give specific reasons, take it to a Business Link adviser or other consultant for a second opinion. If there is a fatal flaw to your plan it is much better to discover it before you borrow and spend the money.

Private funding

A recent survey of British small businesses showed that the majority of funding for both new enterprises and second round finance came from private sources. That is the owner, his or her family and friends. The reasons for this are not difficult to discern. Private funding will usually accept more risk, because the business involved and its owners are personally known to the cash providers, whether they are lenders or investors. These people are less likely to have to provide a return; so they will be less picky and less experienced in analysing small businesses. This makes them easier to get money from. The downside is that you will not necessarily be receiving any expert third party opinion on your plan; it will not be being benchmarked against other opportunities, so you will not be able to gauge its attractiveness. Finally if you cannot pay back the money you may well be ruining more than just a business relationship, which, when the chips are down, can be doubly damaging.

It is imperative that the terms of the private funding are contracted as carefully as a bank loan would be. Make sure that everybody concerned understands the downside risks, the time the loan is for, and the potential maximum upside return as well. You should get your accountant or solicitor to advise you on the documentation and terms applicable to your situation.

Grants and soft loans

Another source of funding for your business, whether it is at start-up stage or established, is through local authority and central government grants and special funds. It is worth contacting your local authority small business advisory team, your local Business Link branch, the local Chamber of Commerce, and also enquiring at your bank if they know of any such funds that might be available to you. Your local reference library may also be able to provide some useful ideas.

The problem with grants is that they are often very specific (for perfectly valid reasons) as to how, where and when the funds can be used. As such, your plan may not fit with their requirements. Do not alter your plan just to get funds. In the majority of cases you will be required to provide a substantial part of the money yourself in order for the granter to release its percentage of the planned costs. If the plan and the grant fit, you should assess the grant's value, including the bureaucracy often involved in applying for and receiving funds, in just the same way as you would assess the offer of a bank loan.

Outside investors

This source was once the glamorous end of the funding search. When the technology bubble was fizzy with excitement, a lot of the froth surrounded the ease with which venture capitalists and business angels showered new business ideas with capital. Now the bubble has burst, reality has gripped the venture capital (VC) industry, and trying to get funds from these providers is extraordinarily difficult.

Typically the VC industry is uninterested in any project smaller than £250,000, and most likely £1 million. Venture capitalists are investing other people's money on the basis of their own business judgement and acumen. Therefore they will be meticulous in their appraisal of your plan – the 'due diligence' required of them will often be the same in time taken for a £250,000 project as a £1 million one, but their percentage return is clearly much more worthwhile for the latter. The British Venture Capital Association (www.bvca.co.uk) will be able to provide you with more information if you think this is the route for you.

Business angels are private individuals who invest their own money in businesses. They tend to be much more flexible with the sums they will invest. The problem is finding an angel willing to invest in your business. Angels tend to only invest in a small number of projects, in sectors about which they are already knowledgeable. A good starting point in searching for angels is the National Business Angels Network (www.nban.co.uk).

With both VCs and angels you will be expected to sell a percentage of your company in return for the funding. You should also expect to find the funds provider(s) sitting on your board as company director(s). Clearly their business advice and experience can be a real bonus, but you must be comfortable with the risk that you will disagree on the company's direction. Through its funding, the investor will have enormous leverage over your company. It is important that you are as comfortable with the investors as with their money.

PROCESS PROBLEMS

The biggest single change to your business model when you find that your business grows is that your ability to control, communicate and change things becomes diluted. When you started your business, perhaps there were three of you in an office or shop. Three years down the line there may be 15 staff in three different locations. If you want to find something out, you cannot just swivel your chair around and ask your two colleagues; you now have to 'speak to the right person'. So from now on everyone has to have a defined role; otherwise no one knows who 'the right person' is or should be.

When there were three of you the risk of someone leaving or being away when you needed them was relatively low; now you do not know everyone's movements or timetables, so you must have a procedure to access their work and files if you need to. When you were all in the same office all deliveries could only come to one place, all stock could only be in one place and all customer information could only be in one place. Not so when you have multiple sites.

In order for you to remain quick, responsive and in control of your business when it grows, you need to create a structure of procedures. It is this necessary imposition of systems and 'processes' that stops your business becoming chaotic, unfocused and inefficient. You grow your business because you wish to enhance the economies of scale: bulk purchasing, more cost-effective advertising, lower per unit administrative costs and so on. But you will also notice that you lose the small team atmosphere, the camaraderie created by having your backs against the wall, and some of the excitement – unless you actively work to create this culture across the business.

The building of processes to ensure that your business works efficiently and effectively is greatly helped these days by computer technology. The existence of networked computer systems that store centrally customer information, product data, sales data and so forth immediately solves many of your information process problems. Mobile technology (laptops and telephones) also allows you to contact staff easily wherever they may be. The more significant process management decisions will cover multiple applications through the establishment of supply chain management, resource applications and a raft of standardized procedures. As the need for more integrated procedures grows, you will become accustomed to the management jargon that they entail, and appreciate the role of recognized national standards such as ISO 9000 and quality standards like 'six sigma'.

It is this movement away from an informal communications and information structure to a formalized one that most characterizes the development from a small business into a mature medium-sized enterprise.

PERSONNEL PROBLEMS

The third element of your business's growing pains is the change associated with an increased number of employees. As the business grows, the original management team will find that it is unable to attend to all the day-to-day decisions and the strategic planning that is required. You will inevitably find that all levels of employment are stretched, from the warehouse staff to yourself.

Increasing the number of people employed at the customer service end of the business will bring with it a number of issues. First, you will want to maintain the business's culture and atmosphere and try to keep alive the customer-led spirit. With a large recruitment drive, it will become increasingly more difficult with each extra employee to find personalities and skills that fit your company. You will also need to keep front-end staff motivated and enhance the team spirit.

Further up the company you will be faced with management issues as well. If you have brought in outside investors you may find the need for a full-time finance director who can liaise with the investors and manage the assets actively, as well as produce the monthly and quarterly reports that investors demand. The growth of different departments may also mean that specialist skills are required. This creates the dilemma of whether to promote from within or seek people who already have the relevant skills from outside the business. In turn, this can create an environment whereby existing employees feel left out or passed over – which can demoralize and cause resentment.

Essentially, you have to look to your growth objectives to determine your method here. If you are looking to grow the company in order to sell it, then you may want to bring in skills quickly to achieve growth as soon as possible. If you are intent on a longer-term organic growth, then promoting and training in-house may be the best way to achieve the cohesive, motivated team spirit. If you intend to grow through acquisition, part of your acquisition strategy may be to buy in companies that already possess the skills you need, as well as the customers you want.

Finally, you should have a plan for management succession. This is as much an insurance policy as anything else, if you have no intentions of letting go of the reins for a while. However, you may find when you have nurtured your company from its start-up to a mid-sized company that your particular set of skills are not suited to managing and promoting such a business, but that they lie in the faster, looser, more flexible and creative world of start-ups. If this is the case it may be difficult to let go, but it may be wise to hand over the detailed management to someone with more mid-size management experience.

With all these growth issues, the earlier they are faced up to, the more easily the transitions will be made. Clearly, you are not going to be seeking out a list of venture capitalists for second round financing, creating a supply chain management framework and employing a finance director while you are still having to do the deliveries yourself. But when the growth phase starts, it is as well to think through the implications of any new processes and assess them for their suitability to further and wider expansion at a later date. If you can build systems that can grow with the business, you will be avoiding a lot of extra unnecessary upheaval and expenditure further down the line. Growing up is traumatic and stressful – laying a solid foundation will ease the process and enhance value.

Checklist

▌ Do you really want to grow your business – or are you happy with it performing at its current level?

▌ Why do you want to grow it? The answer to this will determine how you should grow it.

▌ Focus on cash flow. Do you want to buy it (sell shares to raise cash) or borrow it?

▌ Have you tried your family and friends? Most small businesses get finance privately.

▌ Your bank is your best chance to borrow money.

▌ For amounts of £20,000 to £250,000, business angels and local government enterprise funds are your most likely sources.

▌ For amounts over £250,000, some venture capital funds may help, but in the main they only operate from £1 million onwards.

▌ Focus on process. When your business moves from the point that everyone knows what everyone else is doing all the time, to a more mature structure where responsibility is clearly divided up, you will need to create clear procedures for communicating management ideas, decisions and operations.

▌ Learn about national excellence standards to enhance your processes.

▌ Focus on personnel. As you grow you will need to employ more people.

▌ Is your growth strategy acquisitive or organic?

▌ Will you try to expand your HR from within or externally?

▌ Have you established a management succession plan?

▌ Try to establish a growth framework early on, rather than cobble your exit plan together at the last moment.

18 | Ownership Issues

Paul Waite

When you started your business it is unlikely that you had a highly developed long-term strategic plan. It is more likely that your business plan was founded on a growth policy to achieve a certain level of market penetration within the first three years, defined by levels of turnover and market share. As your business starts to develop and demonstrates that it can continue to generate profits, you will need to plan how to manage it to grow further, and perhaps faster, and as an owner, decide what your longer-term objectives are in terms of wealth creation and the release of capital from the business.

Plainly, the first issue in your strategic planning is to revisit your original growth policy and to decide what changes or refinements you should make to achieve sustained, longer-term growth. Some owners are satisfied with a certain level of profit and personal income and have no entrepreneurial urge to drive the business forward to higher levels of profitability; for them it is sufficient that turnover increases at the rate of inflation, provided that margins and profits are maintained. Effectively, such owners are opting for a 'zero growth' strategy, which sounds prudent but, in practice, is likely to prove highly risky. It is often said that a business either grows and prospers or declines and dies; in general terms, this view is supported by empirical evidence. Most of us can think of small and sometimes larger businesses, often family-owned companies, which seem to have adopted a zero growth strategy and are visibly 'withering on the vine'.

ORGANIC GROWTH VERSUS GROWTH BY ACQUISITION

Assuming that you have adopted a positive growth strategy, as a means to generate increasing profits and add value to the net worth of your shareholding, you will consider how to achieve the necessary levels of annual growth to fulfil your objectives. As a basic dynamic of business, growth can either be created organically or purchased by acquisitions.

Organic growth can be defined as growth through increased sales, which occurs through the development of the firm as an organism represented by its services and products. In this context, 'organic' means structured, organized, systematic, coordinated. Many of the chapters in Part Three, Chapter 16 particularly, focus on the business areas that have to be addressed in order to stimulate and strengthen the organism.

An alternative and faster form of growth than organic expansion is through integration with another firm by merger or acquisition. Integration can be horizontal, that is, between the same type of business, or vertical, that is, between two firms operating at different stages of the supply chain in a business sector or even in different markets.

The two forms of growth are not mutually exclusive, and good decision making by the entrepreneur requires that the horizon is constantly surveyed for both kinds of opportunity, which will better enable business objectives to be achieved. Your survey activity should include spotting new investment opportunities and alternative means to finance the firm. As with the adoption of a zero growth policy, a company failing to seek opportunities is likely to become stale and run the risk of heading into decline.

Organic growth

Drawing on many of the key points from Chapters 6, 7 and 16, we conclude that sales growth can be achieved by several routes:

- gaining market share relative to competitors;
- creating a new market through product innovation;

▌ a strategy to expand the market;

▌ a long term trend of growth in a given market.

When firms expand they are usually responding to increased orders. At first they will use the same buildings, the same people and the same equipment. In the longer term, other decisions will need to be taken, such as capital investment and staff training.

In theory, organic growth should be less risky than acquisition, and is a route likely to be more favoured by lenders. However, the growth programme must be underpinned by a sound business plan with clearly articulated short-term, medium-term and long-term objectives.

Among many considerations, the entrepreneur must consider whether the existing staff are sufficiently trained, or of sufficient quality, to meet the growth demands, the most appropriate sales and marketing strategy and the financial implications of the growth programme, notably in respect of cash flow.

Growth by acquisition

'Mergers' and 'acquisitions' are usually spoken of in the same breath, and the distinction between the two is mainly technical. In the case of a merger the shares of two companies are combined, either by one company (Company A) issuing new shares to the shareholders of the other company (Company B) in exchange for their shareholdings at an agreed ratio, or by forming a new holding company which issues shares to the shareholders of both Company A and Company B in agreed proportions. In the case of an acquisition, Company A makes an offer for the shares of Company B, with or without the consent of the board of Company B; the consideration may be cash, loan stock or shares in Company A or any combination of the three. Often a cash alternative is offered in place of the loan stock or share elements.

In practice, the result of most mergers or acquisitions is that the owners of one company, or directors in the case of public companies where the shares are widely held, gain a dominant, if not controlling, position in the combined and reorganized business. The term 'takeover' is often applied to merger and acquisition transactions, implying a victor and victim. Although used pejoratively, 'takeover' is usually an accurate enough description of what has happened or is about to happen. Equally, the term 'merger', which implies a meeting of minds, is more often than not a euphemism for takeover. Like marriages, few mergers are made in heaven.

Putting yourself in the position of an objective predator, a firm will wish to acquire when it sees an opportunity to make an investment with a positive incremental net present value. However, there are other supporting factors that may motivate an acquisition:

- elimination or reduction of competition;
- safeguarding sources of supply or sales outlets;
- access to economies of scale that a larger business can yield;
- recognition that the target company is under-utilizing its asset base;
- risk spreading and reduction by diversification.

Acquisitions often provide a quick way to enter other markets and industries. Diversification can make the firm safer and reduce the risk of corporate failure, particularly when the markets in which you are operating show signs of stagnation.

However, diversification into areas where your firm lacks expertise can be risky and costly. You should also address the implications of issuing shares in your company as consideration for acquisition in terms of any potential loss of control.

In pursuing an acquisition policy it is important to keep in mind the motivations of the owners whose businesses you are targeting, as well as your own. As we identified in Chapter 1, entrepreneurs in small businesses tend to value one or more of the following:

- satisfaction in building up a business;
- a desire to lead a particular way of life;
- freedom to make management decisions;
- a desire to keep a tradition alive or perhaps ensure family succession.

While larger listed companies may have the incentive of generating increases in earnings per share by taking over companies at prices that reflect a lower price/earnings ratio, smaller companies are more likely to be sensitive to the vendor's motivations when structuring their deals. In any event, decisions that consistently ignore the question of wealth creation cannot be taken by either purchasers or vendors.

EXIT AND INHERITANCE STRATEGIES

Your long-term strategic plan would be incomplete without the inclusion of your personal exit strategy. You may have been driven to consider the end game already, with the introduction of private equity capital to fund the growth of the business (see Chapter 5). Just as private equity investors will be looking for a degree of certainty that they can realize their investment in your company within a three to five year period, you should be looking at the opportunity to release a part of your capital within the same time frame.

Owners of most privately owned businesses seek to either pass the business on to the next generation, particularly if the company is a family company, or sell it to a third party, either by a straight trade sale or management buyout (MBO). The MBO concept can also be applied to the succession plan scenario.

Essentially the exit route alternatives are:

- succession plan;
- trade sale;
- MBO or MBI (management buy in);
- a realization of assets;
- flotation.

Succession plan

Many owner-managers will work closely in a team environment over a long period of time. Therefore, it is natural to want to pass the business down to someone in the management team, particularly where there are younger members. The considerations are similar where there are younger family members, although in this case the business may be handed on for nominal or little consideration. In terms of providing for succession in a family company, the current UK capital gains and inheritance tax regime is probably as favourable as it is ever likely to be.

Insurance policies can play a very useful role in succession planning:

- A 'key man' insurance policy may be taken out to provide a much-needed cash sum for the company in the event of the death of an owner-director.

▌ Where there is more than one shareholder, there should be a formal shareholders agreement which provides that shareholder protection insurance is in place. This enables a director's estate to receive a fair value for his or her shareholding upon death, while ensuring that the relevant shareholding is passed on to the other shareholders.

Frequently, owner-directors continue to maintain control so that they receive a salary or dividend in retirement, sometimes because they don't trust their children/successors to provide them with a secure source of income. For this reason, the owners should plan to build up a substantial pension fund as well as making a sensible provision for savings.

In the event that the chosen successors have little capital, and provided that the company is sufficiently liquid, it can create cash for the departing owner by purchasing its own shares. With an effective current capital gains tax of 10 per cent (see Chapter 13), it is better to exploit this advantage wherever possible rather than receive sums subject to income tax.

Trade sale

In many cases a trade sale is the natural exit route. For third-party private equity shareholders, it will be the preferred route, in the absence of a sustainable flotation within the time frame for the manager's planned exit. At the end of the day, most people have a price that they will accept, and the wealth can be passed down to family members.

A company sale can take one of two forms: a sale of shares, or a sale of assets. It is highly preferable for a vendor to sell his/her shares. This ensures that business taper relief (see Chapter 13) and retirement relief, if applicable, can be claimed. It also avoids the potential double taxation charge arising from a sale of assets.

In an assets sale the company will sell the assets and make chargeable gains subject to corporation tax. The owner will then pay income tax when the profit is extracted. If an assets sale is unavoidable, the most efficient way forward is usually a pre-liquidation dividend. In practice, it is well worth encouraging the purchaser to purchase the shares in your company, even if it entails passing on a discount or giving indemnities and warranties that would not be demanded in an assets sale, provided that the latter are not too onerous.

However, a trade sale of your company's shares may not be quite so straightforward as it first appears. Perhaps the purchaser will ask you to accept shares in its company for a part or the whole of the consideration. If the purchasing company is listed on the London Stock Exchange you may be willing to accept a part of the consideration in shares, given that a share exchange does not attract capital gains tax until such time as the shares received are sold. Nevertheless, before accepting this alternative be sure that there is an active market in the shares and that you are free to sell them over a reasonable period. If you are in any doubt about your ability to convert the shares into cash, be sure to insist on arrangements for them to be placed in the market on your behalf.

Another quite common requirement in trade sales is for the purchaser to insist on an 'earn out' element in the payment of the purchase consideration. Under this kind of arrangement you will receive only a part of the purchase consideration on completion of the transaction, and the remainder in one or more instalments over a further period, with the price adjustable by reference to the audited net profits before tax. This is a reasonable approach if the final reckoning relates to a financial year that has ended before the acquisition was completed, and the audited accounts are not yet available. However, calculation of the outstanding consideration is often referenced to an accounting year that is not yet complete or to one or more financial years ahead, and such conditions give rise to a number of uncertainties.

You may be unable to sell the company without some element of earn-out, but there are several conditions that you should strive to include in the part of the sale agreement that refers to the earn-out period:

1. A sufficient part of the purchase consideration to be paid up front in cash on signature of the agreement. This is your 'drop dead' money of which you can be certain if the rest of the transaction is delayed or fails to be carried out.
2. Your continued employment by the company, if the deferred element relates to a future accounting period, as a director and

on no less than the same terms that you enjoyed prior to the sale of the company. Your employment should be the subject of a written service agreement.

3. An undertaking from the purchaser in the form of a shareholders' agreement that for the financial periods to which the earn-out provisions apply, no parent company management charges will be levied, no additional senior management appointed, no capital expenditure incurred, no loan capital introduced, no new share capital issued and no dividends paid without your express written consent.

The third set of provisions is necessary to ensure that neither pre-tax profits nor shareholders' funds are deflated during the earn-out period, and your remaining shareholding is not diluted by actions of the new controlling shareholder, unrelated to normal trading.

If the purchaser requests that you remain with the company as a salaried director for a minimum or indefinite period of time, irrespective of any earn-out arrangements that may be agreed, do not be deceived into thinking that your trade sale is anything other than a takeover of your business. Whatever the intentions of the parties at the time of the transaction, and however flattering an invitation to stay on may seem, it is extremely unlikely that you will still be employed or play any active part in your company's affairs 18 months after the sale. Of course, there are recorded cases of vendors who have gone on to take increased responsibilities and senior positions in the group of which their company has become a part, but such cases are few and far between. More commonly, the vendor finds it difficult to adjust to a new situation where he or she is unable to take decisions unilaterally, or where the management ethos or business practices of the group are incompatible. Moreover, there are likely to be a band of thrusting young managers to whom the vendor is now exposed, who are confident that they can run the business better.

A service contract will help to ensure that the final parting is financially acceptable but, with the gift of hindsight, you might wish that you had negotiated a higher drop-dead element in the purchase consideration, if there is still an earn-out payment outstanding. As a general recommendation, you should try to ensure that at least two-thirds of the total purchase consideration in a trade sale is paid in cash on completion.

MBO or MBI

A management buyout (MBO) is often a good way of exiting from a business. In fact, an MBO may not involve the existing management at all, and could be a scheme led by institutional investors, involving the insertion of a new management team into the business, thereby creating a management buy-in (MBI).

Similar considerations apply as with a trade sale. However, earn-out provisions and service contracts for the vendors are less likely. In raising institutional financial backing, the new management team will probably have developed a business plan of its own which involves major changes to the way in which the business has been run previously and ambitious growth targets. You are unlikely to be a welcome guest at the feast that follows.

Realization of assets

A realization of assets is often a scenario forced on the owner because of poor trading, and takes the form of a receivership or liquidation. In cases where there are difficulties in making a trade sale on the best terms or there are peculiarities in the business, such as a total dependence on the continuing presence of the original owners, the owner-director(s) may decide to wind up the company voluntarily, following either a sale of the assets and ongoing trade, or a planned closure of the business. In any event, good timing and prompt decision making will help to maximize the outcome.

Flotation

A public flotation on the Alternative Investment Market (AIM) of the London Stock Exchange, or even a full listing for larger companies, can be the ultimate exit route over time, and entrepreneurs may be attracted by the prestige of leading a quoted company. However, the listing process is fraught with complicated requirement pre-flotation, and the post-flotation maintenance of the listing is a continuing burden.

_____

The actual process of flotation is expensive, and involves the appointment of an accredited nominated adviser or sponsor, solicitors to the issue, reporting accountants, a corporate broker and financial public relations consultants. The decision whether to go public should be appraised long before the decision is finalized, after evaluating carefully the alternative strategies and contrasting them with the flotation model.

If all goes well, new capital can dramatically increase your company's potential growth in many different ways, and is the stepping stone to substantial financial rewards through future share sales. However, the best-laid flotation plans can be blown off course by market developments beyond the influence of your advisers or yourself, such as the 2001/2002 'bear' market which has caused a number of companies to defer or break off their flotations.

The main disadvantage of flotation is its inadequacy as an exit strategy for the owner-managers of the company. There will be restrictions on the disposal of the owner shareholdings for several years, and invariably the owner-managers will be required to remain in office for an extended period following flotation.

Checklist

▌ As your business grows profitably, revise your original growth policy to achieve sustained, longer-term growth. Zero growth strategies are risky.

▌ Growth can either be created organically or purchased by acquisition.

▌ In theory, organic growth should be less risky than acquisition, and is a route more likely to be favoured by lenders. Consider whether existing staff are of sufficient quality to meet growth demands, and the cash flow implications of the growth programme.

▌ Where a merger or acquisition results in the owners or directors of one company gaining control or dominance of another, in reality the transaction is a takeover.

- In pursuing an acquisition policy, keep in mind the motivations of the vendors. The question of wealth creation is paramount for both purchaser and vendor.
- Succession plans can provide for exit payments to owners through the company's purchase of its own shares, which are subject only to capital gains at the current preferential rate.
- Owners should plan for retirement by building up pension funds rather than expect to continue drawing salaries or dividends subject to income tax.
- Trade sales through the sale of a company's shares are preferable to a sale of assets for the vendor. The latter is subject to double taxation charges.
- Trade sales can involve 'earn out' elements in the payment of the consideration. Take care to secure a substantial cash payment on completion and written undertakings to ensure that neither pre-tax profits nor shareholders' funds are deflated, and your shareholding is not diluted during the earn-out period.
- MBOs and MBIs involving institutional investors are an acceptable variation on trade sales. If you remain an employee after any kind of trade sale, do not expect your employment to continue beyond the short term.
- Asset realization through a voluntary winding-up of the company may be appropriate following a sale of the assets and ongoing trade. Good timing and prompt decision making will help to maximize the outcome.
- Public flotation of your company may be the stepping stone to substantial financial rewards, but there will be restrictions on the disposal of owner shareholdings for several years, while owner-managers must stay on post-flotation.

Further Reading

KOGAN PAGE TITLES

Kogan Page publish a wide variety of helpful titles for people in business. A full list of titles is available by writing to the publisher at the address given on the back cover, by calling on 020 7278 0433, or by visiting the Kogan Page Web site: www.kogan-page.co.uk

Business communication

CBI Corporate Communications Handbook (1998), eds Timothy Foster and Adam Jolly
Doing Business on the Internet (1998), Simon Collin
How to be a Better Communicator (1996), Sandy McMillan
Marketing Communications, 2nd edition (1998), Paul Smith
Sales Promotions, 2nd edition (1998), Julian Cummins

Start-ups, business plans and new directions

The Business Plan Workbook, 3rd edition (1998), Cohn Barrow, Paul Barrow and Robert Brown
Forming a Limited Company, 6th edition (1998), Patricia Clayton
Great Ideas for Making Money (1994), Niki Chesworth
Money Mail Moves Abroad (1998), Margaret Stone
Net That Job! Using the World Wide Web to Develop Your Career and Find Work (1998), Irene Krechowiecka
Working for Yourself, 21st edition (2000), Godfrey Golzen and Jonathan Reuvid
F-Business Start-Up Guide (2000), Philip Treleaven

Law and company secretarial

An A-Z of Employment Law: A Complete Reference Source for Managers, Companies Act 1985, 2nd edition (1997)
The Company Secretary's Handbook: A Guide to the Duties and Responsibilities, 2nd edition (1998), Helen Ashton
The Employer's Handbook (2002), B Cushway
Law for the Small Business, 9th edition (1998), Patricia Clayton

Finance, accounting and bookkeeping

Accounting for Non-Accountants, 4th edition (1999), Graham Mott
Do Your Own Bookkeeping (1988), Max Pullen
Financial Management for the Small Business, 4th edition (1998), Cohn Barrow
Self Assessment for the Small Business and Self-Employed (1998), Niki Chesworth
Understand Your Accounts, 4th edition (1999), A St John Price

Franchising

Guide to Buying Your First Franchise, 3rd edition (1999), Greg Clarke
Taking Up a Franchise, 14th edition (2000), Cohn Barrow and Godfrey Golzen

Import and export

CBI European Business Handbook, 5th edition (1999), ed Adam Jolly
The EMU Fact Book (1998), Niki Chesworth and Susie Pine-Coffin
The Export Handbook: In Association with the British Chambers of Commerce (1998), ed Harry Twells
Getting Started in Export (1998), Roger Bennett
Getting Started in Importing (1998), John Wilson

Management

How to Be an Even Better Manager: A Complete A-Z of Proven Techniques and Essential Skills ... Reveals the Secrets of Successful Managers, 4th edition (1994), Michael Armstrong

International Dictionary of Management, 5th edition (1995), eds Hano
    Johannsen and G Terry Page
Introduction to Modern Management (1998), Tony Dawson
Transform Your Management Style! (1998), Hilary Walmsley

Sales, marketing and advertising

*Customer Driven Marketing: The Ideal Way to Increased Profits Through
    Marketing, Sales and Service Improvement* (1997), John Frazier-
    Robinson
Do Your Own Market Research, 3rd edition (1998), Paul Hague and
    Peter Jackson
European Direct Marketing Association, 3rd edition (1999), eds Adam
    Baines and Sheila Lloyd
*Handbook of International Direct Marketing: In Association with the 101
    Ways to Boost Customer Satisfaction* (1997), Timothy R V Foster
A Handbook of Marketing and PR for the Small Business (1998), Moi Ali
How to Sell More: A Guide for the Small Business, 2nd edition (1997),
    Neil Johnson
101 Ways to Get Great Publicity (1992), Timothy R V Foster
A Marketing Action Plan for the Growing Business (1999), Shailendra
    Vyakarnam and John Leppard
Measuring Customer Satisfaction (1993), Richard F Gerson
Selling by Telephone, 2nd edition (1998), Chris de Winter
Successful Marketing for the Small Business: The Daily Telegraph Guide,
    4th edition (1998), Dave Petten

Working from home

Running a Home Based Business, revised edition (1998), Diane Baker
*Your Home Office: A Practical Guide to Using the Technology
    Successfully*, 3rd edition (1998), Peter Chatterton

FLOTATION

Going Public: The Essential Guide to Flotation Issues (2002), ed
    Jonathan Reuvid

OTHER SOURCES OF INFORMATION

Official information

Leaflets from government offices provide a further source of information. They are normally available either from the government department concerned or from the Stationery Office.

Barclays Bank publications

Barclays Small Business Survey: Start-ups and closures Quarter Four 2001
Third Age Entrepreneurs: Profiting from experience
Young Entrepreneurs: Tomorrow's business leaders
Women in Business: The barriers start to fall
Thinking of Starting a Business?

Information on employment issues

Butterworth's Employment Law Handbook (2000) 9th edition, Butterworth, London
IRS Employment Review (published fortnightly) Industrial Relations Services, London
Legislation is available from the DTI Web site (www.dti.gov.uk). Relevant Acts include:

Asylum and Immigration Act 1996
Data Protection Act 1998
Disability Discrimination Act 1995
Employment Act 1989
Employment Act 2002
Employment Rights Act 1996
Race Relations Act 1976
Rehabilitation of Offenders Act 1974
Sex Discrimination Acts 1975 and 1986
The Children (Protection at Work) Regulations 1998 and 2000
Trade Union Reform and Employment Rights Act 1992
Transfer of Undertakings (Protection of Employment) Regulations 1981 (TUPE)

Useful Contacts

GOVERNMENT

The Adjudicator's Office

(For complaints against rulings by Customs and Excise)
Haymarket House, 28 Haymarket, London SW1Y 4SP
Tel. 020 7930 2292
Web: www.adjudicatorsoffice.gov.uk

Business Links

Addresses of regional offices are available by phone or Internet.
Tel. 0845 600 9006
Signpost line: 08457 567765 / freephone 0800 500200
Web: www.businesslink.org

CCTA Government Information Service

A gateway to all Government Department Web sites:
www.open.gov.uk

Central Office of Information

Web@ www.coi.gov.uk

Customs and Excise

Addresses of regional / advice centres are available by phone.

Tel. 0845 010 9000
Web: www.hmce.gov.uk

The Data Protection Registrar

Wycliffe House, Wilmslow, Cheshire SK9 5AE
Tel. 01625 545745
Web: www.dpr.gov.uk

Department of Education and Skills

Sanctuary Buildings, Great Smith Street, London SW1P 3BT
Tel. 020 7925 5000
Web: www.dfes.gov.uk

Department of the Environment, Food and Regional Affairs

Nobel House, 17 Smith Square, London SW1P 3JR
Tel. 020 7944 3000
Web: www.defra.gov.uk

Department of Trade and Industry

Enquiries: 1 Victoria Street, London SW1H 0ET
Tel. 020 7215 5000
Web: www.dti.gov.uk

Export Credits Guarantee Department (ECGD)

PO Box 2200, 2 Exchange Tower, Harbour Exchange Square, London
E14 9GS
Tel. 020 7512 7000
Web: www.ecgd.gov.uk

Her Majesty's Treasury

The Public Enquiries Unit, Horse Guards Road, London SW1A 2HQ
Tel. 020 7270 4558
Web: www.hm-treasury.gov.uk

Inland Revenue

The Inland Revenue has a number of helplines for enquiries, a
listing of which can be found on its Web site at
www.inlandrevenue.gov.uk

Office of Fair Trading

Fleetbank House, 2–6 Salisbury Square, London EC4Y 8JX
Tel. 08457 224499
Web: www.oft.gov.uk

Office for National Statistics

Cardiff Road, Newport, Gwent NP10 8XG
Tel. 0845 601 3034
Web: www.statistics.gov.uk

Small Business Service

Department of Trade and Industry, 1 Victoria Street,
London SW1H 0ET
Tel. 020 7215 5000
Web: www.businessadviceonline.org

St Mary's House
Moorfoot
Sheffield S14 4PQ
Tel. 0114 259 7314

Local Enterprise Companies

These have different titles and forms in different areas. Details can
be obtained from regional Business Link offices.
Tel. 0845 600 9006
Web: www.businesslink.org

GOVERNMENT OFFICES FOR THE REGIONS

Various departments have been organized into integrated offices known as Government Offices (GOs) for the Regions.

Government Office for the East of England

GO-East – Victory House, Vision Park, Histon, Cambs CB4 9ZR
Tel. 01223 202000
Fax 01223 202020
and
GO-East – Westbrook, Milton Road, Cambridge CB4 1YG
Tel. 01223 346700
Fax 01223 346701
Web: www.go-east.gov.uk

Government Office for the East Midlands

The Belgrave Centre, Stanley Place, Talbot Street, Nottingham NG1 5GG
Tel. 0115 971 2759
Fax 0115 971 2404
Web: www.go-em

Government Office for London

Riverwalk House, 157–161 Millbank, London SW1P 4RR
Tel. 020 7217 3328
Fax 020 7217 3450
Web: www.go-london.gov.uk

Government Office for the North-East

Wellbar House, Gallowgate, Newcastle upon Tyne NE1 4TD
Tel. 0191 201 3300
Fax 0191 202 3830
Web: www.go-ne.gov.uk

Government Office for the North-West

Sunley Tower, Piccadilly Plaza, Manchester M1 4BE
Tel. 0161 952 4000
Fax 0161 952 4099
and
Cunard Building, Pier head, Water Street, Liverpool L3 1QB
Tel. 0151 224 6300
Fax 0151 224 6470
Web: www.go-nw.gov.uk

Government Office for the South-East

Contact details for numerous personnel and departments are given
on their Web site.
Web: www.go-se.gov.uk

Government Office for the South-West

2 Rivergate, Temple Quay, Bristol BS1 6ED
Tel. 0117 900 1700
Fax 0117 900 1900
or
Mast House, Shepherds Wharf, 24 Sutton Road, Plymouth PL4 0HJ
Tel. 01752 635000
Fax 01752 227647
or
Castle House, Pydar Street, Truro TR1 2UJ
Tel. 01872 264500
Fax 01872 264503.
Web: www.gosw.gov.uk

Government Office for the West Midlands

77 Paradise Circus, Queensway, Birmingham B1 2DT
Tel. 0121 212 5050
 Fax 0121 212 1010
Web: www.go-wm.gov.uk

Government Office for Yorkshire and the Humber

PO Box 213, City House, New Station Street, Leeds LS1 4US
Tel. 0113 280 0600
Fax 0113 283 6394
Web: www.goyh.gov.uk/

Industrial Development Boards for Northern Ireland and Local Enterprise Development Unit

These were dissolved by the Industrial Development Act
(Northern Ireland) and replaced by Invest Northern Ireland.
Invest Northern Ireland
64 Chichester Street, Belfast BT1 4JX
Upper Galwally, Belfast BT8 6TB
and
17 Antrim Road, Lisburn BT28 3AL
Tel. 028 9023 9090
Fax 028 9049 0490
Web: www.investni.com

START-UP ADVICE

England and Wales

Local Enterprise Agencies

Business in the Community, 137 Shepherdess Walk, London N1 7RQ
Tel. 0870 600 2482
Web: www.bitc.org.uk

The National Assembly for Wales

Industry and Training Department, Crown Buildings, Cathays
Park, Cardiff CF10 3NQ
Tel. 029 2082 5111
Web: www.wales.gov.uk

Welsh Development Agency

Client Services, WDA, QED Centre, Muir Avenue, Treforest, Mid
Glamorgan CF37 5YR
Tel. 01443 845500
Web: www.wda.gov.uk

Scotland

Scottish Business in the Community

PO Box 408, Bankhead Avenue, Edinburgh EH11 4HE
Tel. 0131 442 2020
Web: www.sbcscot.com

Scottish Enterprise

5 Atlantic Quay, 140 Broomielaw, Glasgow G2 8LU
Tel. 0141 248 2700
Web: www.scottish-enterprise.com

The Office of the Scottish Executive

Enterprise and Lifelong Learning, Meridian Court, 5 Cadogan
Street, Glasgow G2 6AT
Tel. 0141 248 2855
Web: www.scotland.gov.uk

Highlands and Islands Enterprise

Cowan House, Inverness Retail and Business Park, Inverness IV2
7QF
Tel. 01463 234171
Web: www.hie.co.uk

Northern Ireland

See opposite for details of Invest Northern Ireland.

NATIONAL ASSOCIATIONS REPRESENTING SMALL FIRMS

Association of Independent Business

34 Bow Lane, London EC4M 9AY
Tel. 020 7329 0219

The British Chambers of Commerce

Manning House, 22 Carlisle Place, London SW1P 1JA
Tel. 0120 7565 2000
Web: www.chamberonline.org.uk

British Franchise Association

Thames View, Newton Road, Henley on Thames, Oxon RG9 1HG
Tel. 01491 578050
Web: www.british-franchise.org.uk

Confederation of British Industry (CBI)

Centre Point, 103 New Oxford Street, London WC1A 1DU
Tel. 020 7395 8247
Web: www.cbi.org.uk

Federation of Small Businesses Ltd

Sir Frank Whittle Way, Blackpool Business Park, Blackpool, Lancs FY4 2FE
Tel. 01253 336000
Web: www.fsb.org.uk

The Forum of Private Business Ltd

Ruskin Chambers, Drury Lane, Knutsford, Cheshire WA16 6HA
Tel. 01565 634467
Web: www.fpb.co.uk

Smaller Firms Council (CBI)

Centre Point, 103 New Oxford Street, London WC1A 1DU
Tel. 020 7395 8247
Web: www.cbi.org.uk

The Work Foundation

(formerly The Industrial Society)
Peter Runge House, 3 Carlton House Terrace, London SW1Y 5DG
Tel. 020 7165 6700
Web: theworkfoundation.com

FORMING A COMPANY

The Patent Office

Concept House, Cardiff Road, Newport, Gwent NP10 8QQ
Tel. 01633 814708
Web: www.patent.gov.uk

Registrar of Companies

Companies Registration Office, Crown Way, Cardiff CF14 3UZ

For Scotland: 37 Castle Terrace, Edinburgh EH2 2EB

For London: Companies Registration Office, 21 Bloomsbury Street,
London WC1B 3XD
Tel. 0870 333 3636
Web: www.companies-house.gov.uk

Companies Limited/Rapid Refunds

For purchasing an off-the-shelf company.
376 Euston Road, London NW1 3BL
Tel. 020 7383 2323
Web: www.limited-companies.co.uk

Industrial Common Ownership Movement (ICOM)

Advice on setting up worker cooperatives.
Holyoake House, Hanover Street, Manchester M60 0AS
Tel. 0161 246 2900
Web: www.euro-social-economy.org.uk

Institute of Business Advisers

Response House, Queen Street North, Chesterfield S41 9AB
Tel. 01246 45322

Institute of Directors

116 Pall Mall, London SW1Y 5ED
Tel. 020 7839 1233
Web: www.iod.co.uk

The Law Society

Lawyers for your business.
113 Chancery Lane, London WC2A 1PL
Tel. 020 7242 1222
Web: lfyb.lawsociety.org.uk

BANKS

Barclays Bank plc Business Direct

Octagon House, Gadbrook Park, Northwich CW9 7RB
Tel. 01606 844033
Web: www.barclays.co.uk

HSBC plc

8 Canada Square, London E14 5HQ
Tel. 020 7991 8888
Web: www.banking.hsbc.co.uk

Lloyds TSB Bank plc, Small Business Advice

PO Box 112, Canons House, Canons Way, Bristol BS99 7LB
Tel. 0117 943 3433
Web: www.lloydstsb.com

National Westminster Bank plc, Business One Stop Shop

PO Box 4114, 120–126 High Street, Hornchurch, Essex RM12 4DF
Tel. 0800 028 2677
Web: www.natwest.com/startup

RAISING CAPITAL

Association of British Credit Unions Ltd

Holyoake House, Hanover Street, Manchester M60 0AS
Tel. 0161 832 3694

British Venture Capital Association

Tower 3, 3 Clements Inn, London WC2A 2AZ
Tel. 020 7025 2950
Web: www.bvca.co.uk

British Insurance and Investment Brokers Association

BIBA House, 14 Bevis Marks, London EC3A 7NT
Tel. 020 7623 9043
Web: www.biba.org.uk

EU Money Service

2 Gallands Close, Swanland, East Yorkshire HU14 3GE
Tel. 01482 651635
Web: www.europeangrants.com

Factors and Discounters Association

Boston House, The Little Green, Richmond, Surrey TW9 1QE
Tel. 020 8332 9955
Web: www.factors.org.uk

Finance and Leasing Association

Imperial House, 15–19 Kingsway, London WC2B 6UN
Tel. 020 7836 6511
Web: www.fla.org.uk

Institute of Patentees and Inventors

Suite 505a, Triumph House, 189 Regent Street, London W1R 7WE
Tel. 020 8541 4197

The Prince's Trust

18 Park Square East, London NW1 4LH
Tel. 020 7543 1234
Web: www.princes-trust.org.uk

3i plc

91 Waterloo Road, London SE1 8XP
Tel. 020 7928 3131
Web: www.3i.com

Venture Capital Report Ltd

7 Old Park Lane, London W1K 1QR
Tel. 020 7072 2410
Web: www.vcr1978.com

PREMISES

English Partnerships

St George's House, Kingsway, Team Valley, Gateshead, Tyne and
Wear NE11 0NA
Tel. 0191 487 8941
Web: www.englishpartnerships.co.uk

Estates Today

Online commercial estate agency
Web: www.estatestoday.co.uk

Royal Institution of Chartered Surveyors

12 Great George Street, Parliament Square, London SW1P 3AD
Tel. 020 7222 7000
Web: www.rics.org

MARKETING AND SALES

The Advertising Association

Abford House, 15 Wilton Road, London SW1V 1NJ
Tel. 020 7828 2771
Web: www.adassfoc.org.uk

Chartered Institute of Marketing

Moor Hall, Cookham, Maidenhead, Berkshire SL6 9QH
Tel. 01628 427500
Web: www.cim.co.uk

Direct Marketing Association UK Ltd

DMA House, 70 Margaret Street, London SW1W 8SS
Tel. 020 7291 3300
Web: www.dma.org.uk

Institute of Direct Marketing

1 Park Road, Teddington, Middlesex TW11 0AR
Tel. 020 8977 5705
Web: www.theidm.com

Institute of Public Relations

The Old Trading House, 15 Northburgh Street, London EC1V 0PR
Tel. 020 7253 5151
Web: www.ipr.org.uk

Marketing Society

St George's House, 3–5 Pepys Road, London SW20 8NJ
Tel. 020 8879 3464
Web: www.marketing-society.org.uk

SAFETY AND STANDARDS

British Safety Council

70 Chancellor's Road, London W6 9RS
Web: www.britishsafetycouncil.org

British Standards Institution

389 Chiswick High Road, London W4 4AL
Tel. 020 8996 9000
Web: www.bsi-global.com

Health and Safety Executive

Rose Court, 2 Southwark Bridge, London SE1 9HS
Tel. 020 7717 6000
Web: www.hse.gov.uk

MANAGING FINANCE

Association of Chartered and Certified Accountants (ACCE)

29 Lincoln's Inn Fields, London WC2A 3EE
Tel. 020 7242 6855
Web: www.acca.global.com

Chartered Accountants Directory

Datacomp, 4 Houldsworth Square, Reddish, Stockport, Cheshire SK5 7AF
Tel. 0161 442 5233
Web: www.chartered-accountants.co.uk

Chartered Institute of Taxation

12 Upper Belgrave Street, London SW1X 8BB
Tel. 020 7234 9381
Web: www.tax.org.uk

Institute of Chartered Accountants in England and Wales

PO Box 433, Chartered Accountants Hall, Moorgate Place, London EC2P 2BJ
Tel. 020 7920 8100
Web: www.icaew.co.uk

Institute of Chartered Accountants of Scotland

ICA House, 21 Haymarket Yards, Edinburgh EH12 5BH
Tel. 0131 347 0100
Web: www.icas.org.uk

Institute of Company Accountants

40 Tyndales Park Road, Clifton, Bristol BS8 1PL
Tel. 0117 973 8261

International Association of Book-Keepers

Burford House, London Road, Sevenoaks, Kent TN13 1AS
Tel. 01732 458080
Web: www.accountingweb.co.uk/iab

LABOUR RELATIONS AND PERSONNEL MANAGEMENT

Advisory Conciliation and Arbitration Service (ACAS)

Brandon House, 180 Borough High Street, London SE1 1LW
Tel. 020 7210 3000
Web: www.acas.org.uk

Chartered Institute of Personnel and Development

CIPD House, 35 Camp Road, Wimbledon, London SW19 4UX
Tel. 020 8971 9000
Web: www.cipd.co.uk

Chartered Management Institute

Management Information Centre, Management House,
Cottingham Road, Corby, Northants NN17 1IT
Tel. 01536 204222
Web: www.managers.org.uk

Institute of Management Consultancy

3rd Floor, 17–18 Haywards Place, London EC1R 0EQ
Tel. 020 7566 5220
Web: www.imc.co.uk

EXPORT

The British Chambers of Commerce

Trade Partners UK Support for Export Marketing Research Scheme, 4 Westwood House, Westwood Business Park, Coventry CV4 8HS
Tel. 024 7669 4484
Web: www.britishchambers.org.uk / exportzone

British Exporters Association

Broadway House, Tothill Street, London SW1H 9NQ
Tel. 020 7222 5419
Web: www.bexa.co.uk

British International Freight Association

Redfern House, Browells Lane, Feltham, Middlesex TW13 7EP
Tel. 020 8844 2266
Web: www.bifa.org

Commission of the European Communities

Jean Monnet House, 8 Storey's Gate, London SW1P 3AT
Tel. 020 7973 1992

Department of Trade and Industry

Export Control Enquiry Unit, Kingsgate House, 66–74 Victoria Street, London SW1E 6SW
Tel. 020 7215 5444

Web. www.tradepartners.gov.uk

Euler Trade Indemnity plc

1 Canada Square, London E14 5DX
Tel. 020 7512 9333
Web: www.eulerhermes.com

European Info. Centre, London Chamber of Commerce and Industry

33 Queen Street, London EC4R 1AP
Tel. 020 7489 1992
E-mail: europ@londonchamber.co.uk

Export Credits Guarantee Department

2 Exchange Tower, PO Box 2200, Harbour Exchange Square, London E14 9GS
Tel. 020 7512 7000
Web: ww.ecgd.gov.uk

Institute of Export

Export House, Minerva Business Park, Lynch Wood, Peterborough PE2 6FT
Tel. 01733 404400
Web: www.export.org.uk

SITPRO Ltd

(formerly Simpler Trade Procedures Board)
Oxford House, 8th Floor, 76 Oxford Street, London W10 1BS
Tel. 020 7467 7280

Technical Help for Exporters

British Standards Institution, 389 Chiswick High Road, London W4 4AL

Tel. 020 8996 9000
Web: www.bsi-global.com

TradeUK

Online advice on export issues and e-commerce.
Web: www.tradeuk.com

INFORMATION AND COMMUNICATION TECHNOLOGIES

British Telecom

Advice on communications and information technologies for business.
Web: www.britishtelecom.co.uk

Information Society Initiative

For IT advice and support centres.
Web: www.isi.gov.uk

Nominet

To register Internet names.
Web: www.nic.uk

Exploit

Web: www.exploit.com

Submitit

These companies will submit your Web site address to online search engines.
Web: www.submitit.com

Internet Link Exchange

Exchange advertising banner with other sites.
Web: www.linkexchange.com

Liszt

Description of most mailing lists and joining details.
Web: www.liszt.com

Technologies for Training

Gateway to IT help with links to numerous organizations working in IT.
Web: www.tft.co.uk

WebCounter

Adds visitor counter to your Web site.
Web: www.digits.com

SECTOR INFORMATION

Construction

Federation of Master Builders

14–15 Great James Street, London WC1N 3DP
Tel. 020 7242 7583
Web: www.fmb.org.uk

Crafts

The Crafts Council

44a Pentonville Road, London N1 9BY
Tel. 020 7278 7700
Web: www.craftscouncil.org.uk

Design
British Interior Design Association

1–4 Chelsea Harbour Design Centre, Lots Road, London SW10 0XE
Tel. 020 7349 0800
Web: www.bida.org

Design Council

34 Bow Street, London WC2E 7DL
Tel. 020 7420 5200
Web: www.designcouncil.org.uk

Estate Agents

National Association of Estate Agents

Arbon House, 21 Jury Street, Warwick CV34 4EH
Tel. 01926 496800
Web: www.propertylive.co.uk

Farming
Agricultural Development Advisory Service

Oxford Spires, The Boulevard, Kidlington, Oxon OX5 1NZ
Tel: 01865 842742
Web: www.adas.co.uk

Agricultural Mortgage Corporation plc

(part of Lloyds TSB Group)
AMC House, Chantry Street, Andover, Hants SP10 1DE
Tel. 01264 334334
Web: www.amconline.co.uk

Gardening and landscape architecture
The Landscape Institute

6–8 Barnard Mews, London SW11 1QU
Tel. 020 7350 5200
Web: www.l-i.org.uk

Institute of Horticulture

14–15 Belgrave Square, London SW1X 8PS
Tel. 020 7245 6943
Web: www.horticulture.org.uk

Hospitality
British Beer and Pub Association

Market Towers, 1 Nine Elms Lane, London SW8 5NQ
Tel. 020 7627 9199
Web: www.beerandpub.com

Hotel and Catering International Management Association

191 Trinity Road, London SW17 7HN
Tel. 020 8772 7400
Web: www.hcima.org.uk

IT
Association of Computer Professionals

204 Barnett Wood Lane, Ashtead, Surrey KT21 2DB
Tel. 0137 2273442
Web: www.acpexamboard.com

British Computer Society

1 Sanford Street, Swindon, Wilts SN1 1JH
Tel. 01793 417417
Web: www.bcs.org

Management consultancy
Institute of Management Consultancy

3rd Floor, 17–18 Haywards Place, London EC1R 0EQ
Tel. 020 7566 5220
Web: www.imc.co.uk

Retail
National Association of Self-Employed

Lynch House, 91 Mansfield Road, Nottingham NG1 3FN
Tel. 0115 947 5046
Web: www.n-a-s.org.uk

Tourism
English Tourist Board

Development Advisory Services Unit, Thames Tower, Blacks Road,
Hammersmith, London W6 9EL
Tel. 020 8846 9000
Web: www.visitbritain.com

VisitScotland

23 Ravelston Terrace, Edinburgh E14 3TP
Tel. 0131 332 2433
Web: www.visitscotland.com

Wales Tourist Board

Brunel House, 2 Fitzalan Road, Cardiff CF2 4UY
Tel. 029 2049 9909
Web: www.visitwales.com

TRANSPORT MANAGEMENT

Association of Car Fleet Operators (AFCO)

Rivendell House, Winton Road, Petersfield GU32 3LL
Tel. 01730 260162

British Vehicle Rental and Leasing Association (BVRLA)

River Lodge, Badminton Court, Amersham, Bucks HP7 0DD
Tel. 01494 434747
Web: www.bvrla.co.uk

Glass's Information Services

1 Princes Road, Weybridge, Surrey KT13 9TU
Tel. 01932 823823
Web: www.glass.co.uk

SPECIALIST LIBRARIES

Business Information Service

British Library, Lloyds TSB Business Line, 96 Euston Road, London
NW1 2DB
Tel. 020 7412 7454/9799
Web: www.bl.uk/bis

Chartered Institute of Marketing Library

Moor Hall, Cookham, Maidenhead, Berks SL6 9QH
Tel. 01628 427 500
Web: www.cim.co.uk

Chartered Management Institute Management Information Centre

(for members only)
Management House, Cottingham Road, Corby, Northants NN17 1TT
Tel. 01536 204222
Web: www.managers.org.uk

Export Market Information Centre Library

Kingsgate House, 66–74 Victoria Street, London SW1E 6SW
Tel. 020 7215 4555

Frobisher Crescent Library at City University

Contact numbers for various departments are given on the Web site.
Web: www.city.ac.uk/library

London Business School Library

25 Taunton Place, London NW1
Postal address: London Business School, Regent's Park, London NW1 4SA
Tel. 020 7262 5050
Web: www.lbs.lon.ac.uk/library

London Metropolitan University Library

School of Business Studies, 84 Moorgate, London EC2M 6SQ
Tel. 020 7320 1000

Monopolies and Mergers Commission Library

New Court, 48 Carey Street, London WC2A 2JT
Tel. 020 7324 1467

Office of Fair Trading Library

Field House, 15 Bream's Buildings, London EC4A 1PR

Office for National Statistics

Government Buildings, Cardiff Road, Newport, South Wales NP9 1XG
Web: www.statistics.gov.uk

Trade Partners UK Information Centre

Kingsgate House, 66–74 Victoria Street, London SW1E 6SW
Tel. 020 7215 4555
Web: www.tradepartners.gov.uk

WEB SITES OF INTEREST

CBI 'Fitforthefuture'

New site from CBI on National Best Practice.
Web: www.fitforthefuture.org.uk

DTI

Good links to government-sponsored schemes.
Web: www.dti.gov.uk

Electronic Telegraph

Access to full text of *Daily Telegraph* and directory listing of British business.
Web: www.telegraph.co.uk

Enterprise Zone

Extremely useful resource with useful links for start-ups.
Web: www.enterprise-zone.org.uk

Financial Times

Business directory and up-to-date financial information.
Web: www.ft.com

Keele University Management Web Resources Database

Well-resourced database of business and management Web sites
with good links.
Web: www.keele.ac.uk

Kogan Page

Extensive list of publications for start-ups and SMEs.
Web: www.kogan-page.co.uk

Strathclyde University Business Information Sources on the Internet

Thoroughly recommended Web site with extensive listings of sites
and general sources of business information.
Web: www.dis.strath.ac.uk

WhoWhere

E-mail address, telephone number and street address directory.
Web: www.whowhere.com

Yahoo!

Search engine with extensive business directory.
Web: www.yahoo.com

Yell

Online version of the Yellow Pages.
Web: www.yell.co.uk

TRANSPORT-RELATED PUBLICATIONS

Business Car

Tel. 01733 578 458

Fleet Car Business

Tel. 01733 467000

Fleet Management

Tel. 01733 578458

Fleet News

Tel. 01733 467048

Fleet Operator

Journal of AFCO
Tel. 01730 260162

Motive

Journal of BVRLA
Tel. 01494 434747

Index of Advertisers

Index

NB: page numbers in italics indicate figures or tables